# MAKING ROOM

"*Making Room* is a must-read for anyone who cares about our LGBTQ homeless youth. In the spirit of a true saint, Carl Siciliano has spent a lifetime giving shelter, dignity, and hope to young people off the streets. The story is riveting, emotional, powerful, and an important part of our history. Siciliano has lived a life of service, spirituality, and love."  —DAVID MIXNER, activist, performer, and author of *Stranger Among Friends*

"Carl Siciliano's *Making Room* guides us from the cold, pitiless streets faced by homeless youth to a warmer place, from heartbreak to a place of hope. His deeply personal, spiritual telling intertwines his life with that of Ali Forney—his fierce and fabulous muse—in a way that reminds us that the fate of our queer kids is intertwined with us all."  —CHRISTIAN COOPER, *New York Times* bestselling author of *Better Living Through Birding*

"It is tragic that so many LGBTQ youths are forced into home-lessness, all too often due to their parents' religious beliefs. In his essential new book, *Making Room,* Carl Siciliano tells stories of young people struggling to overcome crushing circumstances. Some are inspiring, others are heartbreaking, but all are told with tender-ness, affection, and respect. As they welcome thousands who've been abandoned, with compassionate and nonjudgmental love, Siciliano and his co-workers at the Ali Forney Center are living out Jesus's parable of the Good Samaritan in our time. I hope that this compelling book will be read by many in the church as well as many who wish that churches treat LGBTQ youth not like lepers but as who they are: beloved children of God."

—JAMES MARTIN, SJ, *New York Times* bestselling author
of *Building a Bridge*

"Within the pages of this endearing journal lies a poignant testament to resilience, compassion, and unwavering commitment. Through the looking glass of the struggle to house and protect homeless trans/nonbinary individuals, the author offers a nostalgic reflection on their own journey, navigating a world often indifferent to their needs. This heartfelt narrative serves as both a reminder of the challenges faced by marginalized communities and a testament to the transformative power of service and love. . . . A must-read for anyone seeking to understand, empathize, and advocate for the most marginalized among us."

—KRISTEN LOVELL, director of HBO's *The Stroll*

"The key to Carl Siciliano's candid, artful, soul-altering book, I think, is that it makes room for the reader. We are right there with him as he faces challenges such as few of us will have to face. We see what he sees, feel what he feels, believe what he believes—and are changed by the experience. I know I was."

—PAUL ELIE, author of *The Life You Save May Be Your Own*

"A gut-wrenchingly poignant real-life saga of how one gay man's radical commitment to the teachings of Christ sparked a sea change in how abandoned LGBTQ youth, most of them poor and of color, are treated and supported in New York City and beyond, *Making Room* is almost novel-like in its rich swirl of events and vibrant cast of characters who appear, disappear, and often, triumphantly, reemerge. Carl Siciliano has written an unputdownable account of what it looks like when compassion is harnessed to funding and policy."

—TIM MURPHY, author of *Christodora* and *Speech Team*

"*Making Room* demonstrates what it looks like to follow your vocation. Carl Siciliano recognized that LGBTQ youth were disproportionately homeless yet had fewer resources to assist them. Drawing on his calling to serve the 'least of these,' Siciliano found a way to provide housing, stability, and dignity for LGBTQ youth. May this book inspire others to recognize the unmet needs around them and find ways to creatively solve the problems that plague this world."

—Ross Murray, vice president of the GLAAD Media Institute

"From the trials of seeking safe shelter and the struggle for identity acceptance to the small victories in forming makeshift families and finding moments of joy, *Making Room* offers a raw, unfiltered look into the resilience and solidarity of queer youth against the backdrop of their greatest challenges. Siciliano explores the complexities of homelessness, the quest for love and understanding, and the undying hope for a brighter future through his personal accounts. *Making Room* is a call to action—a reminder that in the fight for inclusivity and equality, no one should be left behind."

—Emanuel Xavier, former homeless teen, author, and activist

"Homelessness is cruel and vile, and I am haunted by the fact that LGBTQ youth are still being displaced. When I read Carl Siciliano's extraordinary memoir, *Making Room,* I was reminded how one random act of kindness can change the life of someone who's been abandoned, discarded, beaten, dehumanized, and flung into poverty. I am honored to know that the Ali Forney Center is now in Harlem, and across NYC, showing compassion and empathy to many. . . . A must-read for all of us who survived homelessness and its atrocities!"

—Junior LaBeija, trailblazing, pioneering icon of the ballroom community and star of *Paris Is Burning*

"An absolutely beautiful and breathtaking book destined to be a classic . . . Before Siciliano founded the Ali Forney Center, New York City was a city of danger, violence, and despair for homeless LGBTQ youth—a place where killings and abuse were tragically common, and even supposed 'safe havens' were tainted by homophobia. This changed significantly with Siciliano's tireless efforts and advocacy: He didn't just provide shelter; he crafted sanctuaries where love and care were personalized. He didn't just provide direct services but also challenged the existing political structures by bringing the needs of those on the outside into the halls of decision-makers, demanding that they pay attention!"

—Fr. ADAM BUCKO, author of *Let Your Heartbreak Be Your Guide*

# MAKING ROOM

# MAKING ROOM

## THREE DECADES OF FIGHTING FOR BEDS, BELONGING, AND A SAFE PLACE FOR LGBTQ YOUTH

## CARL SICILIANO

CONVERGENT

*New York*

A Convergent Books Trade Paperback Original

Copyright © 2024 by Carl Siciliano

All rights reserved.

Published in the United States by Convergent Books,
an imprint of Random House, a division of Penguin Random House LLC,
New York.

CONVERGENT BOOKS is a registered trademark and the Convergent colophon
is a trademark of Penguin Random House LLC.

ISBN 978-0-593-44424-5
Ebook ISBN 978-0-593-44425-2

Printed in the United States of America on acid-free paper

convergentbooks.com

1st Printing

*Book design by Fritz Metsch*

*You weren't born to be forsaken*
*You were born to be loved.*
—LUCINDA WILLIAMS, "BORN TO BE LOVED"

# CONTENTS

# AUTHOR'S NOTE

Ali Forney was a pioneer in the struggle to break free from rigid, societally imposed gender roles. Their presentation veered fluidly between male and female, between Ali and his alter ego, "Luscious." Today I suppose Ali might have identified as nonbinary, but that term wasn't widely used at the time. Ali alternated between female and male pronouns to self-describe, often from one moment to the next, and I have done the same here out of respect. When quoting others discussing Ali, I have not changed the pronouns they used, which varied between "he," "she," and "they."

Throughout this book, I tell stories involving other young people I've worked with over the years. I have retained the names of those who authorized their stories to be shared, along with the names of those who have died. In all other cases, I have changed names and identifying information out of respect for their privacy.

MAKING ROOM

# FATHERS AND MOTHERS

*Can a mother forget the baby at her breast?*
*Can she fail to love the child of her womb?*
*Even these may forget, but I will not forget you.*
— *The Book of Isaiah*

*December 1997*

did not know if Ali's memorial service was about to descend into
chaos, but as I stood at the doorway to Saint Mary the Virgin
Church, it seemed entirely likely.

A biting wind swept through West Forty-sixth Street on that
overcast December afternoon. I had planned most of the service's
details with the rector, but I hadn't considered who would welcome
the hundred or so mourners as they arrived. Inkera and I scrambled
into place, two pillars standing at the threshold of the grand Gothic
church.

It made sense for the two of us to welcome mourners to Ali's
funeral. While it might have been more traditional for birth parents
to take on such a task, Ali's mother and father had not been a part of
his life for years. Inkera and Ali were the closest of friends; Ali had
confided to me that he considered her—a fellow client at SafeSpace,
our drop-in center for homeless youth—his "House Mother." And
it was Inkera who designated me the "father" of the drop-in center.
(Though the limits of such a description must be acknowledged,
for what sort of father goes home to a warm bed each night while
his children sleep in the street?) I'm sure the two of us bookend-
ing the doorway seemed like an odd pairing—Inkera a young, tall,

statuesque Black transgender woman, and myself a muscular, goa-teed, Italian gay man. But in our world of rejected youths, family was wherever you found it.

As the mourners arrived, Inkera and I greeted them with hand-shakes and hugs. However, when Ali's birth mother and younger sister ascended the stairway and I introduced them, Inkera reared back against the wooden door, eyes afire. This woman had wounded her dear friend. Badly.

"How dare you show up here? *You* don't belong here!" Inkera spat.

Ali's death two weeks earlier had devastated us at SafeSpace. His closest friends, like Inkera and Angie, were beside themselves with grief. Co-workers had been breaking down in tears or looking shell-shocked as they went about their tasks. And how did I feel? Well, I felt assaulted whenever the sun shone. How dare the world look bright when our hearts were buried in darkness?

I was desperate to avoid a repeat of the hostilities that had over-taken Kiki's funeral eight months before. At a service planned by her birth mother, our street family had been horrified to discover Kiki in an open casket, dressed as a man. Knowing all too well the sufferings Kiki had endured to honor her inner truth, I found it grotesque to see her identity erased in death. One of Kiki's social workers calmly asked why a man's suit had been placed upon the body of the fiercely proud young transgender woman. Kiki's mother erupted in rage, shouting that Satan had made her "son" believe she was a woman.

I had only just met Ali's mother. She and her daughter had arrived half an hour before the service, and I invited them to wait in my office next door. The woman standing before me seemed smaller and less formidable than I'd expected after hearing grueling stories of how she abused Ali as a child.

Peering into her eyes as we sat together quietly, I could not per-ceive villainy—only hurt, regret, shame. She seemed nervous, tenta-tive. She clearly felt out of place in this gay white man's office, at this strange organization where the child she had abandoned had been fed and cared for and loved. She must have noticed the photo I'd hung over my desk—an impromptu, grief-stricken shrine—of Ali in an ill-fitting wig, a playful, knowing look in her eyes, tongue curling suggestively out of the side of her mouth. Ali's mother did not recoil from the evidence that the part of her child she didn't understand was so openly celebrated here. Seeing her willingness to be with us despite her pain and discomfort, I reluctantly admired her courage.

Still, her very existence had been a revelation to us. For years, Ali had told us that both his parents were dead. Two weeks earlier, when my co-workers Kristin and Yola had gone to Harlem Hospital to identify Ali's body, they were prepared to see Ali's corpse laid under a sheet on a gurney. They were shocked to walk into the room and find his mother standing next to it—alive.

It was the only lie I ever knew Ali to tell. Many of the young people at SafeSpace tried to conceal their sex work and drug use, among other things, ashamed of the tools they needed to survive life on the streets. But not Ali. Ali was remarkably free of shame. The only secret he was too ashamed to confess was having a parent who left her child to suffer alone in the streets.

This book is about homeless queer youths. It's about the terrible harm done to them when our eyes, and policies, are blinded to their human value. It's about the love and protection that should be every child's birthright.

There are hundreds of thousands of unhoused LGBTQ teenagers in this country, making up about forty percent of all homeless young people. This crisis is a national and global epidemic. It transcends boundaries of country, race, and class, and I have come to see it as one of the most pervasive expressions of homophobia and transphobia in our lifetime.

Overwhelmingly, parental rejection is why an LGBTQ kid is

far more likely to experience homelessness than a straight one. It is a brutal thing for a teen to be deprived of the love and support of their parents. Not only does it jeopardize their access to food, housing, education, and medical care, it undermines a child's ability to believe themselves worthy of love. Our need for family is not easily extinguished. Yet, too often, the kids in our care have been met with eyes and hearts shut tight. Religious leaders frequently condemn LGBTQ people. Politicians often scapegoat us as embodiments of societal evil. Both messages foster environments where parents are more likely to view their queer children as shameful, and end up rejecting them.

One might hope that the LGBTQ-rights movement would have a long history of responding to the crisis. Sadly, this has not always been true. For decades after the Stonewall uprising, the plight of homeless queer youths went unseen by the organizations fighting for our community's rights. When Ali's death moved me to create an organization to house and protect young people like her, removing those collective blinders was among the most challenging tasks I faced.

I have dedicated my career to fighting for the protection of these kids. When I started this journey at age twenty-nine, I never imagined I'd end up founding a housing program that has served tens of thousands of homeless queer youths. It hasn't been easy, nor have all my decisions been perfect. But along the way, I grew close to many people—with one of my most transformative relationships being that with Ali Forney. Throughout her life and after her death, Ali became a kind of spiritual compass for me. In a world determined to shut her out, Ali lived with her heart wide open. As I sought to protect these youths and wrestled with my own fears and inadequacies, Ali's spirit was an incredible inspiration to press on. To honor Ali and our friendship, I named the organization in her honor: The Ali Forney Center.

This is by no means an all-encompassing narrative of Ali's life. Her story is hers and hers alone. But in these pages, I have shared the parts I was privileged to witness firsthand, or to hear from loved ones who knew Ali best. It is my hope that readers might come to understand something of the strength, beauty, and transformative power I saw in Ali.

Ali lived within the maelstrom of forces that made the lives of young queer people so treacherous. She contended with homophobic violence at home, in her neighborhood, and in the foster care and shelter systems. She lived through the AIDS pandemic and the wave of crack addiction that washed over New York City in the 1980s. She faced a storm of gentrification, hyper-policing, and mass incarceration in the 1990s, a time when America's Jim Crow policies morphed into pernicious new forms.

In writing this book, I am not attempting some clinical, dispassionate case study. This is not a scholarly examination of "sociological issues," but a personal account drawn from years of working alongside Ali and thousands of kids who endured similar circumstances. The story is not always linear. Instead, I have explored memories and lessons learned from four decades of working among homeless people, in the hope of unearthing deeper truths.

Ali and I came from different worlds. Yet despite the vast gulfs of our differing races, gender identities, and economic backgrounds, both of us experienced displacement and loss. Both of us were rejected by our parents. And we struggled to uphold deep spiritual values at a time when our religious traditions were hostile toward queer people. These losses and aspirations became a gravitational force that fused our two lives together.

Much of the hatred and opposition marshaled against queer people in our time stems from religious intolerance. Yet Ali and I each found strength in our faith. We believed that living an authentic spiritual life obligated us to defy the religious devaluation of queer people. Neither of us was inclined to impose our faith on others, and the Ali Forney Center is certainly not a religious organization. Nonetheless, we each discovered a proximity to the Divine precisely by asserting the precious, fundamental worth of our queer community and our queer selves.

In the end, this book is a love story. About the love Ali held for his friends in the streets. About the love Ali and I held for each other. And finally, about the radical change unleashed when a community challenges itself to embrace its most marginalized members.

The great author, educator, and social activist bell hooks wrote, "The light of love is always in us, no matter how cold the flame. It is always present, waiting for the spark to ignite, waiting for the heart to awaken." This book will show how, amid a vortex of abuse and brutality, Ali Forney bore witness to that essential truth.

# PART ONE

*Love and hope and sex and dreams*
*Are still surviving on the street.*

—THE ROLLING STONES, "SHATTERED"

# CHAPTER 1

# LIVES OF THE SAINTS

met Ali three years before he died, on November 30 of 1994. It was my first day as program director at SafeSpace, a recently opened daytime drop-in center for homeless teens that provided food, medical care, support groups, and a range of other essential services.

In the very early hours of that morning, Tupac Shakur had been shot five times in the lobby of a Times Square recording studio, only two and a half blocks from SafeSpace. Some of our clients who spent their nights out in the streets had witnessed the artist being carted into a wailing ambulance. During lunch, anxiety buzzed among the dozen dining room tables. *Would Tupac survive? Was Sean "Puffy" Combs behind the attack? Could it have been Biggie Smalls?*

I had determined to spend my first few days immersing myself in the program's activities and meeting the young people in its care. After lunch, I went downstairs to the large community room, where eight long tables were joined together in the shape of a Greek cross. I took my seat there, surrounded by a dozen kids ranging in age from their teens to early twenties, most of them Black and Latino, many decked out in bulky winter coats. I introduced myself and asked if they would speak to me about their experiences at SafeSpace. What did they like? What could we improve?

One young woman wasted no time in taking up my invitation. "This place sucks!" she said, her voice shrill and electric with anger. "The staff don't care. None of you care about us! You're all just here for a paycheck. You talk down to us, you won't lift a finger to help us. And the food *is shit*. You don't care! *None* of you care!"

I looked around the room and saw some of the young people squirming in discomfort. Not wanting to respond defensively, I forced myself to remain calm and asked the young woman her name.

"Tangie," she said.

"Tangie, I'm so sorry to hear you've had such negative experiences at SafeSpace," I said softly. "I'll see what I can do to make it better. But I'm curious, how long have you been coming here?"

"Since eleven-thirty."

"Eleven-thirty *today*?" I asked.

"Yeah, I came in for my intake just before lunch."

It was a few minutes past one o'clock. I didn't know what Tangie had experienced in the ninety minutes she'd been with us, but it was hardly enough time to make an accurate assessment of SafeSpace and the dedication of its staff. More likely, I was listening to the agony born of a lifetime of trauma.

By then, I'd spent twelve years serving homeless people in soup kitchens, shelters, and residential facilities. I had come to understand that entering their lives meant opening yourself to heartbreak, to people battered by poverty, abuse, mental illness, oppression, and the inevitable rage born of it all. It also meant looking past the surface and seeking to understand more of who they were. When I listened to Tangie without rebutting, it seemed to defuse her anger. She sat attentively as other youths talked about SafeSpace's medical care, food, showers, and laundry facilities. None were especially effusive, but they made it plain that we met some of their most urgent needs.

Afterward, reflecting on Tangie's eruption, I thought about how the hagiographies that led me to this work had not prepared me for its reality. As a teenager and a Catholic convert, I had immersed myself in the lives of the saints. Inspiration poured through me when I read of Saint Martin of Tours cutting off half his cloak to give to a naked beggar, or Saint Francis of Assisi physically embracing a rotting-fleshed leper. In both legends, after the saint gave aid, the person in need subsequently vanished, and the saint realized that they had actually been God. In real life, however, I quickly learned that people in distress rarely disappear for any good reason, and their needs are far too vast to be resolved with half a cloak or a hug.

Over the next month, Tangie returned to SafeSpace sporadically, until one day she vanished. She had gotten herself a boyfriend, though the word around the center was that she'd just been hooking up with him for a place to stay out of the cold. A couple days later, we heard from her friends that Tangie and her boyfriend had gotten into a huge argument. Tangie was dead. The boyfriend had killed her.

I learned little of her story in the month I knew her, but if Tangie's experiences were similar to those of other displaced youths, there's a good chance she would have been abused by parents struggling with poverty, addiction, mental illness, or all three. She might have been sexually assaulted while living in foster care. She could have been forced to do sex work to survive in a city that terrorized its homeless youth with its police force, whose primary offering of shelter was incarceration. In the end, her being killed was something else she shared with far too many of our clients. Tangie's death appalled me. How could someone sizzling with so much life force be extinguished so easily? But as I look back, I realize that Tangie was one of three young people I met that day who would go on to be murdered.

After my meeting in the community room, I went downstairs to sit in on the transgender support group. As I crossed the crowded lobby, Inkera, whom I hadn't yet met, loudly remarked that the new program director was "the sexiest white man alive, *except* for Jean-Claude Van Damme." My face grew hot. I continued on to the basement, wondering what I was getting myself into.

The group got off to a colorful start. Six transgender youths lined up along the opposite wall, and each took turns sashaying across the room like they were strutting down a runway. Whenever one of them reached me, they would strike an elegant pose and announce their chosen name—"Inkera," "Regine," "Kiki," "Coco"—before plopping themselves down in a metal folding chair.

The last young person was different. She wore masculine clothes and no makeup, though her head was crowned by a wig. As she walked the imaginary runway, her wrists and elbows bounced about, at once gangly and elegant, and her head swayed slowly back and forth. Pausing in front of me at the end of her walk, she fixed her gaze on me with a conspiratorial smile, like we were in on some cosmic joke. Then she introduced herself in a deep, melodious voice: "My name is Ali Forney."

When the flamboyant introductions were done, I asked the kids for their impressions of SafeSpace. "This is just about the only program in the city where we are treated with respect," said Coco. A few years older than the others, she seemed to have appointed herself the spokeswoman. The other young people nodded in agreement, and I was relieved to hear of their approval. "But the food sucks," Regine added. (She was correct about that. Later that week, our clearly inexperienced chef served up plates of undercooked, bloody chicken, and I realized he needed to be replaced.)

I'd come out of the closet eight years earlier and moved fluidly through many spaces of New York City's gay world, but had only met transgender people in passing. That this was my first deep encounter speaks to the segregation the LGB community imposed upon its "T" members, how back then they were still held at arm's length, like unwanted stepchildren. As I got to know our young transgender women, I also began to recognize how gay organizations back then often refused to include them in their advocacy.

There were persons in that room who would come to shatter my heart's constraints. They would greatly expand my understanding of what it means to be queer and of how to be an authentic human being. At that point, I had no idea how these kids would change my life.

One afternoon during my first weeks at SafeSpace, I was summoned to the case management office. Tyrone, a thin young man, was shaking uncontrollably and unable to respond to his case manager's questions. Afraid he might be having a seizure, we called for an ambulance. When the paramedics arrived, they recognized Tyrone was hyperventilating from a panic attack, gave him a paper bag, and instructed him to breathe into it slowly. Once he stopped shaking, he explained his situation.

Tyrone had been couch-surfing for six weeks at various friends' places, a common practice of teens when they first become homeless. Now he'd come to the dreaded day when no more couches would welcome him, and he was panicked at facing the night with nowhere to go. As Tyrone described his predicament, I was struck by the difference between his clothing and his demeanor. He was dressed in a baggy black sweatshirt and a tilted black baseball cap, projecting toughness like a member of the Wu-Tang Clan—yet he wore unmaskable terror on his face. As hard as he needed to appear to the outside world, his clothes couldn't disguise his painful vulnerability.

Tyrone's case manager made some calls and was able to locate a grandmother in Washington, D.C., who offered to take the young man in. I agreed to foot the bus fare, and one crisis that day was resolved.

But the vicious reality was that New York City failed to provide anywhere near enough shelter beds for its thousands of outcast youths. Many had grown up in foster care, but once they turned sixteen, the foster system didn't want them unless they were already grandfathered in. Young people over eighteen were permitted to sleep in the adult shelter system, but almost all our youths were fearful of the violence and abuse in those titanic warehouses. Most spent their nights trying to sleep on stiff park benches, at the bus terminal, or while riding the subway. At the end of each day, I would watch them leave SafeSpace to spend the night outside, unsheltered.

I learned quickly that the deprivations went even further. Our drop-in center was open Monday through Friday, from 11:00 A.M. through 7:00 P.M. On Mondays, we cooked a huge amount of food for lunch because many of the youths would return for three or four extra servings. In all of New York City, none of the drop-in programs for homeless kids stayed open past Friday. Our clients went hungry all weekend while SafeSpace was closed.

Family holidays were particularly depressing. A few weeks before Christmas, I discovered that we were the city's only drop-in program for teenagers that remained open for the 25th. Unable to bear the idea of our youths being left alone in the cold on these days of love and togetherness, my colleagues and I chose to keep the drop-in center open for half the day.

On Christmas morning, we rolled out all the festivities. We decorated the dining room with wreaths and garlands, colored lights and flowers, and two dozen volunteers came to help from the church next door. These keen, strange new faces lined up behind steaming pots and platters, serving up a feast of foods and cakes and pies, and freeing up the staff to sit and eat with the young people.

But the young people were uncharacteristically subdued, made shy by the many guests in the room. Most days, meals were boisterous affairs, with clients calling out across the tables, provoking endless bursts of laughter and verbal taunts. But now even Ali spoke in quieter tones, without much of her usual bawdiness or shade-throwing. Having witnessed this phenomenon at many holiday meals since, I've realized that their shyness is a function of adolescence. Teenagers place huge stock on how they are evaluated by others, and generally feel terribly self-conscious about being pitied. Homeless teens are no different. Being observed by a large crowd of unfamiliar faces made our young people acutely aware of their destitution. Whether welcoming volunteers into youth shelters is always a good idea remains an open question. Nonetheless, on my first Christmas at SafeSpace, I was glad the kids were indoors for a few more hours, eating their fill.

But it was awful when three o'clock arrived and we had to close the center. I marshaled everyone down to the lobby and watched Ali, Kiki, and all of the others make their way out of our warm building and into the snowy streets. Later, after I'd locked the doors, set the alarm, and walked to my mother's apartment on East Twenty-fourth Street, I couldn't shake the kids from my mind. We'd given them backpacks and gloves and hats and scarves as Christmas presents, and they stood there in the lobby, wrapping their necks and covering their heads and fingers. Then they made their way into the street, most with nowhere good to go, little tufts of their hot breath forming icy clouds as they shuffled outside into the frigid air.

We were caring for the violated children of Ronald Reagan's America. Our clients had grown up in the 1980s, when tax cuts yielded extravagant lifestyles for the rich and gutted the lifelines of the poor. Blue-collar jobs became harder and harder to find, but drugs were readily available. Meanwhile, gentrifiers descended upon once affordable urban neighborhoods, displacing poor families from their homes and pushing them into shelters. All their young lives, the teens in our care had been subject to avarice, governmental dysfunction, racism, violence, and chaos.

In those days, there was only one overnight facility for people under twenty-one in New York City: the notorious Covenant House. An enormous building that had been intended to house a New York State prison, it could be harrowing for *anyone,* and especially for queer youths, who made up a third of the young people in our care. Almost all of them were afraid to seek refuge at Covenant House. Others had braved it and returned with horror stories of being harassed and beaten for being "faggots."

Of all of them, the young transgender women faced the most difficulty in the city's shelters, though "difficulty" seems far too gentle a word. We saw numerous blackened eyes and busted lips, heard too many accounts of rapes. Even tasks as basic as applying for welfare, food stamps, and identification cards could be a nightmare for these women. Our case managers would accompany them to social services offices and report back that the city workers rarely restrained their hostility, insisting on addressing the transgender youths with male pronouns and refusing to use their female names. Often, kids would end up running from those offices humiliated and in tears, denied even the pittance offered to destitute people to stay alive.

And, dear God, the police. Once, when a fight broke out in our library and we couldn't subdue it, we had to call 911. A large white cop responded to the situation by snarling at one of the teens— a young Latina transgender woman—that she was a man, and threatening to throw her out the window by her "fucking ponytail" if she didn't shut up. When I filed a report with the Civilian Complaint Review Board, it was deemed "unfounded." What does it say when those who are supposed to "protect and serve" can threaten to murder you with impunity?

The threat of violence was ever-present. In the week before I arrived at SafeSpace, two transgender women, both clients of ours, were found drowned in the Hudson River near the Christopher Street piers. Tragically, this was not uncommon. During the prior three years, several transgender women had been found dead in the river nearby—among them Marsha P. Johnson, a heroine of the Stonewall riots. The police seemed to have little interest in investigating their murders. No one was ever held accountable for any of those women's deaths.

Given all these perils, many homeless transgender women had taken survival into their own hands: They constructed a shanty-town from scraps of wood and plastic and cardboard boxes on an abandoned pier reaching out into the Hudson River, just below the salt storage mounds on Thirteenth Street. George and Tisha, our outreach workers, went on foot to the shantytown each weeknight, bringing condoms, food, and clothing. I joined them one December night, a few weeks after my arrival, and was aghast to see people living in such desperate conditions, out in the cold, sandwiched between the roaring West Side Highway and the windswept Hudson.

Inkera was with us that night, helping with the outreach. I remember her laughing nervously after we left the pier. "I'm *never* going to let myself end up there," she insisted. But the reality was that many of our transgender clients deteriorated when they hit their mid to late twenties. After aging out of the youth programs, they found little available in the way of material support. Even their sex work became less lucrative as time and the hardships of home-lessness took their toll.

Often, they weren't even given the relative dignity of being ignored. Instead, they were treated as freakish objects of fascination and disgust. A 1995 *New York Times* article titled "The Shantytown of the He-Shes" focused completely on their sex work, addiction, and squalid living conditions. The reporter ridiculed their clothes and makeup while failing to mention the bigotry and hatred they faced daily, or their lack of equal access to services.

Before joining SafeSpace, I had thought of myself as an engaged, aware, progressive person. I'd been working with homeless adults in New York City for almost a decade, yet I'd been clueless to the vicious treatment the queer youths were dealt. It was distressing to realize how blind I'd been.

* * *

SafeSpace was located half a block east of Times Square, in a three-story mission house owned by the adjacent Saint Mary the Virgin Episcopal church. Affectionately known as "Smoky Mary's" because of its extravagant use of incense during the high services, the church had many gay men in its congregation, drawn by the campiness of the lush liturgical worship. Often, as we cared for our youths, the aroma of incense and sounds of the organ would wash over our walls.

Not that you needed an organ or incense to feel the presence of God at SafeSpace. You could sense it everywhere.

I perceived an aura of divinity among all our clients, but especially the young transgender women. I was in awe of their courage; of the price they were willing to pay to be faithful to the depths of their selves. Or, as I saw it, the depths of their souls. They were not exempt from the character flaws common to our humanity, but they seemed afire with a holy authenticity. In my readings of the lives of the saints, I'd been struck by the radical measures many had undertaken to honor the truths of their faith, renouncing family, money, social standing. The young women I found myself with were no less devoted to their inner truth; they likewise had given up everything. It was a privilege to be among them.

If there was anyone who most embodied for me the raw spirituality of SafeSpace, it was Ali Forney.

The first thing that struck me about Ali was how his relationship to gender diverged from that of other transgender youths at SafeSpace. His presentation veered fluidly between masculine and feminine, between Ali and his alter ego, "Luscious." Compared to her transgender friends, many of whom took hormones, presented consistently as female, and adhered to their identities as a matter of life and death, Ali's way of inhabiting gender seemed mischievous— like she delighted in transgressing expected roles, as though gender was some kaleidoscopic, ever-shifting venue for self-revelation.

Ali described himself as "a man in a dress and a wig." Typically, he spent the day at SafeSpace dressed as a boy and presenting as Ali. After dinner, though, he would descend to his basement locker and change into feminine clothes, wig, and makeup, like Clark Kent transforming into Superwoman. Then Luscious would come striding up the stairs in all her glory, exuberantly heading out to a night of sex work in the streets.

During my first week I noticed Ali filling his knapsack with great handfuls of the condoms we kept on hand for clients. I asked a co-worker what Ali could do with so many. "Ali is famous for that," was the response. "He cares so much about his friends on the stroll that he stuffs hundreds of condoms into that knapsack every day. He wants to protect them from HIV."

Around our building, I'd watch Ali chatting up our staff, joking playfully about their clothes and sexual prospects. A radiant smile would be plastered on her face, and she'd lean her head toward them, taking in what they said in a way that exuded joyful companionship. Many of the kids were far more guarded—they'd been hurt and failed so often by adults that it was difficult for them to trust us. Ali had been hurt no less severely, but there was something remarkable about her ability to be so generous with her affection.

Ali glowed with hints of divine compassion in these personal interactions, but it was at the first SafeSpace talent show that I truly felt like he took us all to church.

We held the first show in the spring of 1995, in an auditorium two blocks west of SafeSpace. For weeks the young people rehearsed their acts, the usual high-school conglomeration of sung performances, rapping, and spoken word recitations (though with a lot more drag and voguing than ever would have been seen in my suburban Connecticut high school). The evening was fun, exuberant, celebratory, lighthearted. Until Ali took the stage and unexpectedly guided us into more profound territory.

Ali closed the show with a gospel song, "His Eye Is on the Sparrow." He sang painfully off-key, but the performance was overwhelmingly heartfelt—his eyes closed, hands gesturing expressively, head turning slowly side to side as he crooned, "I sing because I'm happy, I sing because I'm free." He seemed to be summoning some deep part of himself.

Then Ali "caught the Ghost" and segued into a free-form sermon, no doubt inspired by the church services she'd attended as a child. With a miraculous combination of abandon and self-possession, she began preaching in a rhythmic half-chant:

> *I believe that one day, the Lord will come back to get me.*
> > *Hallelujah.*
> *If I live right, hallelujah, I will go on to that righteous place!*
> *I believe that one day, hallelujah, all my trials, all my*
> > *tribulations, they will all be over.*
> *I won't have to worry about crying and suffering no more.*
> *I won't have to worry about being disappointed, because my God,*
> > *hallelujah, is coming back for me.*

Ali strode back and forth with jaunty gravitas at the front of the stage, one hand occasionally slapping her leg or resting for a moment on her hip. Each line was punctuated by a bluesy chord on the electric organ. Every so often, Ali stopped walking and leaned toward the audience to emphasize a certain syllable, sometimes drawing it out, more song than speech.

> *Whether I'm a man with a dress and a wig,*
> *My God will love me for who I am!*
> *I might not walk like I'm supposed to walk. I might not have sex*
> > *with who I'm supposed to have sex with.*
> *My God will love me for who I am!*

Then Ali ripped her wig off, exposing short twists of hair.

*So don't worry about me, worry about yourself.*
*Because as long as my God believes in me, I'm not worried about*
  *what folks say.*
*Hallelujah.*

"My God will love me for who I am . . ." I had never witnessed such an adamant proclamation of God's affection for queer people. It hit me like sweet water pouring into a mouth parched with thirst. Watching Ali, I could hardly breathe. I felt awestruck, but also challenged as hell.

It was a time in my life when my own faith was fading, scarred by the Catholic Church's rejection of gay people. An insistent question burned inside me: How does one absorb profound rejection and loss without being buried alive under its weight?

Ali's eruption at the talent show gave me hope for an answer. Here was a kid who had faced more adversity, abuse, and rejection than I could imagine. Yet she had not been destroyed by it. She refused to be mired in bitterness. She was anchored in a love vast enough to make the hostilities and rejections that uprooted me seem insignificant as specks of dust.

I realized then that I was in the company of someone utterly remarkable. As Ali closed out her performance, I understood there was something unbreakable in her heart. What I had no clue of then was the power Ali's heart had to repair so much of what had been broken—in the lives of other exiled queer youths, and the world's response to them. And the power it had to transform some of what was broken in me.

# CHAPTER 2

# CATCHING THE GHOST

Years after Ali's death, I had the fortune of meeting Darrell, one of his younger brothers. Ali had never talked much about his upbringing, but I yearned to understand how he became able to proclaim his trust in God with such rapture and freedom. Darrell opened a window into the beginnings of an answer.

Ali's family attended the True Worship Church, Darrell said, right across the street from the housing project where they lived in East New York. I've seen online documents that identify the church as Southern Baptist and others designating it as Pentecostal. The family went to service every day. Darrell remembers the music—a choir backed by electric guitars, drums, and tambourines. But what he remembers most is people "catching the Ghost." During worship songs, some of the congregants would feel overwhelmingly connected to the Holy Ghost—another name for the presence of God—and begin jumping up and down, speaking in tongues, and writhing on the floor.

"I was just a little kid," Darrell said. "It scared me when people caught the Ghost. Sometimes they'd get hurt rolling around on the floor. It seemed like they weren't themselves, like they were possessed or something." Darrell wondered if the congregants were faking it, putting on a performance to appease pious eyes. "But then one day it happened to me. I felt a rush of excitement during a hymn, and the next thing I knew, I was laying on the floor."

"What's going on?" Darrell asked Bishop Keaton as the pastor lifted him from the ground.

"Son, you caught the Ghost!"

According to Darrell, Ali was the one in their family who caught the Ghost most frequently. It happened almost every day. Whenever Darrell asked about it, Ali would just smile and say, "It sure was a good service today!"

Having known countless homeless kids who grew up attending churches where they were taught that their queerness made them hateful to God, I asked Darrell how Ali's flamboyant femininity was received at the True Worship Church. To my surprise, he told me church was the one place Ali found acceptance.

"All were welcomed in God's house, welcomed without judgment," Darrell said. Ali felt safe there, embraced. "It was the people in the projects that didn't go to church who tormented my brother."

It made me happy to hear Darrell recount such positive memories of Ali's formative religious experiences—though I must admit to wondering if his memories might be idealized. The last time I heard from Ali's sister, she sent me an aggressively spirited email, alleging Ali had been possessed by the devil. I am not sure how to reconcile Darrell's account with hers.

What is irrefutable, though, is that Ali experienced something formative in that religious community. Ali's faith became a bedrock that she would cling to for the rest of her life.

I did not grow up in a religious home. Far from it. I cannot recall even stepping inside a church when I was a child, except to visit Notre Dame in Paris as a tourist. And while our area of affluent, suburban Connecticut was certainly home to many churches, it seemed that what people worshipped most was money. Our highest reverence was reserved for big colonial houses with manicured lawns, abundant acreage, and rambling stone walls, BMWs and Mercedes-Benzes proudly stationed in their garages. I doubt many caught the Ghost in Darien and Wilton, the towns where I lived as a teen. Ecstasies were more likely to be prompted by children accepted into Ivy League schools and stock portfolios that yielded abundant returns.

When I came to religion at the age of fifteen, it was on my own, suddenly and overpoweringly.

I was crossing a bridge near my home one April evening when, just a few feet from where I was walking, a Canadian goose flew straight into a passing car. The bird let out a brief scream before plunging into the river, presumably dead. I was shocked. I had never seen such a large creature die. I sprinted away down the street, completely freaked out.

After fifty or so yards, I stopped in front of a convent to catch my breath. On the street-facing wall was a mosaic, illuminated against the evening's darkness, of an Italian nun surrounded by impoverished children. I'd seen this mosaic a hundred times. My friends and I had even laughed at it—its campy, early twentieth-century immigrant Catholic aesthetic so jarringly different from the standard New England minimalist reserve. But tonight, something about the image drew me in. Out of nowhere, I felt like I was struck by a lightning bolt of consciousness. For maybe ten minutes, my eyes blazed open to a vision of every fragment of creation held in total love.

It is difficult to describe what happened. My consciousness seemed to detonate; my little, self-absorbed being opened to an immensity. Part of what makes describing it so challenging is that the aspect of my awareness that customarily stands outside of experience—evaluating, interrogating, describing to myself that which I am experiencing—seemed to have been suspended. I was utterly, completely inside the experience. The only moments in my life that begin to approach the loss of self-consciousness I fell into that evening have been during sexual encounters, when delight in my partners' lovemaking transported me to pure ecstasy. Or conversely, during some moments of extreme violence that occurred in my work in homeless shelters, when I was physically attacked and the raw terror of thinking I'd be killed overwhelmed any reflective ability.

Nor was the experience a "vision" in the sense that I saw anything other than the church wall before me. The best I can say is that I stood there, in front of that tacky mosaic, and it seemed as if everything—my heart beating hard within me, my pounding breaths, the soft blades of new spring grass on which I stood, the darkening sky above, the people driving past in their cars with beaming headlights—all of it opened out into this unfathomable depth. It was as if all my life I'd only seen the barest surface of things, and now my eyes could see an infinite dimension of truth buried within. And this seeing was rapturous, because I understood that everything around me and within me was somehow on fire with love. It was amazing, wondrous. But all I can do is stammer helplessly when trying to describe it. Putting words to something so vast feels like trying to stuff the sky into a box.

When the rapture ended after a few minutes, I was confused, disoriented, even terrified. I had no way of understanding what had just happened in my body and in my soul. In the aftermath, my conception of life's purpose was shattered. I could never again be satisfied with the selfish, materialistic values of my upper-middle-class upbringing. I would need to find a new way of being alive.

For months after that night, I was restless, desperate to reawaken to something I didn't know how to name. Then I read Thoreau's *Walden*, and something connected. He described a transcendence that I'd been yearning for, showed me how to begin to put words to my stammering. I began to explore spiritual paths with the excitement of a long-caged dog bounding through open fields. I learned to meditate. I studied Hinduism, Buddhism, and Taoism, seeking a way of reigniting what occurred that night in front of the mosaic. Initially, I didn't connect with Christianity, a faith that struck me as boring, stupid, and mainstream. To me, Christians were the oddly self-satisfied and judgmental people I saw singing lame songs and asking for money on Sunday morning TV. Then a friend gave me a small book on Christ's Sermon on the Mount, written by a Hindu monk. In the introduction, he described how a nineteenth-century Indian mystic, Sri Ramakrishna, was staring at an icon of the Madonna and Child one day when he heard, in the depths of his heart, *This is Jesus, who poured out his heart's blood for all of humanity. He is the embodiment of love.* As I continued reading that day, in a cubicle in my high school library, tears of wonder poured from my eyes and bliss pulsed down my spine. I found in the person and teachings of Jesus the deepest articulation of that radical, self-surrendering love I'd experienced during that first mystical rapture.

As soon as I finished that book, I ran to find a Bible and devoured the Gospels, the four books that narrate Jesus's life and teachings. What I encountered was revolutionary—nothing like the smug, bourgeois messages that previously shaped my impressions of Christianity. Jesus preached that the Kingdom of God was among us, not waiting somewhere in the clouds, and we could enter that kingdom now, by giving ourselves over to unconditional love toward everyone. We were to put aside money and status. We were to forgive, and to renounce violence. We were to live by faith and trust and prayer and mercy and justice. And if we did so purely, if we loved with our whole heart, we would see God.

In the following weeks, I immersed myself in religious texts, ravenous for examples of people who had wholeheartedly lived out Jesus's teachings. A wonderful discovery was Thomas Merton's autobiography, *The Seven Storey Mountain,* which I ploughed through in a single weekend, helpless to put the book down. Merton riveted me with his journey from being a dissipated, unbelieving Columbia University student in the 1930s to feeling called to give himself entirely to God. He joined a Trappist monastery in Kentucky, where he lived a life of silence, prayer, penance, and poverty more in keeping with medieval times than the twentieth century.

Merton opened new worlds for me. I learned of the mystical strain that ran through Catholicism's past, of monks and nuns and hermits and others who sought Christ passionately, and often led countercultural lives. Saint Francis especially thrilled me, with his dedication to living out Christ's teachings without compromise, his renunciation of wealth, his loving service and devotion to the most impoverished and persecuted individuals, and his responsiveness to the beauty of God's creation.

Likewise, I was dazzled by Saint Thérèse, who lived with a tremendous spiritual fire. A provincial French girl born in 1873, Thérèse had entered a convent when she was just fifteen—the same age as me—and died of tuberculosis at twenty-four. In her autobiography, *Story of a Soul*, she wrote that she desired a life of pure devotion: to love God, to place complete trust in God's love, to give every part of oneself to God. I felt a great sense of closeness, recognizing my own yearnings in the words of this nineteenth-century saint.

Thérèse wrote of a spiritual path she called her "Little Way." She strove to respond to everyone she encountered with as much love as she could. She believed that grace lay hidden, pregnant with potential, in every moment of our lives, and that we could uncover it by responding to others with love and tenderness. While she was a deeply committed Catholic, this access to the Sacred didn't rely on priests and religious structures. She believed that to access divinity, all we needed to do was unlock our hearts.

One year after the night of the goose, it was Holy Thursday, which in the Christian tradition is the night that commemorates Christ's suffering in the garden of Gethsemane before he was arrested and crucified. I sat beside a little gorge in the Norwalk River, about a mile from our home. Melting snow had filled the river with surging water, and I watched as the occasional wooden branch descended into the rapids and dashed violently against the rocks.

I was meditating on Jesus's self-surrender, the terror he felt as he consented to the shedding of his blood. I tried to consider what it would mean to surrender myself to love, letting go of the fears and desires that held me back from God. I imagined it would be like throwing myself into the waters, allowing the hard, egotistic shell of my being to be pummeled and battered. It sounds masochistic recounting it now, but the thought of such self-abandonment made my heart swell.

I began to spend countless hours in hidden spots in nearby forests, dedicating time to prayer and meditation. I also started volunteering at a group home for teens with physical and mental handicaps, helping to bathe kids who were unable to do so for themselves, reading them stories, and spoon-feeding them ice cream. Every Monday and Friday during my senior year, I'd cut out of school during the final class period and hitchhike ten miles to a neighboring town to serve people food at a local soup kitchen. I was eager to throw myself into any opportunity where I might practice and encounter the enormous love of God.

Then I discovered the Catholic Worker Movement. In the 1930s, the author and activist Dorothy Day gathered a group of people who were committed to following the most demanding of Christ's teachings about self-renunciation and sharing with the poor. At the height of the Great Depression, a half dozen of them chose to live in poverty in an East Village tenement and welcomed homeless people to live beside them as they offered resources, companionship, and care. At the time I read of Day, she had just died, but there were now more than thirty Catholic Worker communities around the country

CATCHING THE GHOST        31

where people continued to live out her vision of radical solidarity and aid to the dispossessed.

I was thrilled to discover people in my own time who were living like the saints I'd read about. I couldn't wait to leave suburban Connecticut behind. I graduated from high school half a year early and, on the day I turned eighteen, left home to join the Catholic Worker. For much of the next four years I lived in their shelters, first in Washington, D.C., and then in New York City.

At the Catholic Worker I came to understand that it was not enough to feed and shelter the destitute. Love had a political dimension as well, which meant finding ways to resist the economic and political systems that created such poverty. As catastrophic numbers of people became unhoused in the 1980s, we slept in the streets in protest and solidarity with our homeless friends. In 1983 we went high into the war-torn mountains of northern Nicaragua, to a town under siege by American-funded counterrevolutionaries, and helped dig trenches where the townspeople could hide from our nation's bullets. We protested against racism and had the remarkable honor of marching alongside John Lewis, Coretta Scott King, and Audre Lorde at the twentieth anniversary of the great March on Washington for civil rights. We took direct action against Ronald Reagan's escalation of the nuclear arms race, blocking entrances to facilities that developed the weapons. By the time I was twenty I'd been incarcerated three times for these acts, spending a month total in jails.

The sweet myth I'd been fed about America as I grew up— how it was the world's shining beacon of freedom and justice—was torn to shreds. Bringing food to people sleeping on heating vents yards from the White House; observing Nicaraguan children playing among ruins as they dodged the attacks of our president's paid assassins; hearing how some of my housemates had been scarred

and brutalized growing up in the Jim Crow South—these rev-
elations were excruciating. During times of prayer, I'd often feel
overwhelmed with sorrow and anger as I reflected on what my companions had endured. But paradoxically, it was an invigorating time
in my life. I would rather stand in painful truth than in comforting
delusion. Our life at the Catholic Worker seemed the most faithful
expression of Christ's teachings I could find. I was grateful to have
found a community that supported my quest to live a life guided
by love.

That period in the mid-eighties was a time when Ali and I each
seemed relatively secure: Ali with his family and the True Worship
Church, and me at the Catholic Worker. Yet the two of us soon discovered that we inhabited a terrible contradiction. Both of us were
wholehearted lovers of God, and both of us were queer.

The dozen years between the Stonewall uprising and the AIDS
pandemic were a time when queer people created oases of acceptance in neighborhoods like the West Village in New York and the
Castro in San Francisco. Now we were struggling to bring our freedom and truth beyond those ghettos—to our families, our schools,
our workplaces, our spiritual communities. When I think about
those who were out in the 1980s, like Ali and me, I consider us an
early flank of attack in the coming battle for queer equality. We were
among the first to openly place our queer selves, with all our naïve
hopes and vulnerabilities, into spaces where they might be rejected.
Our paradox was this: The very God whose name was used to per-
secute us was simultaneously the bedrock of our strength and hope
as we fought for survival.

CHAPTER 3

# FIDELITY

---------------

W hen Ali was three or four, his father died, and his family
moved from North Carolina to New York City. They
ended up in the notoriously dangerous Louis H. Pink
Houses, a large housing project in Brooklyn's East New York section.
Darrell, Ali's brother, described life in the Pink Houses to me with
a mix of frustration and fondness. The elevators were often broken,
the stairwells left unlit by a City Housing Authority that couldn't
be bothered to provide the most basic services for residents of the
eight-story building. Drug dealing was rampant, and shootings
frequent. It wasn't all bad, though—Darrell recalls a sense of community, with frequent cookouts, lively block parties, and residents
who looked out for one another.

Ali stood out. As he grew, it became clear that he didn't fit the
image of a typical boy. He liked playing with dolls and dressing up
in girls' clothing. "It is frustrating trying to hide something you have
to let out," he wrote in an essay when he was eighteen. "I tried for
years. But my mother knew something was there."

By age twelve, Ali began finding the courage to express her true
self. No longer willing to hide the femininity so intrinsic to her
being, Ali and her one openly gay friend would kiki and vogue and
carry on with their young queer selves in the courtyard in front of
their building. Ali paid for this effusive self-expression with a torrent
of bullying and abuse.

"Lots of people hate what they don't understand," Darrell said sorrowfully, "and they hated on Ali."

Ali was mocked and sometimes made into a human punching bag by toughs in the projects. One attack was especially harrowing. "Ali was coming home, walking down Linden Boulevard, when those assholes attacked him," Darrell recounted. "One of them grabbed Ali and pushed him out into the fast-moving traffic. My brother was run over by a delivery van that almost crushed his skull. They did it on purpose—they were trying to kill him. They came real close to succeeding." For the rest of her life Ali bore a deep dent in the side of her forehead, the mark of others' hatred stamped upon her face.

Ali's mother was unable to cope with the situation. I learned this from Ali's sister, Chaka, when we reconnected ten years after Ali's memorial service. She explained that their mother couldn't bear the violence Ali's queerness provoked. Parents rarely look for their children to be trailblazers, breaking through guardrails of social conformity—and there were certainly no guidebooks in 1987 to assist the mother of a queer twelve-year-old voguing in full view of the neighbors. We are hardwired to protect our children from a dangerous world. When her child was nearly murdered, it must have only reinforced Ali's mother's fear that queerness was an invitation to catastrophe.

Yet this protectiveness took a tragic form. Ali confided to several of his friends, as well as his therapist, that displays of femininity provoked his mother to become physically abusive toward him.

Chaka told me that their mother had named Ali in honor of Muhammad Ali, hoping her son would grow up to be a champion, a strong Black man. While Ali did not conform to society's idea of strength, I do see a clear connection between the teenager I knew and the icon who disrupted his career, risked arrest, and endured public vilification for refusing to fight in the Vietnam War. That is what made Muhammad Ali heroic: the courage to adhere to the truth burning in his heart. I could just picture Ali on his stoop, all long legs and booming voice. With no one in his corner and bullies all around, he stayed true to himself. Whether or not his mother could see it, Ali was a champion.

One afternoon when Ali was twelve, a social worker from the city's child welfare agency visited the family. Apparently, some officials had been monitoring the children's safety because of their mother's crack addiction. During the visit, one of his brothers grew restless and began to taunt Ali with a barrage of homophobic insults. After having contended with relentless abuse in the streets, Ali snapped. He wasn't about to endure that in his home. He slugged his brother in the face, right in front of the social worker. The brother ran into the kitchen and returned with a fork and knife, threatening to stab Ali in retaliation.

According to Darrell, that was the final straw. The social worker had the children removed from their mother's care and scattered the family, placing them in an assortment of foster care group homes. Ali was thrown to the mercy of a foster system that was a nightmare for most youths—and especially so for queer kids.

Ali soon ended up at Project Enter, a group home in Spanish Harlem. That was where he first met Angie, whom I knew later as another regular at SafeSpace and one of Ali's closest friends. Angie, a dark-haired Italian–Puerto Rican girl, was one of our most visible clients, with a loud, commanding presence whether she was participating in support groups or joking with her friends at meals. Years after Ali's death, Angie recalled how he'd shown up at the group home looking unkempt and uncared for, with matted hair. But then she doubled over in laughter, gagging at Ali's shadiness. "Carl, his mouth was *severe!*" Angie said. "I liked him from the start. I liked Ali's style and took him under my wing."

Ali only told Angie fleeting details about his life before they met. His father had been killed, but he didn't know how. He'd been put into a foster home after being removed from his mother's care, but ran away after being abused there.

Like me, Angie was struck from the start by Ali's depth of spirituality. During their early days together, Ali loved to sing gospel hymns, especially "His Eye Is on the Sparrow." "But whenever Ali sang those gospel songs he usually broke down in tears," she said. "Ali cried a lot in those days. Ali wanted to be loved. It hurt him really bad that his mother wouldn't love him. It was like he sang those songs to drive away the bad feelings."

It pained me to picture Ali crying so often back then. How lost she must have felt, how alone and desolate. The ensuing years of struggle must have toughened her; the only time I ever saw her cry was at a friend's memorial service.

Soon after landing at Project Enter, Ali started doing sex work in Harlem. I heard that after earning her first forty dollars, she felt rich. Maybe it was a way to have a sense of agency when so much of her life felt out of her control. Around this time, she began using crack, later confiding in an interview that the drug lessened "the fear and degradation of getting into strangers' cars."

When Ali told Angie what he was doing, she lectured him about the dangers of drugs and prostitution. He retorted, "Girl, I'm not telling you so you'll give me a speech. I'm confiding in you." Angie was livid at first, afraid Ali was making choices that could destroy him. But she came to understand that Ali was doing what he needed to cope with his situation.

Over the next several years Ali lived in more than a dozen group homes, repeatedly forced to flee because of homophobic violence. Once, when the other residents at a home had beaten and threatened to kill him, Ali barricaded himself in a room, afraid for his life.

For that "volatile behavior," he was sent to a state mental institution. I learned this from an Associated Press article published two years after his death.

Ali never mentioned the hospitalization to me. I suppose it was such a painful episode that Ali chose to keep it private, unwilling to revisit the most hellish parts of his life. We saw evidence of that adamant refusal to relive past traumas during a support group at SafeSpace. When the issue of sexual abuse came up, Ali exploded with uncharacteristic rage and would never again agree to participate in the group. To survive, it seemed, there were doors to his life that Ali needed to keep bolted shut.

By the age of sixteen, Ali had despaired of foster care and had nowhere else to live but the streets.

I first realized I was gay when I was thirteen. It wasn't hard to notice that only men's bodies excited me. This scared me to death. "Faggot" was ubiquitous as an insult back then, hurled constantly by boys at my school. And around the same time, my father forbade my siblings and me to watch the popular TV sitcom *Soap*, because it featured a gay character. (My father needn't have worried. Billy Crystal, who played the character, did nothing for me. The censorship would have been more on point if he'd banned me from watching heavyweight boxing matches.)

I didn't act on my desires; I was too afraid. My mother had left our family when I was a small child, and though I was hardly conscious of it then, the self-doubt I carried from that abandonment made the prospect of inviting more rejection seem intolerable. When I became absorbed in my spiritual quest two years later, I gained another convenient excuse for pushing my sexuality to the side. Many of the great mystical practitioners—not only in Christianity, but even in Hinduism and Buddhism—chose to be celibate, viewing sexual desire as an obstacle to the single-minded pursuit of union with the Divine. I eagerly sought to center my attention on God rather than on those men whose bodies I craved.

But one day when I was twenty, praying on my knees in a shrine to Saint Thérèse, a path out of the closet unexpectedly opened up. At the time I was living in South Norwalk, Connecticut, managing a soup kitchen and an overnight shelter. By then, I'd spent a year at the Catholic Worker in Washington, D.C., and six months living as a monk in a Benedictine monastery. All those endeavors had been engrossing, but I still felt restless, with a sense I hadn't found my deepest calling. I was praying for guidance; I wanted clarity on how I might best serve God, like I was a lost traveler staring confusedly at a tangle of roads, uncertain which would bring me to union with the Divine love.

As I prayed silently, my twenty-year-old conscience began to make demands that astounded me, demands I was terrified to obey. Inside my head was a voice saying I could not fully serve God until I was honest about my queerness. Nor could I stand with integrity among oppressed people if I hid the part of myself that was subject to oppression.

This summons to honesty greatly perplexed me. Catholicism had become central to my identity, and I assumed that wherever I found my lasting home, it would be in a Catholic environment. But the Church held homosexual acts to be sinful. And, more immediately concerning, some of the closest friends I'd made in the soup kitchen and the first Catholic Worker house were prone to making casual homophobic remarks—painting gay people as shallow, hedonistic, obsessed with sex, dirty. I was terrified that if I came out of the closet, I'd become a pariah to my friends. And I had no idea how to integrate this inner summons to honesty with life in the only spiritual home I'd ever known. But I couldn't ignore it. The call to truthfulness burned inside me.

While pondering my next steps, I picked up an issue of the *Catholic Worker* newspaper, published by the outpost in New York City where Dorothy Day had lived. Two of the articles detailed how some in the Catholic Worker community were grappling with the reality that many of its members were gay. They discussed how the organization's acts of solidarity, compassion, and justice for marginalized people might be extended toward the LGBTQ community. This fascinated me. Here were people who'd lived side by side with the woman who'd inspired me to join the church, working out a way to integrate queerness with serving God. I decided to spend a few months living there, hoping to find human road maps who might help me resolve my own struggle.

I moved into St. Joseph House in February of 1986, arriving one night as the community was finishing dinner. Gary Donatelli, a resident who'd lived there for a decade, was waiting to welcome me. Gary had almond-shaped brown eyes and short curly brown hair like lamb's wool. His right arm bore a tattoo of the Sacred Heart crowned with thorns and dripping blood. A devotional medal dangled from his pierced ear. I'd met him on previous visits and thought he was adorable, just about the coolest person I had ever met. He was also openly gay.

After giving me a plate of leftover food and sitting beside me in the emptying dining room, Gary surprised me by asking me my stance regarding homosexuality and the Catholic Church. Never having been questioned about this before, I didn't have a thought-out position.

"Well, I, I, believe in a God of love," I stammered. "The Church should teach us to love each other."

Gary said that he hoped the Catholic Worker would take a stand against the oppression of gay people. He spoke of this as an issue of raging controversy in the community, painting a more complicated picture than the articles that had drawn me there. (The next day, I met Peggy Scherer, the editor who published the two articles. She described that process of openly addressing gay issues as torturous, involving months of highly fraught meetings. "It was like crawling on my hands and knees through broken glass," she said.) The matter was especially pressing, Gary said, because it appeared a gay-rights bill was on the verge of being passed by the New York City Council. The new law would make it illegal for people to be fired from their jobs or denied housing for being gay.

To my distress, Gary indicated that the bill's most vocal opponent was the local bishop, Cardinal John O'Connor. He was using his powerful influence within the city to stir up opposition, even holding a press conference on the steps of St. Patrick's Cathedral, where he implied that queer folks were all pedophiles. He threatened to shut down every Catholic school and orphanage in New York City if forced to hire gay men.

"How dare he slander us like that?" Gary asked with fury. "As if being gay is the same as being a child molester!" Rolling his eyes, he added that if Cardinal O'Connor couldn't tolerate employing gay men, he would need to fire most of his priests.

The bill, combined with the wider hysteria around AIDS, had provoked a strong backlash around the city. Over the prior few months, Gary explained, there had been an upsurge in homophobic attacks. Some gay and lesbian people had even been murdered. "Cardinal O'Connor knows we are being gay-bashed, and yet he continues to vilify us." Gary told me he had even seen a wall of neon graffiti on the street with the message: KILL A FAG TODAY, CARDINAL O'CONNOR SAYS IT'S OK.

I was overwhelmed listening to Gary, as if the spiritual ground on which I'd been standing was suddenly crumbling under the force of his words. I blurted out something about how Dorothy

Day always spoke of the Church as being our mother, how we had to love it even when its leaders acted wrongly.

Gary paused, looked at me sorrowfully, and said something that would leave me speechless. "When a mother endangers and hurts her children, responsible people need to step in and get those children out of her care."

I had no way of knowing that I'd shown up in New York City just before the door was slammed shut on the Catholic Worker's exploration of tolerance toward gay people. Dorothy Day had been a radical figure within the faith, criticizing the Church for its wealth and accommodation of war-making, but she was never willing to question its sexual restrictions. In fact, her go-to response when challenged to address the persecution of queer people had always been to quote Saint Paul's admonition: "Let such things not so much as be mentioned among you." Six years after her death, some leaders in the community were horrified that her mandate of silence was now being challenged. They issued a decree that no leader of the Catholic Worker would be permitted to publicly question any Church teachings. And that was that.

The Catholic Worker was extraordinary in so many ways. It was the cradle of progressive American Catholicism. Its members had spent decades forging an ethos of living in solidarity with our society's most disenfranchised members. That's what made the leaders' refusal to challenge homophobia so heartbreaking. It was crushing to see such good people act so close-minded and cruel, as if LGBTQ people were somehow uniquely unworthy of the love and care extended to everyone else. Or more like we were only worthy of love if we kept ourselves in the closet and buried our truth in silence. Almost everyone pushing for openness and acceptance departed after the homophobic edict—as would I, after hanging on for another year.

That year, rejection of queer people swept across the Catholic Church like a windstorm. In October of 1986, Cardinal Joseph Ratzinger, later to become Pope Benedict XVI, issued a public church document that proclaimed homosexuality to be "an intrinsic inclination towards evil." He demanded that Catholic institutions cut ties with groups that affirmed the worth and value of gay people. I belonged to such a group—Dignity—which held masses for LGBT Catholics at Saint Francis Xavier Church in Chelsea. Every Saturday evening, Gary and I would go with a group of our friends to attend the night service. But in the wake of Cardinal Ratzinger's edict, Cardinal O'Connor ordered the pastor of Francis Xavier to stop allowing Dignity to hold services there.

The final Dignity Mass at Francis Xavier was excruciating. On March 7, 1987, a thousand people packed the pews of the cavernous baroque church. Echoes of weeping reverberated through the space as a dozen or so priests stood together at the altar, concelebrating the Mass. Afterward, we somberly marched out of Saint Francis Xavier, led by a man carrying a large cross, through the streets of Chelsea toward the LGBTQ Center, where future Dignity Masses would have to be celebrated. At the time, many queer people who attended the Dignity Masses were dying of AIDS. I'll never forget the sight of one who was obviously sick—his emaciated frame already feeble despite his youth, his skin disfigured by lesions—slowly descending the steps of the church and making his way into the dark winter night. He was so weak that he needed to lean into his boyfriend's shoulder to remain upright. Both were shedding tears. In their hour of desperate need their church had kicked them to the curb. I realized I was looking upon something truly evil. All these years later, the memory of that vision hurts so much that I wish I could rip it from my brain.

It was against this backdrop that I was finally compelled to come out of the closet, while still living at St. Joseph House. Gary was the first person I told. To my surprise and delight, he soon began to pursue me, and we fell in love. So, in one sense it was a truly joyous time. Being free to be honest and open was a wondrous liberation. After years of lonely deprivation, I was amazed at the delight of being able to lie naked beside a man and love him.

But on another level, that season of life felt crushing. I'd come to the Church seeking a community of love, looking for support as I sought to immerse myself in the boundless love I'd encountered in God. For a time, those hopes seemed to have been realized. But then I discovered the Church had built a wall of barbed wire around its collective heart—intent on keeping honest, openly queer people outside of its sanctuary. I'd go to Mass only to find myself ravaged with grief.

One morning in 1989 I headed for a subway station to get myself to a service, like I always did. But I stood there for what felt like ages, as one train after another came and left. I just couldn't do it anymore. I couldn't endure one more inner battle in the pews, feeling all twisted with rage and sorrow while trying to commune with God. Something inside of me had died, some ability to place trust in the Church, to see it as my home. And so, I became spiritually homeless. The disappointment lodged inside me and remained for years—a stubborn bruise on my soul.

Ali and I bared our queer selves before the snarling guard dogs of heteronormativity. Some of those guards were decked out in bucket hats and PRO-Keds sneakers, others clad in Roman collars and mitres—but while their uniforms and modes of attack may have differed, the underlying rage against us was the same.

Despite the obvious gulfs in our racial and material privilege, I'm struck by the commonalities Ali and I shared during that fateful year in the eighties, long before we met. We were two queer youths, one on the cusp of adolescence, the other just embarking upon adulthood; each unmoored by emotional loss and spiritual exile; each wondering how our broken hearts might be mended.

I think of that year of 1986 into 1987 as the moment our paths turned toward each other. Our respective displacements—I from the Church, Ali from his family—set us on a course that would see our lives converge.

# CHAPTER 4

# FAILURES

One cold February day, a few months after my arrival at SafeSpace, a new client came to us. Tim was a very feminine, plumpish, seventeen-year-old white boy with shoulder-length blond hair. He was also HIV-positive. His case manager, Andi, was afraid of him sleeping outside, as, with his weakened immune system, the winter cold could be life-threatening. She referred him to Covenant House for shelter, reluctantly disregarding her trepidation about the place.

Tim returned the next morning deeply shaken, insisting to Andi that he would never go back there. He'd rather sleep on the subway, in the Port Authority Bus Terminal, in the streets. *Anywhere* but Covenant House.

Later, Andi showed up in my office weeping.

"Carl, listen to what they did to him," she said, her outrage apparent through her tears. "They put Tim in a dorm room with fourteen guys. After he fell asleep, the others gathered around his bed and *urinated* on him because they didn't want to share their room with a gay boy."

"Oh my God," I muttered. I, too, found myself fighting back tears.

Our case managers had already heard a litany of outrages regarding Covenant House. Queer and transgender teens were routinely harassed and brutalized. Their staff frequently looked away from these gay bashings, or blamed the victims for provoking the attacks by failing to disguise their femininity. Priests and nuns at the facility humiliated them, proclaiming that being gay or gender nonconforming was against the will of God. The staff tended to give inordinately long punishments, banning kids for months for relatively minor infractions, such as talking back to staff.

At lunch that day I saw Tim sitting alone at a table, his hair dangling over his face. He'd washed himself off in our shower, and Andi had gotten him new clothes. Still, his shoulders were slumped over his food, and he seemed obviously depressed. I went to sit beside him. "I'm so sorry about what happened to you," I said. "You didn't deserve that. *Nobody* deserves that."

"I don't want to talk about it," he said, his eyes fixed on his plate.

Working with destitute people, you confront layer upon layer of failure. The systems that perpetuate their poverty are cruel and overwhelming. The resources for alleviating their suffering are often inadequate; the authorities charged with protecting them are sometimes shortsighted and, in the worst cases, corrupt. If you have any commitment to inner honesty, you will also be forced to look frankly at yourself—at the collusions and failures inherent in your own work—and how the structural responses you participate in are inevitably imperfect, how your personal limitations become apparent when confronted with limitless need.

SafeSpace was a daytime drop-in center, open Monday through Friday. We served lunch and dinner, provided showers and laundry, had a medical clinic and mental health services, conducted street outreach, and hosted multiple HIV education and prevention programs. But we shut down each night at seven o'clock. We didn't provide our youths with the resource they needed most: housing.

Those of us in the little youth service world tended to regard Covenant House as the evil empire, a vast immovable force. When we heard accounts of violence and abuse there,* we filed them into our overflowing mental folders, angered but helpless to change the situation. It was the only emergency shelter for homeless youth in all of New York City. Queer kids had to endure such degradation there, but where else were they supposed to go?

I couldn't file away what happened to Tim. Though I doubted I could change anything, I felt, at the very least, that what he'd suffered there demanded an expression of outrage. I called Covenant House and requested a meeting to discuss Tim's ordeal.

A few days later I made my way to their shelter, walking through the streets of Hell's Kitchen with its low-rise tenements, until I reached Tenth Avenue and Forty-first Street. The area felt like a no-man's-land of old warehouses and heavily trafficked roads leading to the Lincoln Tunnel. How different the environment felt from the Catholic Worker houses where I'd worked among the homeless—which, though located in poor neighborhoods in Washington, D.C., and New York City, were in actual *neighborhoods*, with children playing on the sidewalks and neighbors we could befriend. Here I felt like I was on the outskirts of the city, a place meant only for people to pass through in their cars, a zone of exit.

The feeling of desolation magnified when I walked up to Covenant House itself: a forbidding narrow courtyard edged by high concrete walls, fronted by a security stand. I had to be cleared by uniformed guards to enter the hulking facility.

---

*It is not possible to comprehend the peril faced by Ali and the rest of NYC's homeless queer youths around the turn of the millennium without recognizing the violence and abuse they were subjected to in the city's only youth shelter. However, it bears noting that all the incidents of anti-queer abuse I report here occurred between 1995 and 2003. In recent years Covenant House NY has made significant strides in becoming more protective of LGBTQ youths, and I applaud those efforts.

I'd steeled myself for a combative meeting, but to my surprise, I found myself thoroughly disarmed by the woman who welcomed me—a middle-aged Black woman with a gentle, thoughtful manner. She'd worked at Covenant House for more than a decade and held a senior position. She seemed uneasy as she greeted me, but rather than denying queer youths faced abuse there, or growing defensive, which I'd expected, she admitted that some of their staff struggled to accept LGBTQ youth and did a poor job of protecting them. She thought it stemmed from Covenant House's infamous founder, Father Bruce Ritter. Five years earlier he had resigned in a massive public scandal when several young men came forward alleging Ritter had sexually abused them.

"Father Ritter never wanted obviously gay, feminine boys or transgender girls anywhere near him," she confided. "He was in the closet, and it was obvious they made him nervous. The only gay boys he could deal with were those who passed as straight. And, as for transgender girls, he couldn't stand them. From the very start, Father's fears set the tone at Covenant House."

She was clearly distraught about what happened to Tim. She asked if I would assist her in organizing a day of training to help the Covenant House staff better understand the needs of gay youths. This was far more than I'd hoped for, and I eagerly agreed to her request.

Walking back to SafeSpace, I started thinking about the moral complexities that were so often involved in caring for the poor. Many times, I've come across good, warmhearted people who were trying to do their best within corrosive structures. There is a real ambiguity in deciding whether we can align our efforts with a flawed organization. Can we stay and make a change for the better? Or must we walk away, washing the dirt from our feet and resolving to build something new?

For the training day at Covenant House, I recruited Rosalyne Blumenstein, a transgender woman who ran the Gender Identity

Project at the LGBTQ Center. I also invited Maggie Brennan, the director of the AIDS and Adolescents Network of New York. A few weeks later we sat in a huge upper-floor meeting room speaking to more than a hundred people affiliated with Covenant House. The wall of windows to our right offered a soaring view of the Hudson River and New Jersey, its beauty matching my hopes for what we could accomplish at this training. As we spoke, some in the audience leaned intently toward us, listening with sensitivity. But you couldn't miss the closed resistance among others in the room. Arms were crossed tightly. Expressions of anger, even disgust, were littered across the chairs.

At one point I was explaining that queer youth were doubly exiled—driven from their homes by unsupportive families and driven from shelters by violence and bigotry. I stressed how important it was for employees to set an example of acceptance and nonjudgment, and urged them to prioritize hiring openly LGBTQ staff.

There were a handful of priests in the room, dressed in black suits and Roman collars. As I spoke, one became increasingly red-faced and agitated. It wasn't long before he interrupted me.

"With all this talk of acceptance and nonjudgment, what you are really telling us is to ignore sin!" he bellowed. "You're even telling us to endorse it!"

I had a sick feeling in my chest as I listened to him. I forced myself to respond calmly.

"Father, Jesus did not teach us to respond to the hunger and homelessness of the poor with moral theology sessions. He taught us to feed and shelter them. These kids are not coming to you for instruction in church teaching. They're coming in desperate need of someplace safe to sleep at night. *Please* don't make them targets or drive them away by casting judgment."

His face turned even redder. The priest clearly didn't relish being reminded of Christ's teachings by a faggot.

After the training, I continued hearing horror stories. One gay boy came to SafeSpace and reported that he was made to sleep on the floor by his dormmates. "Faggots don't get to sleep on beds," they said. A transgender girl spoke of being placed in a boys' dorm, where a roommate wrapped batteries in a sock and used it as a weapon to bash her in the head. Another transgender girl said she was sexually assaulted in a boys' dorm, her screams for help ignored by staff. Overwhelmingly, our LGBTQ youths continued to be too afraid to seek shelter there.

Around that time, I read a recently published book, *Broken Covenant* by Charles M. Sennott, the reporter who broke the first story about Father Ritter's sexual abuse for the *New York Post*. The book detailed Covenant House's history of defying best practices for homeless youth residential settings. At the federal level, the Runaway and Homeless Youth Act called for homeless youth to be housed in small, homelike settings with no more than twenty beds per site—a reaction to abuse scandals in large institutional youth facilities. Researchers found that youth were safer and treated with far more dignity in smaller facilities. They also achieved substantially better outcomes.

Father Ritter had no interest in such a humble model. His ambitions were those of an empire builder. He assembled a mailing list with millions of donors and pitched them aggressively for funds. He told stories of blond Midwestern boys, usually thirteen or fourteen years old, who sought care at Covenant House. After being kicked out of their homes, they had journeyed to the Port Authority Bus Terminal, only to be set upon by homosexual pimps who forced them into lives of immorality. That is, until they were delivered to the safety of Covenant House and restored to the path of righteousness. By then, Congress had shifted its support to smaller shelters that were opening across the country. But Ritter's massive fundraising operation enabled him to forgo the federal funding, along with its restrictions and guidelines. He began opening enormous warehouse shelters in major cities, even extending into Canada and Central America.

Other homeless youth providers were alarmed by Covenant House's facilities, seeing them as a degradation of widely accepted standards of care. Their concerns only escalated as they began hearing reports of violence from young people.

Father Pat Moloney, a priest who operated a ten-bed shelter in the East Village in the eighties, was quoted speaking to those reports in Sennott's book. "[Covenant House] was a monster," he said, "Kids in the New York program were getting beaten up and raped inside there." Providers testified at hearings, seeking to prevent their cities from allowing these warehouses. But unfortunately, Covenant House, with its massive war chest, became branded as *the* response to homeless youth. Whenever Ritter opened a location in a new city, it was like when a Walmart opens in a rural town. Smaller programs would struggle to raise funds and invariably go out of business, further cementing Ritter's dominance.

By the early nineties, all of New York City's smaller youth shelters had closed, unable to compete. The city and state, embarrassed that the nation's largest municipality was left without a licensed youth shelter, gave Covenant House a waiver, allowing it to receive a license and government funds despite its operation of a warehouse shelter. Thus, when I arrived at SafeSpace, Covenant House was the only emergency shelter option for the young people in our care. Which, in practice, meant most of our clients had no place to go. Meanwhile, the horrors of the night—the damage done by johns, police, drugs, sickness—undid any good we created in our daytime center. The most fundamental need of any homeless person is housing—a need SafeSpace failed to address. Because of that failure, we were often helpless to alleviate young people's suffering or prevent their lives from deteriorating.

Several months after my arrival, I went to my supervisor and insisted that we had to find a way to provide a protected space for these kids to sleep. He was supportive, but I was low on the totem pole of power, and he said I needed to persuade a chain of higher-ups at our parent organization, the Center for Children and Families. I pressed on, and my efforts made it to the deputy executive director, a rather cold and haughty man. Sitting across from him in his fancy Soho office, with windows looking down upon the luxurious penthouse apartment belonging to David Bowie and Iman, I started to explain how imperiled our young people were in the streets at night. He cut me off midsentence.

"We hired you to manage SafeSpace as it is," he said with curt finality, "not to tell us how we ought to change it. You need to stay in your lane."

I left his office with my hopes deflated.

I look back on that day with shame. It's easy for me to indict the city, or Covenant House, or even my own superiors for their failings. But I *knew* our kids needed safe housing and suffered terribly from its absence. I should have fought for them. Instead, I backed down and spent the next two years focusing on raising funds to stay open on the weekend. At least that way the young people wouldn't starve between Friday nights and Monday mornings. All the while, I told myself that if I was too adamant, too demanding, I'd get fired and be replaced by someone less willing to advocate for young people's needs. How would that help anyone?

It's so easy to find justifications for our failings. But I know this to be true: The kids needed someone who would fight for them, someone who wouldn't back down from the truth. On that humiliating day, I was not that person.

# CHAPTER 5

# ATTENTION AND GENEROSITY

A t SafeSpace we trained some of our young people to be peer outreach workers for other homeless kids. We found that youths in the streets were more willing to have frank discussions about their sexual practices with kids like them than with adults. The peer workers helped our staff distribute condoms, dental dams, and brochures on safe sex. Inkera and Ali did outreach together on many occasions. As I'm sure you can imagine, they made for quite a pair.

Inkera told me she could still picture Ali's outrageous appearance. "He'd have a wig, a three-day growth of beard, feet not done, open-toe shoes. I loved that about Ali. He didn't give a fuck. You had to take him as he was."

Of course, Inkera also remembers Ali gagging at her own fashion choices. "He'd be, like, 'Bitch, *who* does street outreach in heels? Not just heels, *STILETTOS!*'"

But don't let the outrageousness fool you. Ali was a warrior against AIDS, both in his efforts to protect other homeless youth from the disease and in his insistence on remaining HIV-negative himself. He was always begging his friends to use condoms, and unfailingly used them himself, even when johns offered more money to relax that rule. I can still hear Ali's squeals of joy that would reverberate through the halls of SafeSpace every six months, when he got the results of his HIV tests. He would bound up and down the stairs and into the offices of all his favorite staff, waving the results in our faces, crying out, "I'm still negative! I'm still negative!" It was no small accomplishment. Statistically, crack addiction and nightly sex work ought to have condemned Ali to AIDS, but he was determined to avoid infection and ensure that his friends did the same.

Ali's enthusiasm struck me as an act of resistance. He was asserting his precious value in the face of a society that wrote him off as utterly disposable.

AIDS loomed over us at SafeSpace, as inescapable as the enormous, illuminated advertisements towering over Times Square. In the nineties, studies began to show that homeless youths were one of the subpopulations in which HIV was spreading most rapidly. Much of our funding was AIDS-related, from the CDC program that funded our HIV prevention efforts to a federal contract for providing medical and mental health treatment to HIV-positive youth. Without those infusions, it's unlikely SafeSpace would have even existed, so paltry was the availability of any other funding for New York City's homeless youth.

Most of these government funds were dedicated to basic interventions; in particular, giving out condoms and information about safer sex. One of our outreach workers complained that kids doing survival sex would be approached multiple times a night by folks giving them condoms and pamphlets. "The city will give each kid ten thousand condoms," he said, "but won't give them a bed." This strategy was grossly ineffective. Having nowhere to stay at night was the desperate engine that drove our young people's risky behaviors. When you have nowhere to go, and a john will give you more money to have sex without a condom, that extra twenty dollars could be the difference between sleeping in a cheap hotel or curling up on the street. Twenty dollars was the difference between getting a fix that night or suffering through the agonies of withdrawal. Twenty dollars was the difference between being able to take the hormones that integrated your outer being with your inner self or losing agency over your body. These were their stark choices. Few street kids passed on the extra cash.

While at any given time several dozen of the youths at SafeSpace were HIV-positive, most were asymptomatic, having been infected too recently to have developed full-blown AIDS. However, there was a young woman who came to us obviously very ill: weak, exhausted, struggling to breathe. Her awful living conditions exemplified the public health disaster of the government's failure to provide homeless youth with housing.

Monica, a straight Black girl, had been unhoused for years. Forced into sex work to survive, the teen fell prey to pimps who got her addicted to crack and eventually infected with HIV. By the time Monica came to SafeSpace, her addiction was out of control, and she was nearing death. John Nelson, our nurse practitioner, and Cheri Hamm, our HIV services coordinator, worked closely with her, trying to keep her as safe and healthy as possible. But Monica would often vanish for days at a time, slipping back to crack houses where she would trade sex for drugs. During those binges, she failed to take her AIDS medications. John and Cheri were close to despair, watching helplessly as Monica grew sicker and sicker, her T cells plummeting and infections spreading like wildfire.

Walking through the center, I would look over and see Monica collapsed on a bench in our lobby, too weak to make it up the stairs to the medical office. The full weight of the world seemed to be pressing down upon her ravaged little body. It was just awful. And then, when it was time to close the building, I'd see her stumble out to the streets. I wanted to scream, *"How can this be happening? How can we allow this?"*

"Attention is the rarest and purest form of generosity," wrote Simone Weil, the French social activist and philosopher. If we are to give authentic attention to someone who suffers, we are obligated to interrogate the causes of their suffering and seek to remedy them.

The unhoused kids who came to us for help had been overwhelmingly denied such attention by our city. But thankfully, that wasn't the entire story. Against this backdrop of callous neglect, our young people and staff were capable of being remarkably attentive to one another as our community navigated the heartbreaks brought on by AIDS. In my eyes, those acts of care and kindness, and the heroism they brought forth, were at the heart of SafeSpace's ethos during those final years of the pandemic's most deadly period.

SafeSpace regularly conducted HIV testing. It was important for our young people to know if they were infected, so they could take proper care of their health and, hopefully, protect their sex partners. But we were always concerned when a test came back positive. AIDS was seen as a certain death sentence, and for many of our youths, the realm of sex was one of the few places in their lives where they found pleasure and joy. They bragged with delight about their conquests, and it was impossible to miss the efforts they put into looking fly and desirable, as if it was one of the few things they could count on to make them feel wanted. A positive result put all of this at risk.

Inkera was the first client of SafeSpace to receive a positive HIV diagnosis after I began working there.

"I was worried that whole day," she recently told me. "Finally the nurse and my case manager called me into the medical office and told me my test results. They told me what they could do to help me stay healthy." At first, Inkera handled the news OK. But then the adults asked how she planned on telling her boyfriend, Twin.

"That's when I lost it," Inkera remembers. "I knew that my relationship was over. I was going to die alone. I cried and cried and cried some more. They wouldn't let me out of the office until I stopped crying.

"And Ali was the first person it fell out of my mouth to tell I was

positive. He knew I was getting my results and was waiting for me."
Ali held Inkera and told her she was going to be OK. "But all I could
think of was Twin. I knew that man was going to leave me. Twin was
going to *fucking leave me*! I had AIDS, and I was going *down*, alone."

But Ali kept telling her she was going to be OK. "Twin loves
you," he said. "He's not going to leave you."

When Twin showed up later, Inkera took him outside and broke
the news. Twin didn't abandon her. Instead, hoping to cheer her up
and prove his love, he took her shopping at Macy's. He knew the
way to his woman's heart. Inkera returned to us calmed and hopeful.

"Ali was there for me that day," Inkera says. "That was my sister
brother! He was always there for me. *Always.*"

The staff member who was most attentive to the needs of our HIV-
positive clients was Cheri Hamm. She led our HIV prevention
education classes and worked one-on-one with young people who
were HIV-positive, making sure they took their meds and counseling them through their terrors. Though she was in her mid-thirties,
Cheri had a disarmingly childlike spirit and an unguarded vulnerability that stirred in me a tremendous urge to protect her.

The thing is, Cheri *knew* terror. Cheri herself had AIDS. And
of the dozens of people I knew with the disease, she was by far the
most obviously petrified of what lay ahead.

One afternoon during an orientation visit a few weeks before
my start date, Cheri grabbed my arm in the hallway and pulled me
into an office. She collapsed against my chest, completely dissolving in tears.

"Oh my God, Cheri," I said. "What's wrong?"

Tears pouring from her eyes, she gulped for air between her
heaving sobs: "Pedro died."

As Cheri continued to press her weeping body against mine,
I wondered who this Pedro was. I thought he might be one of

SafeSpace's clients. "I'm so sorry, Cheri," I said. "I'm not sure who Pedro is."

"Pedro Zamora!" she wailed, shaking and clinging to my arm.

Pedro Zamora was the handsome young man who'd captivated millions of people as he openly struggled with AIDS while starring as a castmate on MTV's *The Real World.* For people untouched by the disease, Pedro's weekly fight for survival made AIDS relatable in a way it had never been before. Cheri identified with Pedro. Like him, she was a person of color working as an HIV educator, and like him, she was battling the wretched illness. Cheri saw in Pedro's death a preview of her own.

Fearing judgment and rejection, Cheri only told a handful of her most trusted co-workers that she was sick. Despite the fact that several other staff were openly HIV-positive and fully accepted, Cheri was frozen with fear that someone might look down upon her. I never saw any glaring signals of Cheri's illness: no obvious weight loss, no lesions, no coughing. To uninformed eyes, she appeared fine. Just the occasional sick days taken—perhaps with increasing frequency, but even then, not usually longer than a day or two.

Finally, a year after Pedro's death, a day I'd dreaded arrived. Cheri walked into my office and, through tears, told me that she would be resigning from SafeSpace. "Carl, I'm getting sicker. I won't be able to hide it much longer. It would scare the HIV-positive kids to death to see me deteriorate." So Cheri decided she would tell her co-workers why she was leaving us on her final day at SafeSpace, at our weekly all-staff meeting.

I remember sitting in the large community room with the rest of our staff, waiting for Cheri to arrive. I was feeling a bit agitated, my knees jumping nervously beneath the table. Just before we were scheduled to start, Andi arrived and whispered into my ear, "Carl, Cheri is up in the kitchen, bawling her eyes out. She says she needs to talk to you. Please, can you come help?"

Upstairs, two caseworkers were huddled around Cheri, trying to support her. She stood between them in front of the industrial-size refrigerators, weeping inconsolably. When she saw me arrive, Cheri ran and buried herself in my arms.

"I can't do it, Carl," she sobbed. "I can't tell them I have AIDS."

"You don't have to, Cheri," I whispered in response. "You don't have to do anything. It is entirely up to you."

Through her tears, she said, "I owe it to them. I cannot allow them to only find out when I die. I have to tell them. But I'm *so scared*."

It tore at my heart to see Cheri like this. I hugged her and told her there was no right or wrong way to leave. She could tell people she had AIDS; she could tell people she was ill without giving a diagnosis; she could say she was burned out; she could even depart without coming to the meeting.

Finally, I had to leave the room. The meeting was supposed to have started ten minutes ago, and the rest of the staff were waiting, wondering where I was. I left Cheri crying in Andi's and Liza's arms, repeating that whatever she chose to do was OK.

Five minutes later, Cheri walked into the community room. She took her seat and, with the most self-assured poise imaginable, calmly explained why she was leaving. She had AIDS, was growing sicker, and did not want the young people to be traumatized by witnessing her decline. Many of her co-workers began to cry. Cheri gently consoled us.

I'm still astonished when I remember Cheri's transformation. The extraordinary strength and dignity of her goodbye still flashes in my mind. It was the most graceful thing I ever saw. And the bravest. Our society tends to equate courage with fearlessness, with Hollywood fantasies of men conquering scores of evil opponents with violent weapons and relentless self-confidence. But you could fuse Tom Cruise, Vin Diesel, Jason Statham, and The Rock into one gigantic testosterone-oozing macho superbeing, and it couldn't begin to touch the courage this small, terrified woman showed that afternoon, when she rose above her fears and obeyed the voice of her heart.

Cheri died soon afterward, and we held a memorial service next door at Smoky Mary's. Ali sat next to me that day in one of the pews. Cheri had been one of his favorite staff members. He'd relished her kind, caring, maternal energy and was a faithful participant in her HIV educational workshops. Now he wept with choking sobs. It is the only time I remember seeing him cry. All I could do was reach over to hold his shoulder and cry quietly beside him.

There was no way to know this at the time, but Cheri would be the last person in our community to die of AIDS. Within months of her passing, antiretroviral therapy became available, and people with the illness were brought back from the brink of demise. For those with access to treatment—and of course, the dividing line of access was often drawn by race and wealth—AIDS was transformed from a death sentence to a chronic, but usually manageable, condition. Fortunately, SafeSpace was able to provide medication to all our clients who needed it.

At Cheri's memorial, I remember feeling petrified that AIDS would pull one after another of my co-workers and our youths into the grave. Twenty-five years later, almost all of them are still here. It still feels like a miracle that so many were spared. But, oh, the pain of losing Cheri at the very edge of daybreak.

After the service, I walked out of Saint Mary's and stood on the steps, feeling just demolished. I looked at all the people passing by— the pedestrians and taxi drivers and bus passengers in the evening homeward rush. It grieved me that the rest of the city seemed to carry on as normal. I wanted to see Cheri's death announced in bold headlines across the local papers, wanted to see flags flying at half mast, wanted to see everyone in the streets dressed in black.

I'm so grateful to have been among Ali and Cheri and my co-workers when submerged in such grief. Their attentiveness toward one another in those awful years when death was relentless, their sparks of love, were like life rafts as we endured wave after wave of horror and loss. The community we created together, the joy and delight we were able to find in one another, allowed us to remain afloat.

# CHAPTER 6

# LONGING AND HUMILIATION

As a general principle, Ali was not one for boyfriends.

"Boyfriends hold you back from being yourself," Inkera recalled him saying. "He said they were party poopers. Don't want you out smoking crack or turning tricks. Ali was a free spirit, wasn't nobody gonna put him in no box!"

However, for a time in 1996, Ali made an exception to the "no boyfriend" policy. He met a man I'll call "Terrell" who began working at the New York Peer AIDS Education Coalition (NYPAEC), a harm-reduction organization where Ali was a peer outreach worker. According to Angie, who also worked there, Terrell was a handful. Pushing thirty, he was handsome and flirtatious, especially with the transgender women in their circle.

"He flirted with Inkera, he flirted with Regine. I don't think they took it any further. But when he started flirting with Ali, it turned into a sexual relationship." Ali was twenty-one by then, but Angie didn't approve. "They were toxic together. They were both into crack, so when Terrell wanted someone to smoke with, he'd call Ali. They'd get high and have sex."

Ali fell hard for Terrell. "Miss Thing . . ." he confessed to Angie, "I'm in love. He's my man."

But Angie worried her friend wasn't seeing the relationship for what it was. "Ali was all googly-eyed, but to Terrell, Ali was just a booty call." Terrell had a "sugar daddy" who paid for his one-bedroom apartment on the Upper West Side. "When the sugar daddy was gone for a few days," Angie explained, "Terrell would have Luscious up in there." But once the sugar daddy came back, Ali was out.

"I remember one day the sugar daddy called Terrell unexpectedly, saying he was on his way over. When Ali didn't leave fast enough, Terrell just threw him out into the hallway, and tossed his stuff out there too—Ali's knapsack filled with condoms, his change of clothes, his crack pipe."

Humiliated, Ali had called Angie to come pick him up. She hailed a taxi and found Ali outside the building, totally dejected.

"Miss Thang, why people gotta be so fierce?" Ali said. "That child done had me up in his sugar-daddy-paid pad, smoking and fucking, and then threw me out and shit, like a used newspaper!"

What most struck me about Ali's desires was her yearning for tenderness, for intimate relationships, for deep human connection. I saw it so clearly in the way Ali cherished her closeness with her friends and with her favorite staff. She made us feel loved. And made us know how much our love meant to her. I have no doubt that Ali brought that longing to her relationship with Terrell, and it is painful to consider how deeply humiliated she must have felt to be discarded over and over again. In so many ways in her short life, Ali's loving heart had been unable to locate a place of welcome.

It took a while, but slowly Ali woke up to the reality that her feelings toward Terrell weren't reciprocated. She felt emotionally battered by the on-and-off nature of the relationship. When Ali discovered that Terrell was HIV-positive, he stopped answering the booty calls. Terrell preferred having sex raw, and that was a line Ali refused to cross. Somewhere deep in Ali was this ferocious instinct for self-preservation, and it finally enabled him to extricate himself from the demeaning situation.

* * *

When Gary and I first started dating, I read a quote by the French existentialist Albert Camus. He said that love can either burn or last, but it cannot do both. When I first read this, I stood up and went running to the other room to find Gary.

"Do you think that could happen to us?" I asked. "I'd die if it did."

Gary smiled. "Camus was not God, nor was he graced with infallibility," he answered bemusedly. "You don't need to feel doomed by his edict."

For all my prayers, though, the flames between us did begin to subside. I had tremendous admiration for Gary, especially for his hard, compassionate work at Bailey House, where he cared for many homeless people with AIDS during the worst years of the AIDS pandemic. He was a guide for me as I did my own work, and I greatly valued his example of carrying forth the spiritual values we'd shared at the Catholic Worker into the fiery zones of desperate human need. Yet for all my admiration, I was still in my mid-twenties and my chaste adolescence had left me with a sexual voraciousness that hadn't calmed at all. I began to wonder if I should break up with Gary, but the thought paralyzed me. Even if I no longer had a romantic connection with him, he had given me a home, a tangible sense of belonging. I had never had that before and felt terrified to give it up.

After months of wondering what I should do, I confided to Gary how I was racked with curiosity about other sexual experiences. I didn't want to break up with him, nor did I want to destroy the home we had found together. But with these feelings swirling in my body, I feared monogamy would doom us. Gary agreed to give me freedom to explore as I wished, only asking that I spare him the erotic details.

For the next five years, that arrangement seemed to work. I kept telling myself that our partnership was sacrosanct, that I would give my body to other men but reserve the depths of my affection for

Gary. But I was beginning to long for what Gary and I had at the beginning: a love of body and soul, an integrated devotion. I was growing tired of all the shallow sexual games, unsatisfied with all these parts of me strewn across different men.

One warm Saturday night in the summer of 1997, I took myself to The Spike, a bar across the West Side Highway from the still-ungentrified Chelsea Piers. As I surveyed the jam-packed crowd, someone caught my eye: a large, burly, handsome, brown-skinned man. He gave off such a vibe of unforced masculinity that I wondered if he might be a clueless truck driver or worker from the nearby meat markets, unaware that he'd walked into a gay bar. It would've explained the somewhat angry look on his face, the unapproachable aura about him, even the loosely fitting T-shirt he wore, when most everyone else was stuffed into their clothes like sausage casings. I was intrigued and seized with desire.

I stared at him for what seemed like forever, with a look that I hoped would invite him over. When he finally met my eyes, there was an enormous smile on his face, completely transforming his guarded aura. I walked over and introduced myself.

His name was Raymond. I told him I'd had my eye on him the whole night. "Me too," he said. When he saw me enter the bar, he had almost ripped his friend's arm off, tugging on it to point me out. He'd assumed I was staring at someone behind him, not even imagining I could want him. His humility was refreshing, and adorable. I was wildly attracted by this unexpected versatility, this combination of burly masculinity and shy vulnerability.

I called him the next afternoon, and we made love later that night. I was beside myself with delight. When we kissed and held each other, the passion between us was electric. But beyond the realm of the physical, there was a depth to Raymond, a gravity, a soulfulness that moved me in places I had forgotten existed. During the years of my promiscuous sexual exploration, something had iced up inside me. Raymond's tender, longing soul broke through the ice and plunged me back into the depths.

Though he was forty—eight years older than me—Raymond had only come out of the closet a few years before we met. (I've repeatedly been struck by how torturous the coming-out process can be for big, masculine men.) Like many of the young people I worked with, he had suffered a childhood of poverty and annihilating trauma. When Raymond was seven, his four-year-old brother had gotten run over by a car when they were playing outside the housing projects where they lived. Their mother blamed Raymond and punished him through years of violent abuse. And yet now he was alive, intact, thriving. I saw in him a great strength, not merely of body, but of human spirit. In that season of my life, when I felt so shaken—by the tension between my sexuality and spirituality; by the deaths brought about by the AIDS epidemic; by the conditions of the homeless kids I worked with—I needed strength. I could sense that Raymond could be a refuge for me, that with him I might learn how to survive trauma.

Falling in love created a huge problem. I'd been with Gary for a decade. I loved him, even if that love had evolved into one of friendship and companionship, rather than of passion. He'd never been anything but good and kind to me. I wanted to rework my understanding with him, hoping we could continue to live together as friends, but with me being honest and open about my love for Raymond. (In retrospect, it was a rather colossal attempt to have my cake and eat it too.)

Gary found the situation excruciating. He did not reject my proposal, but I could tell it pained him whenever I left to spend time with Raymond. He seemed to prefer to suffer in silence, maybe hoping that my love for Raymond would fade and our situation would go back to "normal." Eventually, even though it broke my heart, I had to accept it made no sense to continue living with Gary. I told him I had determined to find my own place to live. To my disappointment, Gary decided to move back to Ohio instead of staying in New York. I would miss him terribly but did not see it as my place to try to prevent him from leaving town. I will always be immensely grateful to Gary, grateful to him for helping me find the courage to come out of the closet, grateful for his luminous example of caring for homeless people with AIDS, and grateful for his love and friendship. But it is a dreadful thing to hurt someone you love. I know I hurt Gary.

In the Catholic tradition, celibacy is thought to be a helpful tool in developing humility. The hope is that restraining our desires will humble us and make us reliant on God's help. In practice, I've found that sex can also be a school of humility. Our deepest longings have the power to break us apart. They smear our would-be perfections in the mud, they reveal our hidden places of need and contingency, the parts of ourselves that our idealized self-regard would prefer to ignore. Sex can shine a ruthless light upon our broken places. Yet, it is my experience that God meets us where we are weakest, most broken, demolished.

Ali longed for his love to be reciprocated but found himself "thrown out like a used newspaper." Anyone who has endured the torture of unrequited love will understand how hard that was—let alone for someone who'd also been rejected by his mother. Unwanted love must have felt like Ali's middle name. As for me, falling in love with Raymond has been one of the greatest joys of my life, and we're still together, nearly thirty years later. But at the time, I couldn't separate the experience of loving him from the hurt it caused Gary.

Which made me terribly ashamed. Both Ali and I endured humiliation because of our longings and desires. And I humiliated others in the process.

In Catholic theology, God is sometimes described as the "Unmoved Mover": all-powerful, perfect, unchangeable, rigid, utterly sufficient unto himself. A being with no vulnerability whatsoever. I don't see God like that at all. In my eyes, God is astoundingly vulnerable. And consumed with longing.

In the New Testament, Jesus depicts God as the father of a reckless, ungrateful heir who demands his inheritance early, only to squander it on sex workers and debauchery. Reduced to poverty and desperation, the son returns home to plead for his father's help. "The father saw him coming from a great distance," Jesus says, "felt deep feelings of love, and ran to his son and fell upon his neck and covered him with kisses."

It is my favorite passage in the whole Bible. I thrill at the image of a God who longs for us to the point of abandoning his dignity. (In ancient Semitic cultures, it was considered disgraceful for a grown man to run.) A God who helplessly falls upon us and covers us with kisses. What a wild departure from the pathetic god we create from the projections of our egos—that immovable, all-powerful, hierarchical monster in the sky. No, the true God, the living God, is reduced to helplessness by love.

I believe that all of creation emerged from the throbbing heartbeat of God's longing. The chaos, the violence, the suffering, the beauty, the tenderness—all of it, even its roughest, most jagged edges—every particle of our mad, gorgeous universe is shot through with Divine love.

I imagine that every one of us, with our desperate, humiliating desires to love and to be loved, carry that longing like God's spark within us.

# CHAPTER 7

# A MEANNESS IN THIS WORLD

S habba," the young man whispered, looking Shavonne's way.

She rolled her eyes, ignoring him.

"Shabba," he whispered again across the table.

Shavonne huffed and pointed her shoulders toward the book-filled shelves.

"OK, now, leave her alone," Patrick said.

Patrick, one of our case managers, was leading a discussion group with a handful of young people in SafeSpace's library. The young man in question, Jerome, was harassing Shavonne by suggesting she bore a resemblance to the Jamaican dancehall artist Shabba Ranks. It was cruel, both because Shabba Ranks possessed a face as rough as concrete and because Shavonne did kind of, sort of, look like him.

"Shabba," he whispered one more time.

"Shut *the fuck up!*" Shavonne exploded. She grabbed her pencil and lunged at her persecutor, intending to stab him with it.

Acting on instinct, Patrick threw himself between the combatants, hoping to prevent injury. In a blur of motion, his head crossed the line of fire, and Shavonne inadvertently ended up stabbing him with her pencil a fraction of an inch from one of his eyes. A hair's breadth to the left, and Patrick might have lost his sight.

Patrick was shaken by the incident. So was I. I felt responsible for protecting the young people, but also for safeguarding the staff. Often this felt like a losing battle.

Looking back, I'm surprised there wasn't even more violence at

SafeSpace. There easily could have been. Researchers routinely find that we are statistically most likely to commit violence as teens and young adults. That's before you layer on the stresses of homelessness: chronic sleep deprivation, a lessening of impulse control brought on by alcohol and drugs, the powerlessness and humiliation of being relentlessly hounded by cops—the list goes on. Everything conspired to push those kids to the edge.

And as usual, the queer youths had it the worst by far. Violence was omnipresent in their lives. In their homes, in the streets, in the subways, in shelters, everywhere they turned, anti-queer contempt was locked and loaded and ready to strike.

It happened even at SafeSpace. As much as we strove to foster an environment of acceptance and mutual respect among the youths, there was a steady stream of new kids always coming in, many of whom had never been in a place where queer kids were accorded respect. Bill Torres, one of our staff members, remembers an afternoon when three new "street-tough" arrivals stumbled upon Ali in the community room. "*Oh shit!* Look! A faggot! It's a he/she!" they said, moving to surround her.

"It could have gotten real ugly real fast," Bill remembers. "Ali was outnumbered and knew it. I saw terror in her eyes."

Bill and another staff member leapt in to intervene, forcing the three aggressors to leave the building. Later, Bill went outside for a smoke, trying to calm his nerves. Coincidentally, Ali was there on the sidewalk, also having a smoke.

Bill asked Ali about how he dealt with homophobic violence.

"Well, if they make me bleed, I hurl my blood at them and scream that I have AIDS. And if I'm not bleeding, I spit at them. Straight boys are scared shitless of AIDS. Faggot body fluids are straight-boy kryptonite." Gallows humor aside, I hated hearing this was the only protection Ali thought she had.

When violence occurred, we'd remove the offender from the

building. In our lingo, we "OPR'd" them, which meant they were "Out Pending Reentry." As soon as possible, I'd hold a reentry meeting in the library, aiming to have the offending client's case manager and therapist present, as well as staff who'd witnessed the violent incident. I'd ask for detailed descriptions of the violence that occurred and the conflicts that preceded it, and then ask the case manager and therapist to help us understand the broader struggles the offending client was experiencing. Did they have a history of trauma? Mental health issues and addiction? What was their sleeping situation like? Collectively, we would try to reach consensus over the timing for welcoming them back.

Covenant House loomed large as the example we didn't want to emulate. They were famous for banishing kids for a minimum of six months at any occasion of violence. We strove to welcome them back far sooner, usually within a week. Only someone who'd repeatedly been violent in the space would face a banishment of a month or more, and that was rare. Furthermore, we felt it was important to interrogate whether our rules were too stringent and give our clients the tools they needed to cope with stress and prevent conflicts from escalating.

I wanted the staff to be bighearted, to advocate for the young people, to point out that it was unrealistic to expect kids going through a living hell to behave like angels. Most did. And frankly, when the rare staff person was too rigid, too punitive, it was good for me to hear it directly in the reentry meetings. It was a telling sign that SafeSpace wasn't the right place for them.

At times I envied the caseworkers who stood up for their clients in those meetings. I had a different role, as I wasn't just responsible for the good of the person who'd been OPR'd. I also needed to keep the safety of the other clients and staff in mind, and make sure we were applying standards fairly, not giving in to favoritism. It felt like being stuck between a rock and a hard place.

People often imagine that those who spend their lives in service to the poor must feel really good about themselves. But that's not what the work is about. In fact, I've noticed that people who come to the work with a need to feel good about themselves don't last long. The reality is that when you sign up for a job like this, you're entering a ground zero of brokenness, of badly wounded people who sometimes lash out and wound others. You will make decisions that you hate making, and you'll inevitably need to set limits that feel cruel. There will often be an unresolvable tension between your intentions and your responsibilities.

I think of Wanette, a vivacious young woman who preferred the nickname Chocolate. A regular at SafeSpace, she had recently begun working as an intern in our kitchen. One winter morning Chocolate showed up hungover and exhausted after a night dancing in a nearby strip club and promptly got into a fight with another young woman over some triviality that's since evaporated from my memory. She inundated the other young woman with threats and verbal abuse for what seemed an eternity. We needed to protect the poor girl from the onslaught, and when our efforts to calm Chocolate failed, we finally had to remove her from the building.

I remember standing outside with Chocolate next to mountains of snow. There had been three storms that week, and West Forty-sixth Street looked like the arctic tundra. You couldn't even see the cars parked along the sidewalk; they were just mounds of piled-up whiteness.

I explained to Chocolate that she was OPR'd. I promised that our staff would meet that day to discuss her reentry and asked her to return when she was sober to learn the plan.

I'd been in countless similar situations over the years. Often I would be cursed out, called a coldhearted hypocritical bastard, a dirty-assed motherfucking racist, or some variation of the above. With Chocolate, it was far worse.

We stood there together in a narrow path dug through the snow, the young woman wrapped in a white knee-length coat, me shivering in a flannel shirt. Instead of lashing out, Chocolate began to cry.

"My grandmother's right," she sobbed. "I'll never fucking amount to *anything*. I'll ruin everything for myself. It's like she says: I'll end up just like my mother, *nothing but a fucking stripper*."

Then she fell to her hands and knees and began to puke in the snow.

I can assure you I did not feel good about myself that day.

One afternoon, early in 1997, Ali showed up in my office looking unusually grave. "Carl, I need to tell you something very serious," she said.

"What is it, Ali?" I asked as we sat together at my little round table.

Ali informed me that she'd just been in the basement, where the showers and lockers were. When she arrived, turning the corner from the stairway, she'd come upon a staff member and one of our young clients.

"Carl, they were both straightening up their clothes in a hurry, looking all freaked out that I saw them. I could tell they had just had sex."

My heart sank into my stomach. "Did you see any physical contact between them?"

"No," Ali replied. "But it was obvious."

Ali took a deep breath and looked at me sadly. "We need the staff to be here for our good, *not* to use us." I had never heard such a determined, forceful tone in Ali's voice.

I told Ali he was right, that we would never tolerate any sexual activity between staff and clients. I promised I would investigate the allegation.

In succession, I summoned the staff member and then the youth to my office. Each denied anything sexual had occurred—the young person saying he had just been straightening his clothes after showering, and the staff member explaining he was merely adjusting his shirt upon rising from a chair. I called the agency's attorney, who, after I had described each person's story, told me it would be illegal to fire the staff person. Both the client and the staff member denied anything happening, and Ali, the only other person present, had not witnessed anything downright incriminating. I still felt uneasy. Ali was not a mean or vindictive person, hardly one to go around making groundless accusations. However, the final decision belonged not to me, but the agency's executive director. She followed the attorney's guidance.

When I told Ali I couldn't fire the staff person, it was the only time I can recall her being clearly disappointed in me. I can still see the hurt in her eyes, still see her looking down in despair and then slowly walking away from me.

Subsequent developments only increased the pain of that incident. When I told the staff person I couldn't fire him, I went on to say I would be watching him like a hawk, and any sign of sexual misconduct would lead to his immediate termination. Seeing the writing on the wall, he quickly found himself another job and resigned from SafeSpace. A year or so later, two clients—including the youth from Ali's allegation—confessed they'd had sex with that particular staff member before he left.

I have little doubt that Ali had been sexually abused in foster care. I knew how important it was for her that SafeSpace be entirely different, that it be a place of goodness in her life. It frightened me to realize how many sources of danger I needed to be on guard against if SafeSpace was to live up to its name.

One warm evening in June 1996, I got a call from our receptionist. "Carl, you're going to want to come down here quickly," he whispered. "It looks like half the police force is here in the lobby. They're demanding to see you."

Alarmed, I rushed down to find more than a dozen plainclothes detectives ominously crowded in the small entryway. This was not a good sign; I'd never seen more than two or three police show up at SafeSpace for any reason. Wanting to keep them away from our young people, who would soon be finishing dinner and heading downstairs, I brought the officers to our library and invited them to sit with me around the meeting table.

The head detective produced a mug shot of one of our youths, John Royster, and asked if he was in the building. I explained that since we were a licensed mental health clinic, I was legally unable to confirm whether someone was a client without a court order.

The detective wasn't pleased. "He is the prime suspect in the murder of Evelyn Alvarez at the Park Avenue dry cleaner, and also of the sexual assault and beating of a woman in Central Park who's in a coma," he said, glaring at me with visible annoyance.

News of both crimes had dominated the city's attention for the past week. First, a young piano teacher was brutally beaten in Central Park and left unrecognizable. Then, a few days later, a sixty-two-year-old woman was attacked outside her Upper East Side dry cleaning business, her head pummeled repeatedly into the ground until she was dead. Mayor Rudy Giuliani, with his reputation for law and order, pledged that no expense would be spared in finding the attackers. But until then, there had been no suggestion that the attacks were perpetrated by the same person—much less someone in our orbit.

"We also suspect he attacked another woman last night, up in the Bronx, near Yonkers," the detective continued. "She's also in the hospital, in a coma. We lifted a bloody fingerprint from the Alvarez crime scene, and it matched Royster's. He gave SafeSpace as his address when he was arrested for jumping a subway turnstile a few months ago."

As I listened, a knot of dread twisted my stomach. Hundreds of teens passed through SafeSpace each week. It wasn't possible for me to know all of them personally. But I knew John Royster. Thin, with dark skin, big eyes, and a sort of peanut-shaped head, John kept to himself, and always had a book or two in his hands. Quiet, studious kids were hardly the norm at SafeSpace, so he stood out.

One day John had appeared in my office, sat down, and proceeded to gaze at me searchingly, like he was studying an exotic animal at a zoo. The oddness of it made me laugh, and I tried to think of something we might talk about. Noticing he carried a book by the self-purported shamanic mystic Carlos Castaneda, I commented that I'd read several of the author's books when I was a teen.

This information made a big impression on John. Afterward, whenever he saw me in the halls or the dining room, he invariably smiled and said, "Carlos Castaneda."

However, despite John's friendly attitude, I wasn't shocked by the detectives' allegations. Our case managers' supervisor, Nancy, had shared concerns about John a few months earlier. She'd assigned him a case manager and a therapist, both young women. Each told Nancy there was something about John that deeply unnerved them—a look in his eyes as he spoke to them, as though he was seething with hatred. His rage seemed only directed toward women. While he'd never been violent at SafeSpace or even raised his voice, our team had decided that nobody would meet alone with John without leaving the door open.

I asked the officers to excuse me for a few minutes. I didn't want to assume John's guilt, but if the young man really was in the middle of some out-of-control violent rampage, what if he was in SafeSpace at that very moment? I lurched out of the room and ran upstairs to our dining room, three steps at a time. Thank God, John wasn't there. I pulled several staff aside and urgently asked when John had last been seen. It turned out he hadn't visited us for several weeks.

When I returned to the detectives, they sternly repeated their request that I share any information we might have, especially an address where John might be found.

"The court is closed for the evening," the scowling one explained. "We won't be able to get a court order until tomorrow morning. You need to help us." His voice was demanding, but his eyes seemed desperate, pleading. "For the last week he's been attacking women almost every night. He might kill someone tonight while we wait for a fucking court order!"

As I'd told the detectives, it was against the law to release information about clients of mental health clinics without a court order. Even without that barrier, it was important that our youths, so many of whom survived through drug dealing and sex work, be able to trust us. But I'd never been confronted with such a dilemma. The last thing I wanted was to endanger another woman. I could feel myself breathing fast. I racked my brain, trying to balance my responsibilities to SafeSpace with my duty as a human being.

"Look," I said. "As the director of SafeSpace, I cannot give you any information without a court order. But as someone who walks up and down Sixth Avenue every day, I can tell you he sure looks like an employee of the computer software store by Forty-fourth Street. Why don't you go there?"

The head detective thanked me and said he'd return with a court order in the morning if they still hadn't found John. The battalion of officers got up and left, rushing toward the software store.

I hardly slept that night, my mind racing with dreadful questions. Had I done the wrong thing in providing the detectives with an opportunity to find John? What would this group of white officers do to this young Black man? What if John was innocent? But also, what if the police caught him in a violent act and shot him?

The next morning, I turned on the news and learned the detectives had obtained John's address from the computer store and arrested him that night. He gave a detailed and lengthy confession. It turned out he'd committed the three violent acts the detectives had told me about, as well as a fourth: beating another woman into a coma as she jogged near the FDR Drive.

Journalists would go on to detail John's sporadic homelessness, his history of being fired from sales jobs—usually for hostility directed at women—and his affinity for watching violent pornographic films. It was hard to reconcile this information with my experience of the studious kid who always smiled and called me Carlos Castaneda.

So many of the tensions and ambiguities we faced at SafeSpace seemed to coalesce in the person of John Royster. We wanted to welcome everyone in need, to believe in their goodness, in their essential value as human beings. Some homeless centers had security guards and metal detectors. Some trained their staff to engage in physical restraint. We avoided such measures, afraid they'd establish barriers between us and the young people who came to us for help. We wanted to provide an environment built upon care and mutual respect, not control and need for dominance. But John Royster's murderous rampage made us wonder if we were being naïve.

"Well, sir, I guess there's just a meanness in this world," Bruce Springsteen sings in "Nebraska." Yes, there's meanness, and violence, and chaos, and brutality. They are threaded through humanity. But how do we combat the threat of violence—by building walls or by tearing them down? If we become fixated on our protection, how do we avoid closing our hearts? If we surrender to fear, isn't our openness to life diminished in the process? We at SafeSpace made a choice not to hide behind security guards and metal detectors.

Two years later, I was subpoenaed to testify at John Royster's trial. His defense team wanted to establish that SafeSpace had concerns about John's mental health during his stay. New York State had just reinstated the death penalty, and they hoped that by demonstrating John suffered from mental illness, they might spare him that fate.

I have only the haziest recollections of being questioned. What I do remember is scanning the courtroom, trying to guess which attendees were the victims of John's attacks, and which were their family members. I saw faces filled with sadness and hurt; faces bewildered by the mayhem that had battered their lives. And what I remember most is how, when I rose from my seat following my testimony, John Royster smiled shyly, waved at me, and quietly mouthed, "Carlos Castaneda."

John was found guilty. The judge called him "an incurably violent and dangerous monster" and sentenced him to life in state prison without the possibility of parole.

As I followed the case in the news, much of the coverage frustrated me. Again and again, John Royster was described as evil, as a savage, as a monster. But by then I'd lived through Ali's murder, and those of two other transgender women in our community. No battalions of detectives showed up at SafeSpace when they were killed. No citywide effort was launched to investigate. In the aftermath of their killings, I was a changed person—more sorrowful, more enraged. I felt less need to perceive evil in an obviously warped individual like John Royster than I did in those who held power yet refused to protect the youths in my care. Evil manifests itself in many different forms.

# CHAPTER 8

# EYES TO SEE

'll never forget an afternoon spent trying to run a discussion group while two young transgender women were caught up in a fierce verbal joust about each other's alleged beauty deficiencies, building up to a moment when one called out the other's wig: "*Ewwww!* Get that *nasty* thing away from me. It looks like *roadkill!*" I held my breath, fearing such a cutting insult would lead to blows. Instead, the two ladies burst into laughter, unfazed.

I was two years into my job at SafeSpace and had started to learn that "throwing shade"—the scorching queer art of delivering cutting, humorous insults—was often a thinly veiled disguise used by our young people to communicate deeper emotion. The youths tended to attack one another's clothes, body sizes, sexual attractiveness, and the "realness" of their gender presentations. Yet in those interactions, I saw a great deal of anxiety being projected outward. You put someone else down for what you felt insecure about in yourself. Sometimes these duels escalated to blows, but not usually. More often, affection was subtly brought into the mix. Shade was like a humorous externalization of the internal struggle to accept and love oneself. What surfaced as cruelty sometimes began to seem like an expression of attention and care from kids who'd been hurt too often to express themselves openly.

Ali's razor tongue made her our ruling Empress of Shade—though hers was (almost) always delivered with an undercurrent of warmth. Once, Ali was about to co-lead a harm-reduction training with his close friend, Angie. When the host introduced Ali to the group, Angie exclaimed, "Oh, that's the love of my life!" Ali, who surely didn't want the gay boys in the group misled into believing he was into women, responded by twisting his face in mock disgust. "*Honey!* I *don't* do fish!" he exclaimed. "The only fish I do is in a can, on a bun, or in a salad, and that's *not you!*"

Angie flushed with embarrassment, but she didn't hold it against Ali. She knew his heart. "You couldn't be anywhere near Ali and not feel some kind of love for him," she explained.

The shadiest thing Ali ever said to me contained a hidden message of love, though I didn't grasp it at the time. One afternoon, about six months after I came to SafeSpace, I was descending the stairway to the lobby, where some two dozen kids were crowded together during a break between our scheduled groups and workshops. Ali took the opportunity of my arrival to focus the glare of his shade upon me.

"*Carl,*" Ali declared with a tone of commanding authority. The kids held their breath and craned their necks to hear. "When you came to SafeSpace, you looked *good.* In fact, you looked *so good,* you could have sold yourself on Christopher Street. But *now . . .*" and Ali paused dramatically to signal the epic put-down coming. "*Now* you look old and busted. In fact, now you look *so* old, if you were on Christopher Street, you'd have no choice but to pay for it."

My face went hot. I wanted to reply that contending with Ali's shady self had surely contributed to my aging. Instead, I hurried back upstairs while the other youths laughed their asses off.

When I recalled that episode to Inkera recently, she said it fit a pattern of Ali expressing concern for my well-being. "Ali would always say to me, 'Girl, those children are running the White Child *ragged.* I'm worried about Carl. He always looks *stressed!*'"

It was unusual for the youths at SafeSpace to concern themselves with how I was doing. It was the staff's role to protect the youths, not the other way around. Besides, in such a chaotic environment, I felt it important to project stability, to be a center of calm within the storm. I didn't want others to see me struggle—neither the clients nor the staff. (Still, the staff quickly picked up on a physical manifestation of my stress. They noticed that when I got upset in our weekly staff meetings, my neck turned various shades of purple. Apparently the more upset I got, the darker my neck became. Perhaps it's an Italian thing—your body discloses your emotions, whether or not you consent.)

Recently I reconnected with Jovon, a perceptive young man who frequented SafeSpace between 1999 and 2001. It was interesting to see myself through his eyes.

"You were Daddy," he said. "And we all had major unresolved daddy issues. You'd walk into the room with your big muscle body and your black T-shirts and set the boundaries. *No violence. No threats. No hate speech.* Total daddy! So, we put a lot of effort into trying to provoke you, trying to get a rise out of you. We must have driven you crazy. But it was almost impossible to get you worked up."

So Inkera is probably right. Ali's comment about my meager sex-work prospects was a veiled expression of concern, an assertion that he saw through my controlled persona. Ali had this uncommon ability to see the actual person I was, not merely the role I performed. That is my overarching memory of Ali: his eyes fixed on me when we were together, looking at me with genuine care.

On a bright, hot, early summer day, we closed SafeSpace, hoping to provide our kids with a day of fun. Our group of some sixty staff and young people gathered that morning in front of the drop-in center, in the shadows of the large Gothic facade of Saint Mary the Virgin. Then we filed half a block to the Times Square subway station and embarked upon the long journey to Coney Island. An hour later, we emerged into the brilliant sunlight and found ourselves a spot on the beach.

As soon as we'd stripped down to our bathing suits, some of the kids asked me to join them in the sea. As we walked toward the water, they all started shouting "David Hasselhoff" at me (David Hasselhoff having dethroned Jean-Claude Van Damme as the favored muscular white man of comparison). They wanted me to run in and out of the waves in exaggerated slow motion, like I was on *Baywatch*. Complying with their wishes, I ran into the waters as though trudging through quicksand, a dozen giggling teens all running slowly beside me.

A raging battle ensued, with four of us ferociously splashing one another. George Santana, our rotund outreach worker, and Chuletta, an amiable big-boned Puerto Rican kid, squared off against me and James Burke—a shy and quiet young Black man who tended to sheepishly attach himself to me like a sibling seeking the protection of his older brother. Our splash battle was a scene of uncontained bliss. Streams of water shot furiously in every direction, encircling us with reflected sunlight like chaotic halos.

Finally, exhausted from our aquatic combat, we rejoined the rest of our group on the beach for a picnic lunch. We'd brought coolers stocked with sandwiches and fruit drinks. Everyone ate, and as the afternoon wore on, the kids and staff began to peel away. By the time the setting sun stretched our shadows across the beach, only a dozen of us remained: me, one other staff member, and ten youths. I had been wanting to take them on the amusement park rides but was obligated to wait until the group was small enough for our miserly budget. We split into two groups, some setting off for the go-carts and the rest of us going on the rickety old Cyclone roller coaster.

Usually, Ali remained close in scenarios like this. However, James Burke was still following me like my shadow, and I suspect that Ali, recognizing James's need, saw fit to make room. James had close-cropped hair and a shy smile. He seemed on the verge of being mute—it was difficult for him to say much more than "yes" or "no." But James was gifted with a friendly, companionable quality. He always seemed so completely happy to be in your presence that you just *had* to like him.

James sat next to me as we were bolted into our Cyclone seats. I shouted with excitement as the coaster plunged down its first terrifying descent, while James silently grabbed my arm, a wide smile plastered on his face. When the roller coaster was done rumbling and tossing us about, our two groups reconvened for a ride in the bumper cars. Finally, we headed to the subway in the last bluish remnant of the day's fading light.

Our train left Coney Island, passed Brighton Beach, and descended into the darkness of the underground tunnel. The group now consisted of four youths and one baby: Ali and James Burke, as well as a young man named Ricardo with the towering height of a basketball player; and a young woman, Milagro, with her baby, Precious Jewel (such a sweet name for this child born into homelessness).

The youths all sat together opposite me in the subway car's L-shaped seating arrangement. I watched them take turns holding Precious in their laps, covering their faces with their hands, crying out "Peekaboo!" until the baby burst out laughing. It was an endearing sight.

There is a numbing effect that happens when you are regularly submerged in trauma and tragedy. We have a psychological need to normalize our situation, to anesthetize ourselves from the intensity of what we're experiencing. It must be like that for soldiers in combat zones or medical practitioners in inner-city emergency rooms. You need to keep yourself from being swallowed alive, so, emotionally, you hold yourself back.

After two years of witnessing our youths' struggles to survive in the streets, seeing them show up battered and bloodied after being assaulted in shelters and on the stroll, witnessing their incarcerations, their HIV diagnoses, their arrests, I was beginning to numb myself to their conditions. The city refused to provide housing, and my superiors weren't much different. I felt helpless to bring about any substantial change, exhausted from being enraged and terrified all the time. I started telling myself that the kids' homelessness was an unalterable fact of life. The only way to cope was to accept the unacceptable.

But something about that beach day, about jumping in waves and riding in bumper cars, tore at my numbness. In an environment where we were not enacting the rituals of homeless services, our young people were the same as any other kids having a day at the beach. Now, watching them play so sweetly with Precious, I began to tremble at the sheer intimacy and protectiveness I felt toward them.

As I looked at Ali, James, Milagro, and Ricardo, I saw that each one of *them* was precious, not just the baby passed from lap to lap. In the core of their beings, beneath their surface behaviors and various coping strategies, I saw that each of them was utterly good. My eyes felt opened in an almost mystical way. It didn't feel like an overtly spiritual speculation. It was more like I glimpsed what was in front of me clearly, without the veils of distraction or the thousands of self-justifying thoughts that usually fogged my vision. I saw Ali, James, Ricardo, Milagro, and Precious Jewel with an immediate, graced clarity. And in that seeing, I knew them to be infinitely beloved.

But as we reached downtown Brooklyn and I prepared to transfer trains, I felt an increasing sense of dread. I would leave them and head home to Williamsburg, where I was awaited by someone I loved, and a meal of warm tortellini and a cold beer. I would collapse on a couch in front of a TV, surrounded by statues and holy images of Saint Thérèse and my other favorite saints.

The night awaiting these kids had no such comforts. Milagro and Precious would be relatively safe in a shelter for mothers and infants, but what sorts of terrors and humiliations were in store for Ricardo, James, and Ali, who would be riding the trains all night, or sleeping on park benches or in crack houses? I took one final look at my companions and felt overwhelmed by the danger they were in.

As I stood to exit the subway car, I called out, "Goodnight, be safe. I'll see you tomorrow."

James Burke beamed a big smile, and Ali said, "Thanks Carl. We had fun today."

Waiting for the G train, I sat down and buried my head in my hands. My body still smelled of the beach, of the sand and salt water from our day of innocent joy.

My first thought took the form of prayer. *Dear God, what am I supposed to do after what I've just seen? How can I go home every night and send them out to the streets?*

Then the monologue turned inward. *Carl, what would you do if they were your children, out on their own, in this dangerous hell pit of a city? Or even if your puppy or your parrot were lost in the streets? You wouldn't sleep. You'd be in a frenzy—running through the streets like a madman, crying out for them with all your might. You'd be papering the city with posters of their faces; you'd be offering every dollar you have for their safe return home.*

And yet, is it possible to sustain frenzy every night of your life? How do you summon the same desperation for hundreds upon hundreds of abandoned kids, most of whom you will never know? How do you create a boundary between a bottomless hole of suffering and your small, finite self? I didn't have the first beginnings of an answer.

How do you behold such a vision and keep your sanity?

How do you see the face of God and live?

# PART
# TWO

---

*Raise a tent of shelter now, though every thread is torn.*

—LEONARD COHEN,

"DANCE ME TO THE END OF LOVE"

---

# CHAPTER 9

# WHITEWASHED GRAVES

I arrived at SafeSpace just before the "revitalization" of Times Square kicked into high gear.

For several decades, the neighborhood, with its peep shows and go-go bars, its strolls and addicts looking to score, was where New York City's street kids worked their trades. It was their outdoor market, their rolling street fair, the economy where they found some limited means to feed, clothe, and shelter themselves. When I walk through the commercialized, tourist-inundated Times Square of today, it is almost impossible to compare it to what I knew back then.

What occurred in Times Square in the nineties exposed me, more than anywhere else I've lived or worked, to the horrors that result when poor and marginalized people are heartlessly driven from a neighborhood.

Times Square had long been portrayed as a symbol of urban failure, a neighborhood besieged by porn and sleaze and crime. As far back as the eighties, the Ed Koch administration had been planning to remake the neighborhood into a glittering destination for out-of-town visitors and the businesses that cater to them. By 1996, redevelopment was in high gear. Rezoning efforts led to the peep shows and sex shops being shuttered. Disney invested some eight million dollars into the decrepit theaters of Forty-second Street, restoring them to their early-twentieth-century grandeur. A three-story Virgin Megastore opened down the block from us.

Corporations and developers gobbled up any available real estate. And the police, doing the bidding of developers, the Times Square Business Improvement District, and Mayor Giuliani, began a massive effort to eliminate street crime from the area.

Our young people began telling us about the new policing tactics. In the dead of night, the police would conduct "sweeps," swarming into Times Square from every direction and rounding up anyone engaged in sex work or selling drugs. Even if our kids were drinking beer or simply not carrying an ID, they'd be arrested. Previously they'd have been given summonses and sent on their way; now a great number of them began spending lengthy amounts of time in Rikers Island or juvenile detention facilities. When they returned to Times Square, the police were like an occupying army, stationing three cops at almost every street corner, stopping and frisking the homeless relentlessly.

The mayor, the police commissioner, and the head of the Times Square Business Improvement District were messaging to the public that this was a noble endeavor. New York was "cracking down on crime," "combating deviancy," "sweeping the neighborhood clean." From the start, I found such terminology detestable. All I kept hearing was how the neighborhood was being "cleaned up." I knew that in the eyes of the gentrifiers, our kids were the dirt.

Ricardo—basketball-tall, thin Ricardo—was one of the first victims of the sweeps.

Ricardo had been on the subway the day we rode back from Coney Island. But apart from that moment, my strongest memory of Ricardo was from an afternoon when he erupted into an argument with another youth at lunch. Hearing loud shouts, I ran to the dining room.

"Please, Ricardo," our chef was saying, "you need to leave."

"You need to back the fuck away from me!" Ricardo snarled.

I stepped in and invited Ricardo into my office, asking him to sit with me while I did some work. Maybe it would give him the opportunity to calm down without having his ego threatened. When he spotted the hip-hop magazine *The Source* lying on my table, he perked up. He was impressed when I showed him that I'd been quoted in one of the articles (coincidentally, and sadly, an article about the displacement of homeless youths from Times Square).

"Damn! That's mad cool," Ricardo said. Then, as an exclamation mark upon his appreciation, he added, "For real." He spent an hour quietly reading the magazine before departing from SafeSpace peacefully.

A few weeks passed. Late at night, several blocks from SafeSpace, Ricardo was leaning into a car's window, engaged in a drug sale. Then, out of nowhere, the police came swarming in from multiple directions. Ricardo's customer must have seen them before Ricardo did. And he must have been a whole lot more concerned with keeping himself out of jail than he was about Ricardo's safety. The driver floored the gas to speed away while Ricardo's head was still inside the window, almost completely severing it from his body. Ricardo died immediately.

Some of our SafeSpace clients saw it happen. Ricardo's death terrified them and drove home how the city's effort to make Times Square "safe" was putting targets on their backs. But where were they supposed to go? Where else were they supposed to survive?

Of all our youths who suffered from the sudden aggressive policing, the homeless transgender women were the most endangered. In the entire city, Times Square was one of the few places where there was some understanding of who transgender women were. It was also home to a handful of organizations that sought to protect them. But now, since sex workers were one of the prime groups targeted by the police sweeps, most of the transgender women had been driven out and scattered among neighborhoods that were far more dangerous.

Dion Webster was our first transgender woman to die after the sweeps began. She had been a client of SafeSpace, but after too many arrests in Times Square, she was forced to move to Harlem to continue her survival sex work. Ali was one of the last to see Dion alive. They were working the streets of East Harlem together one night in October 1996, and Ali remembered watching Dion enter the car of some john. Later that evening, Dion was found discarded on a nearby street. She had been stabbed to death. The next morning, Ali went to identify her friend's corpse in the morgue.

Dion and Ali were close. I remember seeing him after the trip to the morgue. He kept his head buried in his hands, as though his face exposed a sorrow too raw to be seen by anyone else. All Ali kept saying was, "No, not Dion, not Dion," over and over.

The next person in Ali's circle to be killed was Kiki Freeman. Kiki was a tall transgender woman who had been homeless for years. She took a good deal of pride in her appearance, wearing flattering wigs and tight-fitting clothes to show off her towering physique. Kiki was a tumultuous presence when I first arrived at SafeSpace, prone to loud disruptive fits when she was coming down from crack. It makes me sad that I didn't get to know her before drugs got such a stranglehold on her, though I did see glimpses of her inner determination and resolve.

A few months after I started at SafeSpace, Kiki decided to try to break her addiction. Andi Simon, Kiki's case manager, was by her side through an almost impossible effort to find a rehab program that wouldn't force Kiki to wear men's clothes or be addressed as male. But Kiki and Andi were determined. Finally, they persuaded a facility in upstate New York to agree to respect her female identity.

Some of my happiest memories involve Kiki's visits from rehab. Andi often journeyed upstate to visit Kiki and, as her chaperone, was occasionally allowed to bring her back to the city.

"Look at me, Carl," Kiki would announce in my doorway, beaming with pride, "I'm clean!"

"Wow, Kiki, you look amazing!" I'd reply. "I'm *so* proud of you."

I mentioned my surprise that she was allowed to leave the facility.

"It's probably to give the other residents a chance to eat something," Kiki said, laughing. She had gained something like forty pounds in rehab, finally having access to regular meals and free of the crack racing through her system.

"The weight looks good on you, Kiki," I said. "Very Janet Jackson circa *Rhythm Nation*."

I was proud of Kiki, and proud, too, of Andi, who fought through so many obstacles to gain treatment for her client. (It always made me smile to see the two of them together. Andi was a short woman; Kiki *towered* over her.) Victories in the lives of our young people were few and far between; I rejoiced to see this young woman liberated from the grip of addiction.

But what happened after Kiki's release was devastating. Kiki might have won a battle against her crack addiction, but she had no power over the bigotry and governmental negligence that walled off transgender people to almost every opportunity. With no shelters available where a trans woman didn't face violence, all Kiki had was the streets. It was almost impossible for any transgender person to find employment—especially a trans woman of color, and most especially someone like Kiki who'd spent years unemployed. With no means of finding safe housing and no way to support herself, Kiki returned to the stroll before long, forced once more to resort to survival sex. Within a month, Kiki was back on crack.

It was a wretched day when Kiki aged out of SafeSpace. Kiki did not want to go anywhere; she wanted to stay with us. But she was turning twenty-five, the age limit for our program. Andi had been trying to help her find a drop-in program for homeless adults, but

Kiki wouldn't budge. When her final day arrived, she stood in our lobby, yelling her fury and frustration.

"Get out of my face, I'm not going nowhere!" Kiki shouted, looking at once enraged, desperate, and cornered.

"Kiki, I wish we could keep you," I said sadly, "but we can't any longer. I hope you will go to the programs Andi showed you, and I hope you'll keep in touch and let us know how you're doing."

She heard the finality in my voice. Without saying another word, she hocked up a big wad of phlegm, spat in my face, and stormed out the door.

My heart broke for Kiki. So many doors had been shut to her, and now I was forced to close ours. As her spit dripped down my face, I was not angry, only terribly sad. It was awful to see it come to this. The ferocity of her fight, the enormous hurdles she overcame to get clean, only made her defeat more crushing.

I never saw Kiki again after her volatile exit. She was driven from Times Square by the blitzkrieg of police sweeps targeting sex workers. Like others, she fled to Harlem. A few months later, in April of 1997, her body was found there in an abandoned warehouse, a screwdriver stabbed into her head.

Through all of this, it felt as though the world's moral compass had been swept away. In the news, in speeches made by city leadership, the overwhelming public narrative was that something wonderful was being done in Times Square. We Americans are experts at crafting stories to justify our cruelty and greed. We laud subjugation as transformation, savagery as safety. I wonder if we tell ourselves this mess of lies so loudly and insistently because we need to cover up the sound of blood crying out from the ground beneath us.

In those days it was a given that the murders of homeless transgender women would go uninvestigated and unsolved. But after Kiki and Dion were killed, Ali dared to journey to the relevant police precincts in Harlem. She *demanded* that their murders be investigated, offering information about where her friends were last seen alive—even describing in detail the car Dion had entered. Ali wanted the killers brought to justice. She was desperate to honor her friends' lives and protect other transgender women working the streets.

When I learned, after the fact, that Ali had done this, it made me wish he had asked me to accompany him. He might have faced less danger, and likely been afforded more respect, if my big, white, grown-assed self had been beside him. But it was something Ali chose to do alone.

I've often tried to imagine Ali walking into those precincts during the height of "Giuliani Time." I picture Ali, with his innate femininity, his dark black skin, his skinny body, approaching desks like battleships, behind which stood police officers twice as old and twice as heavy as he. I picture Ali looking into those eyes and trembling. And then I see him overcome the fear and speak aloud the names of his beloved sisters. *"Dion Webster." "Kiki Freeman."*

You need to understand the courage it took for a massively feminine, gender nonconforming, homeless, Black youth with an extensive arrest record to venture into those hypermasculine police stations and insist upon her friends' worth. Ali was entering enemy territory. She was hardly stupid; she knew full well the contempt and risk. But in a world turned upside down, Ali had the capacity to stand upright. Because her heart was upright. For real.

I hold awe for Ali's heroism. Nonetheless, when I remember those years in Times Square, my blood boils with rage. What if the "revitalization" of Times Square had included a commitment to provide Ali and Kiki and Dion and Ricardo with safe housing and drug treatment? What if the new businesses descending upon the neighborhood had been incentivized to offer them entry-level jobs? Our young people were not seen for who they were: abused, disinherited children struggling to survive. They were only seen as criminals, fit to be terrorized and jailed, as trash to be swept away.

In the two years prior to his murder, Ali was arrested more than forty times. The most time he spent sleeping with a roof over his head was in a jail cell. The government would promise him nowhere else safe to sleep. Those simple facts tell you everything you need to know about the Giuliani administration's priorities.

In my eyes, it was Times Square's gentrifiers and profiteers who were the trash. As much as the overlords of its gentrification were lauded and celebrated, I see them, in Jesus's words, as "whitewashed graves, which on the outside look respectable, but inside are filled with dead bones and every kind of filth."

# CHAPTER 10

# REVELATION

Tyra Banks had recently begun volunteering as the spokes-model for our parent organization, the Center for Children and Families. She hadn't yet achieved the mega-iconic status that she would reach a few months later, as the first Black solo cover girl of the *Sports Illustrated* Swimsuit Issue, but our young transgen-der women at SafeSpace were abuzz over her ascendance, seeing her as a new challenger to their reigning beauty icons, Naomi Campbell and Janet Jackson.

One evening, I unexpectedly ran into Tyra in the hallway outside our agency headquarters. She took my breath away. If Botticelli had lived in our time, the woman standing in front of me could have been a model for one of his angels. I leapt into action, introducing myself as the director of the programs for homeless teens.

"Tyra, our gay boys and transgender girls *worship* you. I cannot tell you how much it would mean to them if you would visit our drop-in center."

She handled the surprise request graciously, agreeing to pay us a visit.

When I returned to SafeSpace that evening, dinner was being served. I sat down to eat with Ali and her friend Dutchess, a femi-nine, round-faced boy with a haughty attitude.

"You two would not believe who I was with twenty minutes ago," I said. "Tyra Banks!"

"Oh, I can't stand Tyra," Dutchess pooh-poohed with a sneer.

"Her forehead is MUCH too high. They'll let *anyone* be a super-model these days!"

"Well, Dutchess," I replied, "I was completely gagging at how beautiful she was. It was off the charts."

As Dutchess rolled his eyes, Ali offered, "I *love* Tyra Banks. I hope I get to meet her."

Ali then turned to Dutchess. "And Miss Thing, you wish you looked *half* as good as her!"

A month later I was summoned to the Soho Grand Hotel to pick up Tyra for her visit. We rode up from Soho to Midtown in a limousine. She asked me questions about SafeSpace and the young people we worked with. Then, switching gears, she made me quite jealous by revealing how she'd recently shared a post-awards-show limousine ride with one of my living icons, Al Green. "I don't know what he was on," she said, eyes sparkling conspiratorially, "but the reverend was high as hell!" I was surprised by how down-to-earth Tyra was, and how playful and companionable.

When we got out of the limousine, Ali was waiting on the side-walk. Before I could even introduce the two of them, Ali announced, in his most imperious voice:

"*Girl!* Whoever did your hair and makeup for the American Music Awards was *not* your friend!"

I groaned. Poor Tyra hadn't even entered our doors, and she was already caught in the firing line of Ali's shade! I worried she'd turn right around and get back in the limousine. Instead, she just burst out laughing.

"I know . . ." she said, smiling. "Lots of people told me it wasn't my best look." I guess she wouldn't have gone far in fashion if she couldn't deal with shady queens.

Ali's cutting humor seemed to endear him to Tyra, for within minutes you would have thought they'd been close for years. He made her feel like a friend, rather than some idol on a pedestal. Ali accompanied us for the entire tour, describing the services SafeSpace provided and sharing personally how much we meant to him. He was one hell of an ambassador.

Finally, Tyra was about to leave us. Ali and I accompanied her outside and she hugged us goodbye. Just as she was about to return to her limo, Ali blurted out:

"Tyra, SafeSpace puts on a talent show, and it's, like, the highlight of my year." Then, with a sly smile, Ali continued, "We're planning a segment where some of us walk runway, and it would be the best thing *ever* if you walked runway with us. Girl, the children would *gag*!"

It was an audacious request. But it makes me proud, thinking of how Ali felt confident enough in herself and her friends to ask the superstar to join them.

"Ali, I'd love to walk with you!" Tyra responded, without a moment's hesitation. "If the show happens when I can be in New York City, I'll be there. I promise."

In 1995 and 1996, we hosted our talent shows in a church auditorium near SafeSpace that held about a hundred seats. However, by 1997 we were attracting a larger crowd of supporters and needed a bigger venue. We rented a far more spacious auditorium from the Borough of Manhattan Community College down by the World Trade Center.

Several months after Tyra's visit, the momentous day arrived. About a dozen of us—another staff member and I and a group of the kids—pulled up in our van and saw the college's students were massed in huge numbers on the sidewalk in front of the auditorium. My heart sank, imagining what might happen as we made our way through the crowd. The students, decked out in FUBU and Phat Farm, all looked fashionable and relentlessly cishet. Our group appeared quite the opposite: homeless, raggedy, and several quite

conspicuously gender-nonconforming. A few students looked our
way incredulously and mouthed, "What the fuck?"

Climbing out of the van, I unleashed my inner Mike Tyson.
Flexing myself to maximum dieselness, I set a tough, "fuck with us
at your peril" expression on my face and began to walk ahead of our
kids toward the crowd.

Ali was right behind me. She must have scanned the crowd
and perceived my anxiety. In true Luscious fashion, she placed a
huge Afro wig over her head, covered her eyes with a big pair of
supermodel sunglasses, and before I'd even made it across Fulton
Street, strode past me to the front of our group. Ali sashayed up that
sidewalk like she was the *only* diva, the sidewalk was *her* runway, and
the crowd was nothing but insignificant paparazzi minions. It was a
pure weaponization of fabulousness. The crowd parted like the Red
Sea, onlookers gagging in silence at Ali's lusciousness, while the rest
of us meekly shuffled behind.

That year's talent show opened with a riotous performance of
"Proud Mary." Ali and numerous staff and clients—some trans
women, some cis women, and some gay and straight men in drag—
served up their inner Tina Turners, dancing with frenzy in heels,
dresses, and wigs. Next, I had a ridiculously choreographed boxing
match with George Santana, by then our outreach supervisor. In the
skit, I was dethroned as the heavyweight champion by the rotund
George, who proceeded to hold me pinned to the ground while
enjoying a cheeseburger. The act required that I be accompanied to
the ring by my preening "entourage," including my shy roller coaster
partner James Burke. The room was roaring, with kids in the audience falling out in hysterics during the comical acts and shouting
words of encouragement during the more heartfelt performances.

It was finally time for the runway segment. George Michael's
"Too Funky" began reverberating through the speakers, chosen by
our kids because Tyra had appeared in its music video. Dutchess

walked first, sashaying up and down the stage with his customary haughty elegance. Then came Bobby Williams, a handsome youth with a flair for drama. Bobby wore a sheer unbuttoned shirt to show off his abs, which excited the crowd almost as much as what came next. All of a sudden, Bobby dislocated his double-jointed shoulders and vogued with arms like shooting bolts of lightning. The room erupted in cheers. After Bobby, it was time for Ali to walk. Wearing a slinky black minidress and the Afro wig she'd donned outside, Ali strode onto the stage with her trademark flailing wrists, bouncing elbows, and a knowing smile, as if to convey the marvel about to occur.

We hadn't announced Tyra's presence, fearing it would distract attention from our youths. When she appeared next on the runway, clothed in a skin-tight spandex bodysuit, you could hear the auditorium gasp in astonishment. Tyra strode up to join Ali, and they strutted the runway side by side. They kept a certain degree of serious model-esque decorum at first, but Ali became so oversaturated with joy that he finally erupted in spasms of ecstatic giggles, which brought on the same in Tyra. By the time they concluded their walk, each had dissolved into the other's arms in uproarious laughter.

A few days before the talent show, Ali had walked into my office and stood at the door. He asked if we could speak, so I invited him to sit with me.

Ali pointed to a small poster hung on the wall beside us, a prized relic of mine, an advertisement of an Al Green concert from the early seventies. "Carl, I know you love Al Green," he said. "So, I want to sing 'For the Good Times' during the show. To honor you."

He continued, somewhat more hesitantly, "And while I'm singing, I'll be sitting in a chair. I want you to come out and lay your head in my lap, and then I'll drop roses on you, like Al Green does in his concerts."

I looked at Ali, not knowing what to say. He seemed uncharacteristically shy and tentative. On a personal level, I was moved by
the vulnerability of the gesture, by this child offering to honor me
with an expression of love. On a professional level, I was mortified.
This was only a few years after Father Ritter's scandal for having sex
with young men at Covenant House. The last thing I could do was
entertain some false impression that I was at SafeSpace looking for
romance with the youths. It would have been a catastrophe.

"Ali, I'm so flattered," I said. "That's a very sweet offer, to want
to honor me. But there's no way I'm laying my head in anyone's lap
during the show. It would make people think I have terrible boundaries, that I'm the next Father Ritter. I'd get fired."

"OK. I understand." Ali slunk out of my office, his head hanging down.

I was confused afterward, and a little troubled. Though I'd
clearly sensed Ali's caring for me, I'd never perceived it as romantic
or sexual. Some of the other youths made their attraction to me
abundantly apparent. (There was one young man, for example, who
embarrassed me big time by endlessly telling any staff person who'd
listen about his obsession with my butt . . .) I had never gotten
that kind of energy from Ali, and no other client had ever made a
comparable request. Ali never said what she hoped to convey. The
interaction felt mysterious to me, this expression of love without
any explanation.

Only months after that day in my office did it occur to me that
"For the Good Times" is a song about saying goodbye to someone
you love.

# CHAPTER 11

# RUIN

few weeks after the talent show, Tyra returned to SafeSpace, this time with a crew of young female readers of *Seventeen* magazine. Tyra had proposed a day of service, where lucky devotees of the magazine joined her in repainting our staircases. (Though it was well intentioned, the results were a mess. The young women seemed far more excited about being in Tyra's presence than about focusing on their work, and they spilled paint all over the place, including on Tyra's sandals from Bali.)

They arrived as we were finishing lunch. "Where's Ali?" Tyra called out to me from across the crowded dining room. But alas, this time her friend was not there to welcome her.

Ali spent that summer of 1997 locked up in Rikers Island. He was arrested in a police sweep just a few days after walking the runway with Tyra. I'm not sure if he was charged with prostitution or drug possession, or both. Ali had been arrested many times before, but usually was only locked up for a day or two. I can't remember any other time when he was gone from us for months. It made for a depressing summer.

Ali called me numerous times from jail. Knowing I was usually the last person to leave SafeSpace, some days Ali would phone late in the day, after the program had closed. I'd pick up the phone to be greeted with a hushed, plaintive voice announcing, "Carl, it's me, Ali." She'd quietly inquire about various staff and youths and ask if I was being faithful to my workout routines. I'd ask Ali how things were going at Rikers, knowing full well what a degrading and dangerous place the massive prison complex was, especially for someone entirely lacking in butchness. All she kept saying was, "I'll survive."

Ali was released in September, bursting in upon us one day at lunchtime. It made for a festive meal, with Ali rushing to embrace his favorite staff and closest friends, his wrists and elbows flailing about in grand fashion, overflowing with joy at the sight of each person he loved.

But I felt unsettled when I went back to my office following the meal. Ali looked noticeably healthier than before the incarceration, her eyes more alert, skin smoother, body better nourished. When a prison stint improves your condition, it speaks ominously about your life outside. That was one thing that frustrated me about working with homeless kids day after day—I often failed to notice signs of their gradual decline. But as I looked at Ali's improved health after three months of sleeping indoors without drug access, it was impossible to deny what homelessness and addiction were doing to her.

Then, the strangest thing happened. Sitting there at my desk, I was suddenly bludgeoned by an unbearable feeling: *Ali will be the next to die*. It felt like a bomb detonated in my nervous system. Unable to sit still, I jumped from my chair and ran through SafeSpace, barging into each room, searching everywhere for Ali. I finally found him on the top floor, sitting with Tisha and George in the outreach office. Ali gazed up at me, smiling.

I don't know what I hoped to accomplish that day. I didn't usually have care-planning conversations directly with our young people, mindful not to usurp the roles of their case managers and social workers. But this afternoon, in my great anxiety, I made an exception.

"Ali, I need to talk to you," I said, sitting beside him in a folding chair, mounds of condoms and safer sex pamphlets piled up behind us. "I am worried about you. I'm really scared something terrible might happen if you don't get off drugs. Would you let us help you get into a treatment program?"

Ali's face took on the saddest expression. "I know, Carl. I know I need to get clean, but I'm just not ready."

Listening to Ali's sorrowful but adamant refusal, I felt the same damned helplessness I'd become used to at SafeSpace. Helpless to persuade my bosses to provide our kids with housing. Helpless to undo homophobic violence at the city's only youth shelter. Helpless to protect our young people from the swarms of police. Helpless to break through Ali's addiction.

"Ali," I said, my throat clenched tight with a sob, "I'm scared for you. Really, really scared. Please, please, if you even just think you might consider a change, please come to Patrick or me. I need you to be OK. I need you to make it."

Ali looked deeply into my eyes, then looked away. I wonder if she realized what my pleading represented. It was the clearest expression I ever made of how deeply I cared for her.

I don't know why I imagined drug treatment would help Ali any more than it helped Kiki. Ali would have followed my request and then returned to the same old hostile world that wanted nothing for him but death. I guess I hoped that if he got off the streets for a few more months, maybe, just maybe, he might have a better chance to survive.

Reflecting on that autumn, I feel like I'm watching a film of a magnificent lighthouse being pounded by relentless storms. Built high on a cliff, it stands fast against the gale-force winds, until the slope below slowly breaks apart and plunges into the ocean.

For ten years, the storms of loss, of abuse, of homelessness, of addiction, of crushing disappointments had eroded the ground around Ali. Yet so much of her remained intact. Ali continued to love her friends with loyalty and tenderness. She continued to honor her fierce moral code. Even after her many encounters with cruelty and hatred, she continued to treat others with love. How was that not a miracle? But those weeks after her release from Rikers were when the foundation of her life finally crumbled.

Fall is a time when most homeless youths are anxious to get off the streets. Kids who spent the summer sleeping on the piers or riding the subways will redouble their efforts to find shelter before colder weather arrives. Ali was fortunate in those days to have two decent alternatives. Inkera had obtained an apartment through a city program that provided housing to people with AIDS, and Angie had rented a place in Staten Island with her salary as a full-time peer educator. Both loved Ali and invited him to crash at their places. But after Ali's release from Rikers, he stopped showing up.

Inkera noticed an escalation in Ali's crack use, which he had previously been able to keep under control. "Ali was locked up in Rikers for months, longer than ever before," she said. "When he finally got out, he went wild, making up for lost time."

Addiction is a slow, insidious process. For years Ali had used crack, but she'd seemed able to keep it from overwhelming her life. Inkera remembers her and Ali observing the behavior of more severe addicts at SafeSpace—people like Kiki—who were hounded by exhaustion and had a tendency to erupt in tantrums during their comedown. To Inkera and Ali, this level of addiction was frightening. They promised each other not to let their crack use get so all-consuming. After those weeks at Rikers, however, Ali's restraint started to wane. She began to show up at SafeSpace exhausted and volatile after sleepless nights of bingeing. Ali had usually filled SafeSpace with her charismatic, boisterous energy. But now her body language was more withdrawn. She was quieter, almost sullen.

Angie saw the deterioration. Ali would sometimes call her late at night to come pick him up after bingeing at a Harlem crack house.

Angie would jump in a taxi and find him there wearing nothing but boxer shorts. I asked her why Ali would be almost naked.

"Cause Luscious needed to get high. He would sell his clothes to the drug dealers."

I asked what a drug dealer would possibly want with Ali's old secondhand clothes.

"Nothing. It was just so they could laugh at the faggot, laugh at the drug fiend."

As grim as it was, at least Ali reached out to Angie for help, for some kind of deliverance from the degradation. But Ali stopped calling that fall. When Angie tracked him down and asked him to come stay with her, Ali refused. He wouldn't say where he was spending the nights. He'd abandoned the spot where he'd usually slept during the past two years—a bench on 125th Street, below the Metro-North train tracks. Some friends told Angie that Ali was now sleeping hidden among the steep rocky cliffs in Morningside Park, up behind Columbia University. My guess is he didn't want his friends to see him in such a terrible state. But I also heard Ali was buying drugs on credit and failing to pay back the dealers on time—one of the most dangerous things you could do. He may have hidden in the cliffs because he was being hunted, and I'm sure Ali didn't want to endanger his friends.

As for me, it hurts to admit that during those final ten weeks of her life, between that afternoon in the outreach office until just before her death, I hold no memories of Ali. Part of it has to do with this being a rare period when I was simply out of town. We had just been awarded a federal grant designating SafeSpace a "Special Project of National Significance" for our work with HIV-positive teens. On SafeSpace's behalf, I was obligated to spend a week in Washington, D.C., meeting with other grantees. And earlier in the year, I had planned a personal trip to Lisieux, France, for the better part of two weeks, attending the celebration of Saint Thérèse on the one hundredth anniversary of her death.

And then Ali was banished from SafeSpace for two weeks due to an uncharacteristic act of violence, which I'll examine shortly. So for five of Ali's last ten weeks, one or the other of us was away. But that only covers half the time. It breaks my heart to think this, but when I rack my brain for what kept us apart in those other five weeks, I suspect Ali was avoiding me. Maybe he didn't want me to see him crumbling. And maybe I didn't want to see it either.

When I returned from the meeting in D.C., Nancy told me Ali had been banned from the center. I was taken aback by the news; it didn't align with my sense of who Ali was. I can't remember any other time Ali became violent at SafeSpace. But that same week, Ali had also been temporarily banned from NYPAEC, the peer AIDS education program she participated in, because of a similar incident.

Angie remembers the NYPAEC fight. It happened down the block from their office, outside the Fulton Houses in Chelsea. Ali had joined his friend Regine and her boyfriend in a brutal beatdown of another of NYPAEC's peer educators. The young man had borrowed thirty-five dollars from Regine and then refused to repay her—a flagrant violation of the code among street kids. The beating left the young man bruised and bloodied, with a busted lip.

"I hate what drugs did to Ali," Angie confessed. "As his drug use got out of control, he started to become violent. It was like Dr. Jekyll and Mr. Hyde."

The second incident happened at SafeSpace, when Ali saw another client threaten his caseworker, Patrick. Ali exploded with rage, chasing the young man up from the lobby to the first-floor landing, and then repeatedly punching the youth. Staff had to pull Ali off the boy. Both Patrick and Bill Torres remember the reentry meeting being difficult. Nobody wanted to ban Ali from SafeSpace, and some thought the fact that he was defending his case manager should be seen as a mitigating circumstance. But in the end, it was determined that SafeSpace needed to draw a firm, consistent line. Violence was forbidden. Ali couldn't be treated with favoritism.

After the violent incidents, Angie says, Ali was deeply ashamed. "He felt he let his family down."

The first Friday of December 1997, I worked later than usual, remaining in my office until 11 P.M. to write a report for one of our funders. After finishing, I dragged myself to the Forty-ninth Street subway station and found a seat, too exhausted to stand waiting for a train that might be a long time coming at that hour. To my delight, I found Ali there, the lone occupant on the bench.

"Ali!" I called out, "how wonderful to see you!" He gave me a brief, welcoming smile and I sat down beside him. But as we sat there, I grew uneasy. Despite the late hour, there was no sign of "Luscious." Ali was in men's clothes, wearing jeans and a wrinkled, white T-shirt under an unzipped gray parka. His mood was uncharacteristically somber.

That subway station is covered with bright reddish-orange tiles baked in a shiny, reflective glaze. In my memory, those tiles sizzled with incendiary light from the fluorescent bulbs above, as if Ali and I were in an entry station to hell.

"I'm so sorry you were not with us on Thanksgiving," I said. "I missed you." I reminded Ali of our practice of welcoming everyone on Thanksgiving and Christmas, even those who'd been temporarily banned. I had hoped he would join us.

"I missed you, too, Carl," Ali replied.

"Will you be getting on the next train?"

"No," Ali answered. "I'm waiting to meet a date."

Ali seemed lost in some combination of sorrow and stress. Her short, terse responses to my questions were so unlike her normal, happily talkative self. Sensing that our conversation was taxing her, I sat silently beside her for the next ten minutes. Her body seemed to relax. Her eyes softened, and the air between us felt gentle, like she was at least appreciating my company.

When my train approached the station, its headlights flooded the space with their brightness. I turned to Ali and beheld him, a dark, somber figure encircled by the blazing radiance.

Before standing up, I took Ali's hand in mine, wanting to show I held no grudge over the previous week.

"I'm really looking forward to you coming back to SafeSpace next week," I said. "It's never the same without you."

Ali gave my hand a little squeeze. For a moment we looked into each other's eyes. I saw love in Ali's. I hope he saw the same in mine.

"And please be careful on your date," I added.

"I will, Carl," Ali responded.

I arose and entered the subway car. The doors closed, and as the train began to move, I turned around and saw Ali, alone on the bench, waving goodbye.

Four days later, on a Tuesday morning, Nancy entered my office.

"Carl, we just got a call from Harlem Hospital. Ali is there. Someone shot him in the head. They called us because they found Ali's SafeSpace ID card in his pocket. Yola and Kristin have gone to identify the body. Ali is dead, Carl."

All the color seemed to drain from the room. Then, darkness, like I was plunging into a vortex of despair. Not Ali. Not Ali. This couldn't be happening.

I was spiraling, but understood that Nancy and I had to figure out what to do next. I needed to hold myself back from the abyss. For the next few minutes, the two of us made a plan, deciding to tell the staff after lunch, when we usually closed the building for a fifteen-minute break. Today we would close for an hour instead. We made a list of staff who were off that day, planning to call and ask that they join us at the meeting, if possible. We wanted everyone to hear about Ali's death in person. How could we possibly say Ali had been killed and then hang up the phone?

Kristin and Yola called from the hospital. They had arrived to find Ali's corpse lying flat on a gurney, a small bullet wound in his temple. The police said he was discovered at three in the morning, dead on a sidewalk near the housing projects on Fifth Avenue and 135th Street. Whoever shot Ali had walked up and put the gun directly to his head.

Nancy left for her office to begin making her calls, and I asked her to close my door. Once I was alone, the room began to spin. I collapsed. My muscles could no longer hold my body upright. It was hard to breathe. My brain seemed incapable of forming thoughts, save for the word "No," which I wanted to scream. Instead, I just lay there on the floor, gulping for air, my chest heaving with the weight of the suppressed howl.

"Ali," I sobbed. "Ali . . . Ali . . . Ali . . ."

It's hard to say how long I remained there, curled into a fetal position, below the chair where Ali sat when she asked if she could shower me with roses.

An eternity later, I lifted myself off the floor. I reached for the phone and called Raymond.

The week after we met, I had shown Raymond a VCR tape of SafeSpace's recent talent show: Ali and the other kids dancing riotously to "Proud Mary," Ali walking the runway with Tyra Banks, Ali's ritual catching of the ghost and her rapturous proclamation that God loves everyone for who they are. It was my way of saying: *This is what my life is about. This is what I'm most proud of. These are the ones to whom I give my love.*

Raymond would be the first person I'd tell that Ali had been murdered—the first time my mouth would speak those repulsive words. But for the longest time I couldn't do it. I tried to say them again and again until my voice dissolved into a sob. Raymond had never heard me cry. He must have felt the enormity through the phone. He began to cry as well.

After lunch, the staff gathered in the community room, and I had the impossible responsibility of informing everyone of Ali's murder. I don't recall exactly what happened afterward. Everyone around me was weeping. I had not a clue what to say, and a sense of revulsion overcame me when I grasped at any attempt for words. They felt so grossly inadequate in the face of our tragedy.

After forty-five minutes of crying and trying to comfort one another, we had to reopen the building. Other homeless kids were waiting. Their need of us remained constant, even when we were drowning in grief. But I spent the rest of that day on the edge of a dissociative state. Vaguely, I remember Inkera calling and offering to join me when I told the kids that afternoon. By then I felt like a zombie. Like I was outside of my own body, numbly observing my duty to console everyone else, to perform compassion. Inside, all I felt was dead.

After that, my memories of the day recede. I don't remember dinner. I don't remember taking the subway home. I don't remember going to bed. Nothing. The only part of the day that remains burned into my memory is when I was curled up on my office floor, weeping.

Weeks later, when my brain started to come out of its fog, I couldn't stop fixating on the fact that Ali died all alone. If the police were right, nobody would have been with her but her murderer. This tormented me. I wished that I had been with her, that I could have consoled her in her last moments and cradled her head in my lap. To know this sweet, beautiful child with such a tender, loving heart, who had created such a sense of family with us, had to die all alone on a frigid December sidewalk was unbearable. All these years later, it still is.

# CHAPTER 12

# SEEDS OF CHANGE

t had been a decade of death. Cheri and so many others were devoured by AIDS. Ricardo, Dion, and Kiki had been sacrificed on the altar of the "revitalized" Times Square. Each death brought me anguish, but I had still seemed to be able to maintain an inner resilience—to somehow bounce back and carry on with my service. Ali's death was different.

Everything I had to do in those weeks felt impossible. Serving meals to hungry kids, breaking up their fights, leading staff meetings, attending day after day to the traumas of others; it all felt impossible. Even riding the subway each day felt terrible. For months, I couldn't enter a station without dissolving in tears, always brought back to the final moment I shared with Ali.

After Ali's death, I seriously considered quitting my job. I felt utterly unable to cope with the loss. But then something began to shift. Here's what gradually dawned on me: If I could lift myself up off the ground to get through the hell of telling everyone about Ali's death, if I could endure her memorial service—what other impossible things might I be able to do?

My thoughts kept coming back to the need for housing—and the timidity of my previous efforts to make that happen. I began running through a timeline in my head. It had been two years since I went to the executives of SafeSpace and asked to develop an overnight shelter. Back then, I was told plainly that I'd been hired to manage the drop-in center as it was currently configured. By 1996, we'd raised funds to stay open on Saturdays and Sundays, yet the deaths in 1996 and 1997 only reinforced how desperately these kids needed a place to sleep at night.

When Kiki was murdered, I had gone to Beverly Brooks, our parent agency's executive director, and told her if I couldn't develop a shelter at SafeSpace, I'd find another organization that would let me do so. I made it crystal clear I wouldn't take no for an answer. Beverly did not want to lose me, since I had been bringing money and attention to the organization. She reluctantly gave me her blessing. The battle of permission had been won, but there were still no funds for this dream.

But now I had a new sense of mission burning in my heart. If no funds were available, we needed to *force* a change in governmental priorities. I figured the Giuliani administration could be pushed from two points—from the city council, which had the power to change policy, and from journalists who could expose the mayor's deadly neglect of the city's homeless youths.

I reached out to Ken Fisher, a committee member who oversaw the council's youth initiatives, and invited him and his colleagues to join us in our mobile van as we conducted street outreach. I told them most homeless youths in New York had no safe options for shelter, a fact that became obvious when I brought them to speak with unhoused kids in the streets. They were horrified and decided to conduct a hearing to hold the Giuliani administration accountable.

The hearing uncovered something truly shocking: Over the prior three years, New York City had failed to spend more than $3 million in state funds that had been allocated for youth shelters because it was *unwilling* to fork over the matching funds. While Times Square was being gentrified, while displaced kids were being herded into jails and seeking shelter in subway cars, while young people were being murdered in the streets—the Giuliani administration, in an act of sheer contempt, had allowed millions of dollars earmarked for their protection to go unspent.

I was sitting on evidence of yet another scandal. From 1996 to 1997, SafeSpace had participated in a study that the Giuliani administration conducted on the housing needs of youths living with, or at high risk for, HIV. The report had made it clear how dire the conditions were for NYC's homeless youths, and ended up recommending a series of housing interventions. The administration was incensed. Giuliani had no desire to fund the recommended changes, even though $500,000 in federal HUD funds had been spent conducting the study. A mayoral representative warned that we were forbidden from making the report public.

Now, here's the crazy thing: If the mayor's office had simply released the report, it would have likely gone unnoticed as yet another wonky study on a needy population in a city chock-full of unmet needs. But the act of suppressing the report, especially at a time when Ali and other young people were being killed, ramped up its newsworthiness.

I called Melissa Russo, who hosted *Inside City Hall* for New York 1 News, and said I was in possession of a report that the Giuliani administration forbade me to share. I told her I would show it to her, but only if my being the source would remain anonymous. (Giuliani was famous for stripping funding if a nonprofit dared criticize him.) Soon I was in New York 1's offices handing over an unmarked copy of the report. They broke the story, and it was widely reported on by other outlets, including *The Village Voice* and NPR.

Months earlier, I had been able to persuade Tina Rosenberg, an editorial writer for *The New York Times*, to join us at Ali's memorial. In the past, we held services for our clients in a small side chapel of Saint Mary's, large enough to fit the dozen or so mourners. Ali's memorial was held in the main sanctuary, with almost a hundred people joining us. I had not seen so much weeping in a church since

Dignity was evicted from Saint Francis Xavier. Rosenberg was able to see, in a very personal way, the level of tragedy that had occurred.

It took about six months before her reporting appeared, but by then, the scandals were breaking. In July of 1998, Rosenberg wrote an editorial about Ali's death, in which she eviscerated the Giuliani administration for its reckless disregard of homeless youths. It was the harshest spotlight imaginable. For a local politician, having such a critique in the pages of the *Times* was akin to the voice of God thundering down condemnations from Mount Sinai.

Just days after the *New York Times* editorial, Beverly received a call from the city. Suddenly they were desperate to spend that year's allocation of state funds. Unless the administration contracted with a local organization within three weeks, more unspent monies would be returned to the state. And thus, SafeSpace was abruptly given funding to develop a small youth shelter program. At last, a tangible victory!

The new grant would support eighteen beds. This was a great start, but not nearly enough, considering that there were hundreds more unhoused young people in our care. To help keep those youths safe at night, I wanted to extend our drop-in center's hours, so that instead of being open merely eight hours per day, we might remain open for the entire twenty-four hours. But where would I get the money? Surveying the funding landscape, I saw that the federal government had given the city a block grant of tens of millions of HUD dollars. It was up to the New York City Department of Homeless Services to determine where the unmet needs were most severe. I had testified at the previous hearings in 1996 and 1997, trying to make the case for homeless youths, but the funding had gone toward other needs.

Now, in the aftermath of Ali's death, I brought the raging force of my anguish to the third of those hearings. This time, I did not prepare a testimony. Instead, I sat praying in the cavernous auditorium, calling fervently on Ali and Saint Thérèse to enflame my words with the enormity of what was at stake.

When my name was called, my body language shifted. While working, I usually downplayed my bulked-up muscularity, wanting to be a gentle leader. That day was different. I strode up to the podium like a lion, like I was the king of the homeless advocacy jungle. I flexed myself, holding the podium as though it was barely restraining me from attack, and fixed my gaze on the city commissioner.

The words came out of my mouth with slow, deliberate intensity: "I am *sick to death* of coming here year after year and *begging* the city to recognize that the vast majority of homeless kids have nowhere safe to sleep at night." With an escalating ferocity, I continued, "But even more so, I am sick to death of sending my staff to the morgues to identify the murdered bodies of our kids, while the city does *nothing* to protect them."

I brought my fist crashing down upon the podium. There had been a continuous murmur of distracted voices in the auditorium, but now the whole room fell dead silent. The commissioner, an officious, elegant-looking middle-aged white man who'd appeared bored throughout the testimonies, suddenly looked alarmed.

Continuing to glare at him, I said, "You have the power to make a change." I paused. "So do it."

People in the room were shaken. *I* was shaken! It was like I'd been possessed by someone else; I'd never spoken with such strength and authority. Afterward, I heard the drama of my testimony was the talk of the city bureaucrats in attendance. But it turned out to make a difference. That year, the city finally designated homeless youth a priority population, and SafeSpace received a grant award of $500,000 to keep our drop-in center open through the night.

It was a remarkable breakthrough. With these new sources of funding, we'd be able to keep far more young people safe. We would also be able to restore the smaller, homelike youth shelter model that New York City had lacked for the better part of a decade.

The next year, 1999, was dominated by the nuts and bolts of getting new programs opened. We had to renovate our drop-in center to accommodate the rapidly escalating number of kids coming through our doors. We had to find landlords willing to rent us apartments in which we would first start to provide overnight shelter for our young people. (Just try telling a Manhattan landlord that you hope to move six homeless kids into their building. It was a nightmare even finding real estate brokers willing to go to bat for us.) We had to survey the young people and staff to assist in designing the overnight program at the drop-in center and the new residential sites. Each new residential apartment was required to be certified by New York State's Office of Children and Family Services, an onerous process. We had to hire a slew of new staff. I wished I could have been cloned; there needed to be three of me to oversee all that had to be done.

I was so focused on these tasks, it was difficult to take in the magnitude of what we were accomplishing. Yet, by the end of 1999 we had gotten the drop-in center opened overnight and acquired five residential apartments, which we called SafeHaven. Later on, one of those apartments would become the seed of the vision for the Ali Forney Center.

In my early years at SafeSpace, I would have resisted the idea of creating a specialized program for LGBT kids. Our hope was to provide an environment where straight and gay and trans kids could coexist in (a somewhat tenuous) peace. In the mid-nineties, many queer teens were still in the closet and didn't want to out themselves by attending a "queer" program. Kids would arrive closeted and find the courage to come out after getting to know openly queer youths and staff. Unfortunately, the police sweeps of Times Square led to imprisonments where many of our kids were recruited into violent street gangs like the Bloods, the Crips, and the Latin Kings. Virtually all of these groups were virulently homophobic. If a member was found out to be gay, they'd be beaten and maybe even executed. As the number of gang members attending SafeSpace swelled, openly queer kids began to avoid our program.

I first remember noticing the change in demographics the day Ali was killed, when Inkera joined me to break the news to the group. As I looked around at the twenty-five or so people seated in a big circle in the dining room, I realized everyone but Inkera and me was straight. That ratio would have been unimaginable a year or two earlier.

We needed to respond to this new challenge not by banning the gang members, who needed us as much as any of the others, but by cracking down on their violence, threats, and intimidation. We had to think intentionally about how to keep SafeSpace safe for queer kids in this new environment. It was challenging, because while we were able to address the gang issues within our program, we had little control over what happened outside, in the blocks surrounding SafeSpace, where some of the gang members took to threatening and tormenting the openly LGBT youths.

I wanted to try something we'd never done before: reserving one of the SafeSpace apartments specifically for our queer youths. I wanted the LGBT kids to have at least one place in their lives where they wouldn't be exposed to anti-queer harassment.

It was eye-opening, seeing how the queer kids thrived once we made that change. All of a sudden, they had a space where they didn't have to be on guard, didn't have to worry about protecting themselves, didn't have to censor themselves to avoid others' hostilities. The young people who lived there soon became noticeably happier, freer; they became better able to get jobs and reenter school. I realized what an onerous psychological burden it is to always need to protect yourself against others' hatred, and how being released from that burden allowed the queer youths to blossom.

Recently, I caught up with Jovon, who lived at the queer Safe-Haven apartment when he was eighteen.

Jovon was a husky biracial gay youth, often attired in black Armani Exchange T-shirts and jeans. He'd journeyed to us through a teen hellscape: juvenile detention in Ohio, followed by a Bible camp in Pennsylvania that practiced gay conversion therapy, and finally a stint at Covenant House in New York City.

Jovon spoke to me about his time at Covenant House. "You had to fight to use the bathroom. . . . You had to fight to eat. The staff wouldn't let gay kids sleep in the bedrooms 'cause they said we'd fuck each other, so we had to sleep on the hallway floors, and they'd rip the wigs off the trans girls' heads before they'd let them enter the dining room."

"I'll never forget the first day the queer SafeHaven apartment opened," Jovon continued. "All six of us walked in together and we saw the burgundy walls and the stainless-steel refrigerator and the shower with two shower heads (which we all thought was *glorious*), and we saw how it was a space that had been curated *for us*. It was like a promise fulfilled going all the way back from Stonewall, that there would be some kind of equity for us."

Jovon remembered preparing with his roommates for their first Pride celebration. They spent days critiquing and perfecting one another's outfits. Then they marched with SafeSpace in the parade and gathered back at the apartment that evening for a celebratory meal. It was so profoundly different from his previous experiences in youth shelters.

"We'd talk about how lucky we were to be the ones to live there. Like, how incredible was it, that after all the shit so many homeless queer kids went through, we should finally be the ones to have it so good?"

When asked if any other memories stood out, Jovon described a change he witnessed in one of his co-residents.

"Carmen was a trans-identified woman from Honduras. I remember being in the SafeSpace clothing room with her. She was changing into this hot little maxi dress, and I saw her back covered in bruises. Her family was Roman Catholic—like, her father was a deacon or something. They did an exorcism on her, they beat Carmen with a Bible and a crucifix, tried to beat the gay demons out of her. She had three broken fingers from being hit with the Bible.

"In SafeHaven, it was like she could finally stand tall and proud. She'd be like, *Look at me in my wig! Look at me in my makeup! Look at me in my pink fluffy robe!* She'd dance around the apartment in that pink, fluffy robe, and we'd all join her dancing and voguing in the living room. It was magic, it was dignity. It was just incredible."

As I witnessed the small victories that we won in the years following Ali's death, an ambiguity began to gnaw at me. We'd seen substantive improvements in the conditions for NYC's homeless youths, all of them instigated by something truly horrific: Ali's death. I wondered how to hold those contradictory realities together in my heart.

I would ask myself a question that I knew was absurd and stupid, but in the clutch of grief, we cannot expect ourselves to be entirely rational. I'd ask myself if those transformations were worth Ali's death, if they somehow gave that death meaning. The question made me miserable. Nothing could ever justify Ali's lonesome death on that fucking sidewalk. No outcome is good enough to warrant the death of a child.

Anyway, the premise behind the question is fundamentally false. The abysmal conditions of New York City's homeless LGBT youths *had* to improve. Our young people weren't just relegated to the back of the bus—they were hurled off the bus onto a murderous highway, other vehicles crushing them like they were nothing. But cracks had begun to form in the wall that separated the dispossessed queer kids from any societal concern. The energy was shifting. An organization called Green Chimneys had recently opened a transitional residence for LGBT youths. In 1999, Mariah Lopez and a group of other plaintiffs won a lawsuit proving that LGBT youths were routinely harassed and abused in the New York City foster care system. The city opened LGBT group homes as a response. Young people in the West Village formed their own organization, FIERCE!, and began to empower street youths to resist the policing and displacement that was expanding from Times Square to the Christopher Street piers. Seeds of change were taking root.

We humans have an awful capacity to perpetuate systems of injustice. We enable them, we collude with them, we close our eyes and hearts to the lives ravaged by them. But as torturously slow as their dismantling can be, I believe systems of injustice must inevitably crumble to the ground. We cannot keep our eyes and ears and hearts shut forever.

There is not an atom of my soul that can ever be grateful for Ali's death. But how can I not rejoice in having witnessed a space where abused queer kids no longer had the wigs ripped off their heads, where they could finally dance in celebration around a young woman exulting in her freedom to wear a pink fluffy robe? The things I witnessed in those years—in particular, the great goodness and liberation offered by intentional spaces for dispossessed queer youths—would inform my sense of mission for years to come. And in a strange, paradoxical way, I discovered, slowly, that fighting to provide such homes for other young people allowed me to stay connected to Ali's spirit, despite the unbearable loss.

# CHAPTER 13

# THE MOTHERS OF JUSTICE

B y the new millennium, SafeSpace had become a very different organization. Our SafeHaven apartments continued to expand, and with the drop-in center now open for twenty-four hours, we were able to protect seventy young people every night. This ability to provide shelter was transformative. SafeSpace had formerly felt like a waystation where we fed, and tried to protect, young people on an inevitable road to doom. But once we were able to keep them safe at night, our clients were almost immediately able to get themselves hired or enrolled in school, and we saw significant decreases in their drug use and sex work. The results showed.

Another improvement was that we finally made inroads into the new economies of Times Square, securing internships and jobs for our young people at several of the recently opened businesses. (This was a big change from the horrible days of 1996–1997, when I repeatedly reached out to the Times Square Business Improvement District, hoping they might open job opportunities for our young people. Back then, I couldn't get my calls returned.) One young transgender woman even got hired as a customer service representative in one of the big new hotels in Times Square, receiving a salary that exceeded that of Kristin, the life skills coordinator who'd placed her in the job.

Nonetheless, our limitations could still punch me in the gut. For example: the day James Burke aged out of SafeSpace. James was the almost mute, innocent young man who'd been my companion on the Cyclone in Coney Island. With his social limitations, we knew James would continue to need help after he turned twenty-five and left our program. His case manager, Patrick, had been taking him to visit drop-in centers and shelters for homeless adults, hoping to ease the transition.

I was worried about James. He'd been accepted at SafeSpace, but I feared for his ability to navigate adult homeless facilities, many of which were overcrowded, chaotic, and dehumanizing. The Neighborhood Coalition for Shelter operated an adult drop-in center on East Seventy-seventh Street. Having worked there prior to SafeSpace, I knew it to be gentler than most and hoped James might stand a chance there. I called my old boss and asked if she could make sure to give special attention to James when Patrick brought him there to check it out. She rolled out a kind welcome, accompanying them both on the tour, speaking warmly of the various ways they might assist him. But James didn't say a word. He didn't seem to be absorbing the situation, didn't seem able to reckon with what was coming.

When his birthday arrived, it was time to bid James Burke goodbye. Many of us stood together for a long time, hugging him in the lobby, before we showed him to the door. As usual, James didn't say a word. He just stood across the street, remaining there from morning till night, staring up at our windows and sucking his thumb. I could not bear to look out the window. All I could do was close my eyes.

James Burke was the last client remaining from the subway ride where I'd had a spiritual awakening to the depth of my love and responsibility for the young people in our care. Milagro and Precious Jewel had stopped visiting SafeSpace, and Ricardo and Ali were both dead. Having to enforce James's departure felt like a betrayal. A betrayal of James, and a betrayal of my deepest inner convictions.

James camped across the street for three days, and then disappeared, never to be heard from again. I called my old boss, who said

James never returned to the adult drop-in center. None of the other youths knew what had become of him. He simply vanished.

Those were the days when I began to hear the screams.

We had no money for soundproofing windows, so our work at SafeSpace was accompanied by the relentless noise of Times Square—police sirens, heavy traffic, drilling from numerous construction sites. But a jarring new sound had joined the rest. Sitting in my office in the afternoon, I would jolt at the sound of a crowd of people suddenly screaming. The first time it happened, I feared there had been a terrorist attack, or that a crane raising up one of the new high-rise hotels had dropped metal girders onto a crowded sidewalk below. But no, the screams were coming from the recently opened MTV studios, three blocks from us, as crowds of teenage girls glimpsed the Backstreet Boys or Destiny's Child through the windows of the *Total Request Live* set.

It felt strangely dislocating to see Times Square becoming a celebratory destination. How could those young women possibly understand the horrors that had happened in the blocks where they stood? Did they know the price of the party they were cheering on?

As expensive hotels and restaurants began to creep onto our block, I grew more uneasy. Our youths, who a few years earlier had blended seamlessly into the neighborhood, now made for a jarring contrast, their poverty rudely apparent in a sea of affluence. I began to fear it was only a matter of time before SafeSpace itself would be swept away.

In the fall of 2000, Beverly and I were summoned to the church of Saint Mary the Virgin, our landlord, for a meeting with the new rector, Stephen Gerth. Father Gerth had led the church for eighteen months, but this invitation felt significant. He had declined my every invitation to visit SafeSpace up until then.

I had a wonderful relationship with Gerth's predecessor, Father Edgar Wells, who had originally invited us to open SafeSpace in the church's mission house. In those pre-gentrification days, our partnership served us both well. The church didn't have the resources to fund any service programs, even though the purpose of the mission house had been to serve the neighborhood's poor. For SafeSpace, the site was ideal. Times Square was the center of activity for the city's homeless youths, and the church had offered to rent us the space for the nominal fee of $35,000 per year—simply the cost of insurance and our utilities.

The church became one of our biggest advocates. Father David Carlson, a young priest who assisted Father Wells, began offering an optional weekly spiritual support group for our youths. This group was free from any preaching of what anyone "should" believe; it was simply a space where our young people could sort out their personal religious concerns. Ali had been one of its faithful attendees. Many queer kids, who'd been told by their parents that God hated them for being gay, were *astonished* to learn Father Carlson had a husband. After he talked to some of the kids about their experiences, it was sweet to observe that just being in the presence of an openly gay priest could heal many wounds of self-hatred that their previous experiences with religious people had caused.

In the aftermath of Tangie's, Dion's, and Ali's murders, the priests at the church showed such care and concern, you would think their own children had been killed. They led the funeral services and performed those works of mercy with much tenderheartedness— consoling us in our terrible sorrow, showing us love. I came to feel much love for those good, caring, kindhearted men.

But in 1996, Father Carlson left to become the rector of a church up in Westchester County. Then, in 1998, Father Wells resigned as the vicar of Smoky Mary's.

Shortly afterward, we received the HUD funding to open SafeSpace overnight. The increased use of our building would necessitate upgrades to its antiquated heating and electrical systems, but I was anxious about investing several hundred thousand dollars into the building during a time of transition. What if the new rector didn't share Father Wells's commitment to our work? I talked to Gerald, the chair of the parish's board of trustees, who reassured me that the work of SafeSpace was dear to the hearts of their congregation. They wanted our partnership to continue "well into the next millennium," and selecting a rector who valued our partnership was a high priority. With the trustees' blessing, we went forward with the costly renovations.

Father Gerth arrived in February of 1999. When I greeted him after his introductory Mass, the tall, blue-eyed, prematurely white-haired priest seemed thrilled to meet me, giving me a brilliant smile and gushing about how he had heard wonderful things about me and our work. When I invited him to visit SafeSpace, he said that he looked forward to doing so, but that I should first give him some time to settle into his new life.

In the following weeks I called Father Gerth several times to reiterate my invitation, but he kept saying he was too busy. With each call, his tone became less friendly. The weeks stretched into months and Father Gerth still had not found the time to walk the ten yards' distance from the rectory to SafeSpace.

I reached out to Father Wells to discuss my concerns. During our four years of partnership, he'd taken me out to lunch from time to time. So one Wednesday we reunited at our usual Ninth Avenue lunch spot, and I told him of my anxieties about Father Gerth's aloofness.

Father Wells was pained to hear it. "This is not a good sign that the partnership will continue," he warned.

"But Gerald promised me that the trustees would prioritize bringing in a rector who valued our work," I responded, hoping I could will Gerald's assurances into reality.

Father Wells shook his head. "In the Episcopal Church, the rector has sole discretion over the use of church properties. If he doesn't want you there, there's nothing the trustees can do about it."

The next week, Beverly and I anxiously made our way over to the rectory. Father Gerth invited us into a parlor, where we sat with him and Gerald on old-fashioned, high-backed upholstered chairs. Gerald looked stiff and uncomfortable. Meanwhile, Father Gerth was giving us these odd, self-satisfied, reptilian smirks, as though he could not restrain his glee at what was about to transpire.

"Our church is facing a financial crisis," Father Gerth began. "We have an annual deficit of two hundred thousand dollars. If we do not turn the deficit around, Saint Mary's will no longer be viable.

"But we have an opportunity to turn things around," he continued, the Cheshire cat grin still plastered to his face. "There is a marvelous new energy in Times Square, and we need to harness it. The way we need to attract new parishioners is to begin a church-led service program in the mission house."

Then Gerald began to speak. He sternly announced that SafeSpace's lease term was ending in six months, and the church had made the choice not to renew it.

My insides felt like they had turned to concrete. I wanted to cry. My mind began to run through the ramifications of what was about to happen. It had taken us the better part of the year just to upgrade our building's heating and electrical systems. How on earth would we raise the funds, renovate a new space, complete the entire move, and get the licensing needed for our medical clinic in six months? It was not possible. We'd be lucky to pull off such a feat in three years!

I looked at Beverly, but she sat silently in her chair, her face gray and ashen. I knew it was up to me to say something.

"We just invested hundreds of thousands of dollars upgrading the building, with your blessing!" I said, looking desperately toward Gerald, still clinging to the hope that he'd honor his promises. But he just sat there, stone-faced and unresponsive.

I asked if, considering this new information of the church's financial peril, SafeSpace could pay a market-rate rent, which would have covered their deficit. They said no, it was impossible, their tax-exempt status prohibited their profiting from the property. I asked if we could purchase the building. Again, they refused. I asked if we might negotiate a lease extension to give us time to find and ready a new site. Again, that was impossible. Everything was impossible, and it was all delivered with a smile.

I was not a man prone to violence, but at that moment I wanted to punch that damned smile right off Father Gerth's face. Gerald, who had promised a partnership enduring well into the new millennium, couldn't even look me in the eye.

Father Gerth cocked up his coy grin once more and reiterated that the only way the church could survive was to harness the neighborhood's energy by starting its own church-led service program. Lifting his arm, he gestured to the wall behind him: "It needs to be a religious program, with a crucifix on the wall."

It was a chilling moment—and for me, an insult to everything that crucifix was supposed to represent. When Jesus died on the cross, it was to humbly share in our sufferings and reveal the depths of God's love. The love of the crucified Christ was a million times more present in our abandoned kids than in anything Father Gerth might hang on a wall. Jesus once said, "*Whatever you do to the least of these, you do to me.*" Didn't Gerth see that by throwing our kids away, he was turning his back on God?

The priest announced there was nothing further to discuss and showed us to the door. Descending the rectory's steps into the noise and bustle of Times Square's "marvelous new energy," I was reeling—panicked at the possibility that we would be unable to protect our kids.

After that grim meeting, I searched frantically for a new site, while Beverly launched a fundraising campaign for our relocation. But by November I had not found anything remotely promising, and our lease was ending in five months. We tried again to plead for a lease extension, but our religious landlords refused to even discuss it. Our situation was growing more and more desperate.

On Thanksgiving, while heading over to SafeSpace for our big meal, I picked up *The New York Times*. You can't imagine the shock of what I found. Inside was an article in the Home and Garden section about a just-completed renovation to Father Gerth's *eleven-room* house. (A parishioner, ashamed of the spectacle, described Father Gerth's elegant minimalist aesthetic to me as "Martha Stewart Monastic.") How tone-deaf to show off one's beautified digs while simultaneously kicking out a program for homeless children. I thought *The New York Times* might also find the juxtaposition jarring, so I reached out to pitch the story.

Several weeks later, Nichole M. Christian, a reporter from the Metro section, was sitting in my office. I gave her background on the situation: the promise Gerald made before we undertook costly renovations, and the history of our good relationship with the church when Father Wells and Father Carlson had been in charge. When I told her how Father Gerth hadn't set foot in SafeSpace in his two years as rector, her eyes opened wide.

"Could you repeat that?" she asked. She was amazed.

I'd been forewarned the *Times* would present both sides of the story. But when I saw how disturbed Nichole was by Father Gerth's obvious indifference to our youths, I grew more confident her reporting would forcefully depict our misfortune.

The article exceeded my wildest hopes. Nichole's presentation was devastating. A large photo of many of our young people being fed appeared above a bold headline: "Church Evicting a Youth Refuge in Times Square." Below the photo of the kids was a smaller one of Father Gerth, his head tilted up in an arrogant gesture, which made it look like he was recoiling in disgust. I was struck by the racial subtext in the visuals. All the youths in the photo were Black and Latinx, and Father Gerth, by contrast, looked white as hell. Further cementing this subtext, in his first quote justifying his decision to throw us out, Father Gerth spoke of Saint Mary's surviving the "dark days" of Times Square.

The caption above Father Gerth's sneering photo read, "The church's rector since 1999, the Rev. Stephen Gerth, has never visited the center next door."

The article went on to tell the history between Saint Mary's and SafeSpace, discussing Father Carlson's support group and the funeral services for kids who'd been fed and supported on church grounds. It quoted Father Wells, asserting the relationship had been a good one in his day.

When I read Nichole's article, I learned that Father Gerth's plans for the space had evolved. He was no longer talking about a parishioner-led religious service program with "a crucifix on the wall." Now he was proposing a daycare program for the children of corporate executives. What an absurd idea! Daycare programs are rigorously licensed in New York City. It would have taken millions of dollars to make that rickety four-story walk-up building viable for daycare. And anyway, what corporate executives were going to bring their children from Greenwich and Scarsdale and plop them in some religious daycare program in the middle of Times Square? It was obvious Father Gerth hadn't thought out any plans for the space; he just wanted us gone.

All hell broke loose after the article appeared. Local politicians swamped my answering machine with offers to help. Funders soon followed suit. Numerous journalists wanted to report further on the conflict. A great many Episcopalians—some from Smoky Mary's, some from the local New York Diocese, some from around the country—reached out to express their shame and sorrow at Father Gerth's treatment of us. One former parishioner of Smoky Mary's insisted that if Father Gerth threw our kids out of the mission house, then Mary—the church's namesake and the Mother of God herself—would depart from the church in disgust and join our youths in the street.

Suddenly an extension of the lease was open for discussion. Somehow, it was no longer "impossible."

Several weeks after the article appeared, Beverly and I were summoned to the rectory for another meeting. This time there were no smiles. No sooner had all the participants arrived than Gerald and the Saint Mary's attorney began to holler at me about some of the media reports. "How dare you say that Father Gerth is gay!" they bellowed. I was astonished. I'd never made such an assertion. I suggested that they reread the articles and see that it was parishioners of Saint Mary's who'd mentioned he was uncomfortable around queer people, not me. (Some parishioners had alleged to me separately that he wanted us gone because he was in the closet and having gay kids nearby made him nervous. I discouraged them from focusing on Father Gerth's orientation, as I thought their speculations distracted from the central issue of our youths' welfare.)

"I have no interest whatsoever in Father Gerth's sex life," I explained. "My only concern here is the safety of our young people." I hadn't come here to be portrayed as the wrongdoer. Borrowing from the first text that came to mind—Madonna's *Erotica*—I told them, "This is not a crime, and I am not on trial."

The meeting ended, and we still had no agreement on an extension. I was pushing for a minimum of two years, while Gerth and company were talking about weeks. Clearly, we needed to keep up the public pressure before they would engage in a meaningful negotiation. At that point, our ability to publicize their shameful behavior was the only power we held.

A group of supporters—some friends of mine, some disaffected members of the parish, some outraged Episcopalians from other parishes—started meeting weekly to strategize how we might ramp up the pressure to give SafeSpace an extension on our lease. We decided to hold a rally in Times Square, followed by a candlelight march through the streets.

The Rally to Save SafeSpace was held on a cool April evening among the luminous rays of the setting sun. We arranged with the police that a whole block in the middle of Times Square would be shut for an hour to accommodate us. I got a kick out of seeing that, for once, it was the tourists who were pushed aside. To my delight, hundreds of people showed up: queer activists, politicians, ministers, and service providers, all standing side by side with our young people. It was a beautiful mosaic of care, right where the awful sweeps had gone down.

Several ministers spoke to the crowd, as did local politicians, all calling on Father Gerth to show mercy. Some of our young people spoke, telling how SafeSpace was their lifeline and their refuge, and pleading that it not be taken from them. I was the final speaker. I told the crowd that our work with the young people was a work of love and thanked them for coming to our defense.

To be honest, I was anxious about what might transpire next, when we marched past Saint Mary's. How would people react? What if someone lashed out? Would anything happen that might harm our negotiations? I decided to address it in my speech.

"Sometimes," I said to the rallied group, "we find ourselves in situations where there are no words that can do justice. In those times, the most appropriate response is silence. Please, when we pass by Saint Mary's, let us walk in beautiful silence."

When the crowd processed past the church, you could have heard a pin drop. Not even the presence of Father Gerth and Gerald standing guard outside provoked a reaction. When we finally reached SafeSpace, we all massed together at the steps, where one of our staff read aloud the words of the Magnificat, the very words engraved on the church's altar:

> *God has cast down the mighty from their thrones*
> *And has exalted the lowly.*
> *He has filled the hungry with good things*
> *And the rich he has sent away empty . . .*

I was encouraged that some prominent folks were marching with us. Our state assemblyman, Richard Gottfried, and city councilwoman Christine Quinn were there. So was Charles King, who founded the prominent HIV/AIDS advocacy group Housing Works. (He called me the next day, offering to chain himself to Smoky Mary's altar in protest!) But just before the rally ended, I discovered that we'd been joined by someone truly extraordinary.

As we prepared to recite the Magnificat, I scanned the crowd and saw a banner bearing the name STAR. I knew that was the name of an organization Sylvia Rivera and Marsha P. Johnson founded in the first years after the Stonewall riots: the Street Transvestite Action Revolutionaries. My heart started to race, and I plunged through the crowd. To my amazement, I found the legendary Sylvia Rivera there, alongside two companions.

Sylvia and Marsha were among the very first to advocate for homeless queer youths in the years following Stonewall. They are the forebearers of our work, the fierce mothers of justice for our

community's disowned children. By the time of the march, Sylvia
Rivera had been through some tough years. In the mid-seventies,
Sylvia left the streets of New York and moved to Tarrytown, a
nearby suburban community where she and her lover ran a cater-
ing business. But, overcome with grief after Marsha's death in 1992,
she had become homeless again, taking shelter in the transgender
shantytown by the Thirteenth Street pier. For a time, Sylvia was one
of the women our outreach workers brought food and clothing to.

Now Sylvia was off the streets, working in the food pantry at the
openly LGBT Metropolitan Community Church. But it was sad
to notice how the toll of those years showed in her appearance. I'd
seen her in photos looking like this fierce, glamorous force of nature,
but now she appeared frail, her hollow-cheeked face looking small
above a big blue jacket, her graying hair pulled back in a ponytail.
Still, what a trailblazer that stood in front of me. I knew our work
was built on the shoulders of giants, and Sylvia was undoubtedly
one of them.

I reached out to embrace her.

"Thank you so much for joining us, Sylvia," I said. "What an
honor, to have you here!"

With a quavering but deliberate voice, Sylvia looked me in the
eyes and proclaimed, "I would do anything for the children. These
are our children. We must stand up for our homeless lesbian and gay
and transgender children." She looked down and started to shake
her head. "What's wrong with that priest?" she muttered in disgust.
"They are our children."

*They are our children.* Sylvia's words were like a flash of light in the
night. And with that light came a clarity. In my decades of serving
homeless people, I had observed a demoralizing pattern that kept
repeating itself. There is a deformity in human nature. We have the
tendency to become so obsessed with wealth and power that we are
willing to devalue others, even categorize them as lesser, to justify

our inequalities. If there is such a thing as original sin, I do not see it, as Saint Augustine says, as being rooted in sex, but rather in our awful capacity, when we have power, to exploit or discard the powerless. That devaluation had been the defining stance of the deadly police sweeps, and of Father Gerth's willingness to toss us away with a smile.

But I learned there is an antidote to that deformity in our nature, and it lies within those words that Sylvia said to me. *They are our children.* Sylvia Rivera knew that the homeless youths had value. They belonged to us, and we belonged to them. If we organize around that principle, if we invite others to stand in solidarity with those whom the world wants to forget, I know we can find a more humane form of power.

In the years to come, *They are our children* would become my mantra, my slogan as we fought to improve the abysmal conditions for homeless queer youths. I'd write it in op-eds, I'd preach it in churches and synagogues, I'd shout it during rallies and at protests in front of City Hall. I would forever carry forward that simple, but powerful, truth first spoken to me by that great transgender revolutionary, that ravaged mother of our movement, Sylvia Rivera.

Shortly after the rally, Father Gerth begrudgingly agreed to a nineteen-month extension on our lease. Our fight, our advocacy, and our organizing had brought about a rare victory. For once, our young people weren't swept away.

CHAPTER 14

# COLLAPSE

Raymond possessed a subtle, psychic superpower. He could "feel" a person's energy. Occasionally, after meeting one of my staff, he'd pull me aside and whisper, "That one's a mess. They're going to give you lots of trouble." Those predictions proved so accurate that I began wishing Raymond could sit in on our job interviews. His psychic evaluations might have prevented numerous dramas.

Raymond met my boss, Beverly, one night at a benefit. He was seated next to her, but he felt so repulsed by her energy that he switched seats with one of my co-workers. Raymond pulled me aside afterward and said, "I couldn't get away from her fast enough. I *hated* the way she made me feel."

Troubled, I asked what exactly he'd felt.

"She doesn't care at all about your kids," he said, grimly. "All she cares about is money."

I told Raymond how Beverly had given me free rein to expand the services for our young people. Before I reported directly to her, there had been way more roadblocks. "Dozens of young people have a place to sleep tonight because Beverly supported my vision."

"Beverly doesn't give a damn about your vision," he responded. "You need to open your eyes. When she looks at you, all she sees are dollar signs."

When I'd arrived in 1994, SafeSpace's budget was $900,000 per year. By 2001, it had grown to $5.4 million, the fruits of my fighting to provide the young people with housing. I had also built relationships with media and politicians that our parent organization, the Center for Children and Families, lacked. In 2000, hoping to capitalize on that notoriety, Beverly took our name, rebranding the entire parent organization as SafeSpace.

After Raymond's warning, I noticed troubling signs. I wouldn't know the difference between Prada and Thom McAn, but my co-workers had pointed out that Beverly had taken to wearing very expensive shoes and designer clothes. Once, when she was out sick and I needed her to sign a contract application, Beverly had me meet her at her apartment. She directed me to a luxury building just off Fifth Avenue, where the elevator opened to an entire floor belonging to Beverly and her husband. Her assistant also told me that Beverly was seeking a second home up in Putnam County, with a swimming pool and tennis court among her property requirements. All of this was perplexing. While I knew she received a generous salary, it hardly seemed sufficient to finance such an extravagant lifestyle.

One day in late August 2001, I got an odd call from Beverly's chief fiscal officer, Amir. He said our HUD funds had been used up well in advance of their contract term, and because of this, I was going to need to shut our drop-in center's overnight program. We would also have to eliminate several of our SafeHaven apartments.

Over the years, I had become accustomed to errors from the agency's fiscal department, so I figured Amir was confused. Obviously, I hadn't spent down the HUD funds. It had taken so long to renovate the drop-in center and persuade landlords to rent us apartments that I had hardly begun spending down the HUD program budget. Just two months earlier, I'd requested permission from our HUD officer to roll over the unspent funds into the next contract period. We were expecting more than a million dollars to roll over.

The following week I went to our agency headquarters in the Puck Building to set the record straight. Amir was a rather portly, white-haired Egyptian man in his sixties, and he seemed gloomier than usual. After he invited me to sit in his office, he spoke words that chilled me to the bone. "Carl, times are bad. The agency has been suffering from terrible cash flow problems. Homeless had to be sacrificed for the greater good of the agency."

He explained that whenever our agency was in a cash flow crunch, they would, with Beverly's approval, pull from the Homeless Department's federal contracts like an ATM machine, drawing down whatever was needed, despite my Homeless programs not actually having spent the funds. He took out a ledger for the HUD contract to show me what he meant. For the first drawdown, in 1999, I had merely spent $29,000, but they had claimed expenses of $280,000 so that they could meet the agency's shortfalls in other areas. Again, he repeated that grotesque phrase, "Homeless had to be sacrificed."

The money was gone. My heart dissolved into a puddle of misery. Amir was demanding I shut down my programs, but he instructed me not to notify our federal contract managers. (The contracts stipulated that I was responsible for notifying HUD if we were unable to fulfill their terms.) He showed me a memo in which he outlined a strategy to mislead our auditors, with Beverly's signature OK'ing the plan. Clearly, he and Beverly expected me to go along with this. *For the greater good.*

I bolted out of there. According to everything I understood, what Amir described was wildly illegal. But even worse to me was the reality that they had misused money specifically meant to keep our kids safe at night. How could they have done this? I left the Puck Building in shock, my head spinning.

When I got back to SafeSpace, the first thing I did was call Beverly, who was away at her country house. I told her what Amir had revealed about using the homeless youth funds for other agency needs, pointing out that this was unethical and illegal. Cutting me off in midsentence, she shrieked, "You don't know what you're talking about!" and slammed down the phone. I sat there, stunned.

"If you need to steal so you can keep your damn agency going, maybe you should rob a bank or a gas station," I yelled at the disconnected phone. "How *dare* you steal from homeless children?"

While serving dinner that evening, I looked at our young people peacefully eating their food, finally believing they had a refuge from the terrors of the night. I felt sick to my stomach. That dining room was haunted with memories. I could still see Kiki eating at those same tables; Cheri crying in my arms; Ali running through the room and hugging everyone after her release from Rikers; Inkera and me breaking the news of Ali's death.

*What the actual fuck,* I thought, struggling to keep my emotions off my face. *Are these kids like some black hole doomed to absorb nothing but abuse? Does* everyone *need to shit on them?*

I felt myself beginning to hyperventilate again. I asked another staff person to take my place serving the food, then I retreated to my office, where I began to weep.

I knew what I had to do next. I had to resign.

I couldn't go along with the fraud, and there was no way I would fire staff or put kids out in the street because of Beverly's wrongdoing. I felt like I was being torn apart. I loved SafeSpace. Despite everything I have written of in these pages—the suffering of our young people, the cruel acts of homophobia and transphobia endured by so many, the heartrending deaths—I had found a rare form of closeness and solidarity there. These people were my family. I'd never even considered another life. But how could I possibly continue working for Beverly? My trust had been shattered.

In my haze, I spoke to an employment attorney about the situation. He advised that I resign immediately.

"They told you about their fraud assuming you'd go along," he said. "But if they're worried you won't, they'll probably try to pin it on you. I've seen organizations react like that a thousand times. You need to make copies of fiscal documents that show what you actually spent, and then get the hell out of there."

Right on cue, Beverly began sending me emails demanding that I cut "my" $500,000 deficit. This shook me from the torpor. I had to get out fast.

Raymond and I spent hours in my office that weekend, copying financial documents and hauling boxes of them to his car. When Beverly returned from her vacation that following Tuesday, I called her and asked if we could meet. Then I typed up my resignation letter.

I couldn't sleep that night. I kept getting up to pace my apartment, all while my conscience lacerated me. *How can you allow yourself to slither away in defeat? Don't you realize that resigning will only make it easier for Beverly to throw the kids away?*

By 3:00 A.M., I came to a decision. Walking away would be a betrayal.

Whatever power and influence I still had, I would use to pressure Beverly to own up to the misuse of funds and work with the federal government to restore them. I'd be damned if Beverly thought she could discard the youths without a struggle.

Around the break of dawn, I deleted my resignation letter and wrote a new memo. I detailed all that Amir told me about the misuse of funds, and I demanded Beverly join me in informing HUD.

That morning I went to SafeSpace and met with my staff, telling them about the depleted funds and letting them know I was on my way to meet with Beverly to insist we go to HUD. There was a strong chance I'd be fired on the spot. I didn't want to vanish without letting my co-workers know what was happening, or telling them how much I'd loved working with them. Everyone looked shocked. Several began to cry.

Trembling with anxiety, I made my way to the Puck Building. Beverly was a tall, imperious woman in her mid-sixties. Feeling like some queer David about to face off against a matriarchal nonprofit Goliath, I entered her office, sat across from her, and handed her the memo, trying to keep my hands from shaking. Beverly had gotten herself a facelift that summer. (It was a good one, too—took twenty years off her face.) Poor thing, as she read the memo, I saw those thousand-dollar cheekbones collapse.

She lifted her head, visibly infuriated and petrified.

"This is completely wrong," she insisted. "You have no idea what you are talking about."

"Beverly," I responded, "Amir explained the whole thing to me. He showed me the ledgers. I know exactly what I'm talking about."

She continued to insist I was wrong, that I had no understanding of the agency's finances.

I told her that I had not come to argue over my understanding of their fiscal practices. We needed to inform HUD that the funds were gone and let them determine how to resolve the situation. I would not put the kids out in the streets and fire the overnight program staff without informing HUD.

Beverly's eyes narrowed into little slits. "You're nuts!" she spat out. "You're a zealot!"

"Beverly, I don't care how many names you call me. We have to tell HUD." I explained that I was going to inform them with or without her, and that there would likely be a better outcome if she cooperated.

"Well, that makes you a whistleblower," she said. "So I cannot fire you. But what I will do is put you in an office and strip you of all your responsibilities, and you'll just sit there for the rest of your life."

"Whatever," I responded. "You do what you have to do, and I'll do what I have to do."

Beverly stood and walked across the hall to summon Amir. I took deep breaths, trying to compose myself. Our verbal jousting had felt as combative as a physical brawl.

Beverly returned with Amir and handed him my memo. "Everything he writes is accurate," Amir said after reading it. But then, seeing how his response enraged Beverly, and perhaps fearing for his job, he pivoted. "However, the memo is shit and I wipe my ass with it."

Amir tended to speak in a slow, ponderous manner. His scatological comment was so bizarre and delivered with such drama that, despite my stress, I fought the urge to laugh. *What the hell is happening?* I thought.

I stood up. "I've said all I needed to say." As I prepared to leave, Beverly looked at me, and the rage in her face momentarily softened. I guess she wondered if this was the last time we would be together.

"You were very dedicated to the kids," she said softly. "You accomplished a great deal for them."

I walked out of her office without a further word.

I knew there wasn't much time before I'd be fired. Lawful or not, Beverly would not stand for one of her employees openly defying her.

After leaving her office, I met with councilwoman Christine Quinn's chief of staff. I went over the situation with him and asked if he could persuade Christine and her close ally, state senator Tom Duane, to urge Beverly not to close my programs. As we spoke, I became so overcome with emotion that I began to cry.

Then I called Robert Sember, an evaluator who worked closely with HUD, and scheduled a meeting to discuss issues with our contract. I hoped that if I told Robert what happened, he might ramp up the pressure on Beverly, and she would see there was no choice but to tell HUD. With the meeting set, I emailed Beverly, saying that I planned to bring the depletion of our contracts to Robert's attention. She replied saying that if I did so, I'd be fired.

Over the weekend, I was a mess. Monday, September 10, would be a day of reckoning. Raymond was freaked out as I paced back and forth across the apartment like some big, manic Italian Energizer Bunny, wondering if my plans would be enough to protect the youths in our care.

I arrived at Robert's office early Monday morning. A gentle, mellifluous-voiced South African man, he greeted me kindly and told me Beverly had called just before I arrived. Then I sat down and walked Robert through what I'd learned about the misuse of funds, asking that he urge Beverly to go to HUD. He agreed to do so.

"This is just so sad, so terribly sad," he said, shaking his head. As our evaluator, he knew SafeSpace was extraordinary; few programs in the country had so effectively integrated HIV treatment alongside the concrete services like housing that homeless youths needed to survive.

I thanked Robert for meeting with me. Then I headed to SafeSpace. When I showed up at the daily staff meeting, many of the staff spontaneously burst into applause. Everyone had wondered if I would keep my position through the weekend, and most were relieved to see me. It was a sweet gesture, one for which I remain grateful. But then I checked my phone and found a message from Beverly, demanding I report to the Puck Building to work with Amir to cut "my" $500,000 deficit.

Our contract manager, Lynn, and Milly, my assistant, came with me to the purported budget meeting. My plan was to suggest that Beverly sell one of her luxury properties to close the deficit. But when we arrived, I alone was herded into her office.

Beverly looked at me with withering contempt.

"You violated your nondisclosure agreement by meeting with

Robert Sember this morning," she said, handing me the agreement senior officials like me had been required to sign. "You've given me no choice but to terminate your employment, effective immediately."

"Beverly," I said, "don't put our kids out in the streets. Those HUD contracts were meant to protect them."

"Get the hell out of my office," she snarled.

And with those words, my seven years with SafeSpace came to an end.

The next day, Raymond called me at ten in the morning, weeping.

"Don't cry," I said. I assumed he was upset over my firing. "I needed to leave SafeSpace; there's no way I could have worked with Beverly anymore."

"Haven't you seen the TV?" he exclaimed. "Two planes crashed into the World Trade Center. The South Tower just collapsed!"

I ran to turn on the television, and moments later, in a state of shock, saw the collapse of the North Tower in real time.

For me, those horrific days in New York City became inextricably entwined in my memory with the collapse of my life at SafeSpace. People running through the streets covered in ashes; every screen flashing with unbearable images of people hurling themselves from the burning towers; then, later, the thousands of heartbreaking photos of missing loved ones that were posted up all over the city—everything seemed reduced to ruins. The whole world was burning.

I had planned to contact HUD that Tuesday, but when I realized the federal government in D.C. was also under attack, I decided to wait. Two days later, I called David Vos, the director of HUD's Housing Opportunities for Persons with AIDS (HOPWA) division. When I informed him of the misuse of funds, he put me on hold for a few minutes and went to examine the drawdowns.

"You're right," he said upon returning, his voice low and grave.

"The contracts have been alarmingly overdrawn. We will need to initiate an investigation."

"David, my greatest fear is that our homeless kids will be the ones to suffer the consequences of what Beverly has done. They didn't do anything wrong, and they *need* those programs. Please, David," I begged, "please try to find a way to protect them."

David thanked me for bringing the matter to his attention. And that was it. As far as I could see, I had done all I could do, and it was over. I had to move on.

But was it possible? Two weeks earlier my world had seemed intact. How could all my work, all the outpouring of my heart and soul, come to this? I felt totally defeated.

It's hard for most of us to accept the degree to which chaos overlaps with our lives. We convince ourselves that we control our destinies. But things collapse, disasters strike, often through no fault of our own. I thought of the people in the World Trade Center on September 11: the secretaries, restaurant workers, janitorial staff, and all the rest who were there first thing in the morning. They were drinking their coffee, preparing for their day, working to support their families—all before being engulfed in an inferno. Life is full of meaningless, arbitrary chaos. We cannot prevent this.

My spiritual tradition recognizes defeat as being necessary to the process of transformation. "Blessed are you who mourn," Jesus was quoted as having said. And, "Unless the grain of wheat falls to the earth and dies, it bears no fruit." Death is inescapable, whether or not we have a spiritual tradition that helps us integrate loss into our sense of purpose.

But to be honest, spiritual answers seemed hateful to me then. Were the fiery deaths in the Twin Towers necessary to the spiritual growth of those who perished? Of course not. And hadn't the young people at SafeSpace already endured far more than their share of loss and trauma? What good could come from them being once again tossed out into the streets?

There were no answers to lessen the hurt. All I could think to do was to sit before the crucifix in my apartment, staring mutely at the image of a defeated, annihilated God.

# PART
# THREE

---

*You surely know that the Scriptures say "The stone which the builders tossed aside is now the most important stone of all." This is something the Lord has done, and it is wonderful in our eyes.*

—JESUS OF NAZARETH, *The Gospel of Mark*

---

# CHAPTER 15

## ALIVE

*You're alive! You're alive!"*

It was a sunny fall afternoon, six weeks after I was fired from SafeSpace. I was in Midtown, walking across Bryant Park, when I heard the shouts. I looked up and saw the familiar face of Jovon, one of the kids from the shelter, charging toward me at full speed.

"You're alive!" he repeated deliriously as he jumped into my arms, practically bowling me over. "They wouldn't tell us what happened to you. They wouldn't tell us where you went. But you're alive!"

*Just barely,* I thought. I was glad, though, to hear Jovon's updates on his life, enjoying his enthusiasm as he bragged about getting a job with the Big Apple Circus.

Those were challenging times for me. When the word got out that I was no longer at SafeSpace, I received job offers from other nonprofits, but I felt so battered by what Beverly had done, I felt unable to consider them. When it is your job to serve others, you need to bring your best self, to give with enthusiasm and dedication. I wasn't remotely up to the task. Hell, I could barely get myself out of bed each morning.

Fortunately, for the first time in my adult life, I didn't need to worry about supporting myself. I'd always lived paycheck to paycheck, but I had accrued months of unused vacation time at SafeSpace, since I was often too busy to take time off. This meant

I would still receive my salary for three months. Also, my recently deceased grandmother had left me money in her will. With some frugality, I could afford a year without needing employment. I would have time to recover from my wounds and imagine a new life.

I told myself I could take a sabbatical of sorts. I would use the time for prayer, meditation, self-reflection, and, hopefully, some healing. But I was troubled to discover how deeply a sense of hurt had reached its tentacles into me. Searching for some comfort, I went to Mass each morning at the nearby Church of the Good Shepherd and spent time praying and meditating on a bench at Inwood Hill Park, down the road from my apartment.

Then the quiet came crashing to an end. In early December, my phone began ringing off the hook. One after another, former co-workers called to say that Beverly had announced the overnight drop-in program would shut down in two weeks, ten days before Christmas. And then I was told of an unimaginable horror: After the kids learned of the planned closure, a young woman who'd been sleeping at the drop-in center went to the Queensboro Bridge and attempted suicide. Thank God, her big puffy down jacket cushioned her body from the impact. A policeman saw her plunge into the river and dove in to rescue her.

I could tell I was getting these phone calls because my former co-workers hoped I might do something. But what could I do? All I wanted was to be done with SafeSpace. I'd been fired, for heaven's sake. I needed to give up the ghost. Still, I couldn't expel the thought of the young woman throwing herself from the bridge.

Soon, my worst fears were confirmed. SafeSpace publicly announced that the drop-in center and SafeHaven apartments would be shuttered in the spring. The closure of the queer Safe-Haven apartment upset me most. I thought of Jovon, of Carmen and her pink fluffy robe, of Dion and Kiki and Ali. Once again, there would be almost no place in New York City where unhoused queer kids could rest safely.

The response seemed obvious: I should try to open a shelter for queer kids myself. But in my bruised state, it was not something I felt capable of doing. I went through several days of turmoil, racked in combat with my conscience. I'd say to myself, *You are burnt out. Demolished. You don't have it in you to start something new. You poured your heart out for those kids, only to have your efforts trampled in the mud. How can you even find it in you after what happened with Father Gerth and Beverly? You. Don't. Want. To. Go. Back.*

But one memory kept flashing across my mind. It was a phone call I'd made several months after Ali's death. I had called Kate Muldowney, a social worker at the adolescent HIV clinic at Montefiore Hospital in the Bronx, where several of our HIV-positive youths received medical care. When she picked up the phone, she had asked how I was doing.

"It's been a rough time," I admitted. "One of our young people was killed, someone I cared for very much."

She asked who it was. I told her I doubted she would know him because he wasn't HIV-positive, but she said that she'd been a social worker on a mobile outreach van before joining Montefiore, and knew many of the street kids.

"Ali Forney," I said softly. "Ali was shot in Harlem at the beginning of December."

On the other end of the phone, Kate began to cry.

"Oh my God," she said, her voice unsteady. "I used to see Ali on the van. He came for therapy every Thursday night, faithfully." She gulped and whispered, "I loved Ali."

I apologized for being the bearer of such awful news. "We all loved Ali," I said. "That poor kid had a great heart. It's just been so horrible."

And then, after she was finally able to compose herself, Kate said, "Carl, Ali spoke about you every single time we were together."

I didn't know how to take in her words. "Oh, you mean Ali spoke about SafeSpace."

"No, Carl," she said. "Ali always spoke about *you*."

I began to tremble. "What did Ali say about me?"

"That he loved you," she said. "Ali always talked about how much you meant to him, and how he loved you."

After we finished speaking, I laid my head down on my desk and wept. It was the first time I'd heard of Ali saying that she loved me. Kate's speaking those words out loud hit me like a bolt of lightning; they brought Ali's love out of the realms of silence and intuition, made it concrete, undeniable.

As someone who was abandoned as a child, I suffer from a grinding tendency to doubt that I am lovable. I am great at questioning whether someone really loves me, attacking the evidence like a pit bull defense attorney. Yes, I saw Ali looking at me with love; yes, he called me all those nights from prison; yes, he wanted to serenade me with the Al Green song. Yet I still tended to wonder if Ali's love was a figment of my imagination. It was different to hear Kate say those simple words aloud. Ali had told her that he loved me. It put the debate to rest.

What do we owe those who love us? How do we assign limits to our responsibility to them?

Now, as I debated what to do next with my life, Kate's words played on endless repeat inside my head. *Ali loved you . . . Ali loved you . . .* There was a framed photo of Ali on my desk, but I felt afraid to even look at it. I felt unworthy. On a spiritual level, I knew that love holds no measuring scale; it is a gracious gift from God, surging forth wild and free from the heart. Nonetheless, my conscience ate at me: *You did not do enough to protect Ali. You didn't find it in you*

*to fight until the most unbearable tragedy had already occurred. There is
nothing you can do that will ever undo the wrong.*

When I finally lifted my eyes toward Ali's photo, the voice spoke
again: *If you turn away, if you refuse to help, the queer kids—especially
the transgender kids—will once more have no safe shelter, and more will
die in the streets like Dion and Kiki and Ali. It would be like you sur-
rendered Ali to the grave yet again.*

After three days of turmoil, I suddenly felt anchored in the certainty of what I needed to do. I thought it over and realized that
my inheritance money from my grandmother offered a much better
opportunity than I'd imagined. Instead of merely using it to support myself, I could use it to support young people who needed it
far more. I would put my sabbatical aside and dedicate myself to
opening a shelter for homeless LGBT youths.

As soon as I came to this decision, I knew what the shelter would
be called. The Ali Forney Center.

# CHAPTER 16

# ALL WE NEED

O nce I made my decision, I had to take stock of the challenges.

The new shelter would need government support, which would be more difficult to acquire than at SafeSpace. We were in a new millennium. Another political party had taken occupancy of the White House, one whose hostility toward LGBT people became more apparent with each passing day. The Bush administration, overwhelmingly staffed with conservative evangelical Christians, gained a reputation for tossing out any federal contract applications focused on serving LGBT youths. Their religious principles allowed them to collect taxes from us queers, but not to fund core needs of the LGBT community.

But to be honest, I was also worried about my ability to gain support from the queer community. The early 2000s were not a time when the movers and shakers in our movement rallied around the needs of our poorest members. In the five years since AIDS ceased to be the overriding focus, the priority had quickly shifted to marriage equality for LGBT adults.

For all the horrors AIDS had inflicted before the advent of life-saving treatments, it had brought forth a certain solidarity from the LGBT movement. All of us stared death in the face, whether we were sick or healthy, and our universal terror had a unifying effect. In those days, homeless LGBT youths were recognized as a population particularly vulnerable to AIDS. But now any attention seemed to have evaporated. I scoured the websites of the large national LGBT advocacy organizations: Human Rights Campaign, the National LGBTQ Task Force, GLAAD. Not one of them acknowledged queer youth homelessness as a crisis facing our community.

But if I wanted the Ali Forney Center to stand a chance, I knew we would need to turn the eyes of our broader community toward its most destitute members.

By February, I'd gathered a group of people to help establish our shelter. The pastor of Metropolitan Community Church offered the ground floor of her church building, saying we could use it as a temporary shelter while I raised money for a permanent space. Eight weeks later I persuaded Henry van Ameringen, a wealthy gay supporter of SafeSpace, to give us our first donation. We had lunch together at his favorite restaurant in the West Village, and he wrote me a check for $35,000. I heaved a sigh of relief. Henry's immediate gift was the first sign that our efforts would be met with generosity.

We were scrambling to open the Ali Forney Center as soon as possible. SafeSpace was shutting its drop-in center in two months, and they had already closed most of the housing I'd opened. With Henry's donation, the money my grandmother left me, and the space at Metropolitan Community Church, we could at least begin to offer some shelter. I figured the money would last through the end of the year, by which time I hoped to gain more support.

I suppose most people in my shoes would have wanted more security than merely six months' operating funds, but I put my trust in God's providence. I had absorbed an ethos of trusting from the Catholic Worker: If you are willing to respond to the needs of the poor, God will see to it that you have the means to do so.

A week before we opened, I sent emails and faxes to every organization in the city that worked with LGBT kids and homeless youths, notifying them we would be opening an LGBT youth shelter.

Within twenty-four hours, we received more than twenty referrals for our six cots. By the end of the first week, more than a hundred young people would seek shelter from us.

Metropolitan Community Church is situated a few blocks from Covenant House, among the same snarl of roads leading to the Lincoln Tunnel. Our shelter would be on the ground floor, below the sanctuary and church offices. During the day, the space functioned as the food pantry where Sylvia Rivera had worked during the final months of her life. It wasn't close to being a perfect shelter setting—the windowless room was lined with boxes, hardly the sort of homelike space I wanted to provide. But given SafeSpace's closure, it felt urgent to open now, rather than force kids to wait while I raised money for a better facility.

The Ali Forney Center launched on a warm, muggy evening in June 2002. We cleared a large space in the center of the room, assembled the cots, and laid out sheets, pillows, and blankets. At eight o'clock we opened the inner gate, and our first six kids came through, carrying their belongings in old knapsacks and plastic shopping bags. I saw those first young people walk in and take in the humble surroundings: six cots with a kitchen and a large folding dining table in the back. As they unburdened themselves of their bags, I saw the tension in their faces begin to dissolve. They had slept in the streets, in subways, on park benches. They seemed relieved, having made it to this place.

Each young person claimed a cot and gathered with us around the table for our first meal, cooked by my husband, Raymond. I introduced Raymond and the staff members to the youths, and they told us their names. As we ate together, I looked into their eyes, listened to their voices, and felt the reality of their physical presence, the preciousness of their young queer selves alone and abandoned in the big dangerous city.

My heart flooded with warmth for these vulnerable kids. And I felt, far more vividly than I had until then, the magnitude of the responsibility we'd taken on.

Remembering that first summer, I'd love to be able to paint a picture of myself as some valiant, visionary hero, brimming with confidence as I led us into a bright new future. That would be a lie. I still felt utterly gut-punched by the implosion of SafeSpace. And furthermore, as we assessed the vast needs of the youths seeking our help, I quickly became demoralized by our meager ability to respond.

At the height of my time there, SafeSpace had a medical clinic, mental health services, a twenty-four-hour drop-in center, six different sites where we provided housing, and an abundance of food and supplies. Now, in the first days of the Ali Forney Center, I had merely one large room in a church basement. Instead of a $5.4 million annual budget, I had a savings account with $35,000, which was dwindling each week. I wasn't taking a salary, and I paid for all the food and supplies out of my pocket. Each day, dozens more young people sought shelter than we could accommodate. They'd call or show up at our door, and we'd have to turn them away. It was gut-wrenching to watch their hope deflate as they headed back into the night.

I didn't share my discouragement with the handful of staff I hired. They needed to have confidence in me, so I put on a brave face. Meanwhile, each morning, I'd wake up anxious and immobilized, feeling too miserable to get out of bed.

In those first months I did all the food shopping, usually purchasing several days' supplies at a Gristedes supermarket in the West Twenties. One September evening, I arrived loaded down with shopping bags and saw a new youth had joined us. KJ was a seventeen-year-old transgender man who had not yet begun to transition. Their long, dark hair was pulled back in a ponytail, and they wore jeans and a blue and white plaid shirt. They offered to help me unpack the groceries, and we did so together quietly.

After dinner, they remained with me at the table and told me their story in the calm, thoughtful, somewhat sardonic way I would come to know as a hallmark of KJ's personality. The details weren't easy to hear.

KJ had lived in Brighton Beach, the Brooklyn neighborhood that was home to many Russian immigrants—among them KJ, their younger siblings, and their mother. For as long as KJ could remember, their mother had singled them out for abuse. But "things got much worse," they said, "after Mother found Jesus and I found cock." She turned to religion when KJ was fourteen, and her attacks became more frequent and intense. "She'd say I was a sinner, I was dirty, I was shameful before God."

Then, peering intently into my eyes, as if relieved to have their trauma heard, KJ continued.

"One day last month, my mother totally lost it. She attacked me, she grabbed my hair and tore out a piece of my scalp." KJ pulled back their hair to reveal grotesque scabbing that hadn't yet healed. "I had to get out of there. As far as I knew, she was going to kill me."

I felt my throat clench with revulsion. What a corrosive force homophobia is, to make a mother turn on her child like that.

"I pulled away from her, burst out the door, and was running as fast as I could down the stairs of our building, blood pouring from my wounds," KJ continued. "My mother stood at the top of the stairwell and screamed, 'You'll be back! The faggots will never take care of you!'"

For the next month KJ couch-surfed, staying with friends. Things got scarier when they ran out of places to stay.

"I'd hang out at the piers, and other kids warned me about Covenant House, how they'd been attacked there. So I stayed in Central

Park, in the Ramble. But it felt unsafe, too exposed. Then I decided to sleep under the boardwalk at Coney Island, a place I remembered from when I'd volunteered at the aquarium. That was better until September came and it began raining. So, I slept in the subway, which sucked because police were always harassing me. Then a cot opened for me here."

I'll never forget KJ sitting beside me at the dining room table, telling that vile story. I had been given outlines of similar accounts at SafeSpace, but I suspect that being in a deliberately queer shelter enabled this young person to confide in me with a directness and vividness I hadn't heard before.

KJ left a deep impression on me, especially in my own worn-down state. They and the others had absorbed so much hatred and rejection, yet they continued to endure, continued to have hope, continued to rouse themselves from their cots to face each new day. It seemed miraculous to me. Whatever adversities I'd gone through with Beverly paled in comparison. I realized healing would come if I focused more on them and less on myself.

Raymond helped cook the Ali Forney Center's first Thanksgiving meal, preparing macaroni and cheese and collard greens and a tray of smoked turkey wings. We drove the food from our apartment down to the church and added it to other dishes the staff had brought—roast turkey, stuffing, cranberry sauce, and pies. Raymond can throw down in the kitchen, and the kids gleefully heaped seconds and thirds onto their plates. As we all sat together sharing the meal, KJ spoke up, saying how grateful they were that Raymond and I had joined them. Our presence made it feel more like a home, they said, more like a *family*. Then they added, "This is the first Thanksgiving where I've ever been happy, because it's the first where I'm allowed to be myself."

I looked around at this newborn community of outcast kids

eating side by side in a grubby church basement, and realized I, too, felt happy, something I hadn't felt for many months. Our resources might have been meager. Each person around that table might have been battered and bruised. But that night none of it mattered. We had each other and were making it through together. We had survived, we were *alive*. And for an hour or so, I felt I was maybe the luckiest man in New York City.

# CHAPTER 17

# HOME

That fall, I breathed an enormous sigh of relief. Several private foundations agreed to provide support to the Ali Forney Center. Then, in what seemed almost a miracle for an organization so young, we were awarded a government grant from the HOPWA program. (The HOPWA money came from one of the contracts Beverly had defrauded. After SafeSpace's closure, it was redistributed to other organizations.) We finally had the money to rent housing, upgrade from cots to proper beds, and double the number of young people we served. My seemingly foolish trust in God's providence—launching a program with almost no funds—proved not so foolish after all.

I rented our initial three apartments in early 2003. The first was in Hell's Kitchen, just above the bustle of Ninth Avenue, with its little shops and restaurants. The other two we secured a few months later, in a Harlem tenement a few blocks north of Columbia University. The smaller of those Harlem apartments served as our first office, while the other units, taken together, provided beds for twelve kids.

As with the SafeHaven program, it was important for these spaces to feel like homes, rather than institutional shelters. At the core of our young people's trauma was a message that being queer made them unworthy of remaining in their family homes, unworthy of belonging. I hoped that our living spaces would be a tangible statement of the opposite. We rented three-bedroom apartments which fit six young people each—a setup that felt like a family. Each time I visited one, I delighted in seeing kids sitting together around the couch watching TV, gathered at the table for dinner, or even arguing over whose turn it was to use the shower. After all they'd been through, such simple, humdrum acts of normalcy were something to cherish.

Our surroundings speak to us about who we are and what we might become. When we place homeless people in large, frightening shelters, it implies that they are outcasts, fit to be herded into warehouses on the margins of society. I wanted our spaces to speak of the young people's worth: of how they were worthy of being in homes, worthy of belonging to a community, worthy of respect, worthy of love.

I was in our Harlem office during the great Northeast blackout of 2003. When the power went out, I was leaving the building and headed toward the subway for a meeting. I didn't make much of it. The place had poor electrical wiring, and power failures were a common occurrence. But Raymond called my cell saying all of New York City had gone dark.

Our apartments always had at least one staff person present to prepare the meals and attend to the needs of the young people, remaining awake through the night to ensure the safety of the residents. But the person scheduled to be present at the Harlem apartment was stranded out in Brooklyn, so I needed to stay overnight with the youths, which they found quite a treat. A few of them sat down with me to strategize how we'd cope with our lack of light and electricity, and to offer menu suggestions for our improvised dinner. Not wanting us to be submerged in darkness, I ran to a nearby Dominican botanica and bought three big, glass candles with Catholic devotional images printed on them. As we ate and slept that night, we would be watched over by Our Lady of Guadalupe, the Sacred Heart, and San Lazaro having his wounds licked by dogs.

Fortunately, we had a gas stove, so I was able to cook a decent dinner. I set about preparing spaghetti with meat sauce while Ron, one of our youths, "supervised." (I tried not to be snarky when this little white-bread boy saw fit to tell my grown Italian self how to make a Bolognese sauce!) During the candlelit supper, conversation bubbled around the table until the kids became fixated on guessing how old I was. They settled on twenty-eight. When I revealed I was in fact exactly ten years older, they let out a collective gasp.

"Oh my God!" exclaimed Andrew, a former model who had fallen on hard times. "You must do *mad* Botox!" In their minds, thirty-eight was the pit of decrepitude.

I pointed out I was a full seven years younger than Madonna, whom Andrew had recently claimed looked "so flawless" in her "What It Feels Like for a Girl" video. "Well, we all *know* Madonna does mad Botox," he said.

After the kids went to bed, I settled on the couch for a long, sticky night. The city was sweltering through a heat wave. With the loss of power depriving us of an air conditioner, or even a fan, all I could do was sweat and pray that the frozen meats stuffed into our de-powered freezer wouldn't go bad. Our monthly food order had arrived the day before. If the meat spoiled, it would have been a financial disaster for us in those bare-boned days.

As I sat on the couch listening to the faint sound of the young people snoring away in their bedrooms, I was reminded of something I'd realized two decades earlier, when I first worked overnights at a shelter: how entirely lovable people appear when they are sleeping. A person is so unguarded, so vulnerable, while they sleep. For once, the masks and self-protections of their personas are stripped away, leaving their souls in full, unadorned display.

Power was restored in the morning. The young people were relieved to be able to shower themselves, and I said a prayer of thanks for the salvation of our frozen meats.

As the kids got dressed and headed out to their schools and jobs and drop-in programs, I was able to witness a ritual the six of them had created to start their mornings. Before going out the door, they lined up in single file before a full-length mirror I had purchased for the living room. (When we first rented the apartment, it merely contained one little face-size mirror in the bathroom—*totally unacceptable* for a house of queer kids.) One by one, they stood before the mirror and struck a brief pose. Some were flamboyant supermodels, striding to the mirror with haughty elegance. Others served banji realness with their tough little homo-thug gestures. I loved how dignified and respectful they were, each waiting their turn in line, none mocking or being shady toward any of the others.

I saw in those poses a marvel of collective hope and determination. These young people were owning their pride in themselves, shedding the skins of shame before they went out into the world.

It was one of those paradise visions from the lives of the saints, a moment when a veil dissolves and we are able to see the Divine. For a brief, shimmering moment, someplace in this broken world appeared *perfect*.

They were home.

A decade earlier, when I began working with homeless youths and saw how atrocious their conditions were, I was plagued by a pressing question. Who would advocate for them? Schools, daycare centers, pediatric medical providers were far more abundantly supported than programs for homeless youths—largely because taxpaying, vote-casting parents wanted and needed those services for their children. So who would advocate for homeless youths, most of whom couldn't vote and were penniless? Certainly not the parents who wouldn't or couldn't care for them. Who else was there but the ragtag little group of us poorly funded providers? But what power did we have?

However, in those first years of the Ali Forney Center, an answer began to dawn on me. Queer people had the potential to become a voice for homeless kids. Because of our intrinsic collective experience of being exiled, we might have a deeper capacity to empathize with kids who'd literally been kicked out of their homes. We've so often been made to feel alien—a tribe of Dorothys stranded in Oz, dodging attacks from wicked witches (or wicked bishops), exiled from paradise, longing to get back to the garden. I began to suspect that the challenge of finding a true home on this homophobic, transphobic earth could resonate as core to the very mission of queerness.

Isn't the desire for a home among our deepest cravings? A place where we can rest and relax; where we can discard our masks and be our silly, goofy, outrageous selves; where we remove our armor to reveal our tender parts, and even our wounds. In our hearts, we all want a place where the essential parts of our truth are not cause for shame.

A few years after launching the Ali Forney Center, my husband and I moved upstate. Since childhood, Raymond had cherished a dream that when he turned fifty, he would buy a house in the country and raise chickens. As his fiftieth birthday approached, we began to look around.

We were hardly rich, so I tried to figure out how we could afford his dream. I discovered that the area near the border of Orange and Sullivan counties, where the Hudson Valley merges into the Catskills, was rather inexpensive. We found a place on the banks of the Neversink River, about a two-hour drive from the city. Soon we had chickens, followed by turkeys, ducks, and a sweet, hungry pig named Sophie.

Every night when I was done at the Ali Forney Center, I'd

embark on the long drive upstate. As I journeyed through the dark, the stresses of the day would slowly evaporate, until I walked through our front door and was finally *home*. Maxwell, our little dog, would greet my arrival with a dance of ecstasy, jumping in a frenzy until I lifted him in my arms so he could barrage me with kisses. Raymond would greet me more calmly from the couch, where he'd invariably be watching his beloved *Golden Girls*. When Maxwell at last wore himself out, I'd cut up an apple, grab a handful of Goldfish crackers, and head to our garage, which Raymond had converted into a barn, to bring our pig, Sophie, her nighttime snacks. She'd lurch up from her slumber to welcome me with a happy grunt and a wagging tail.

What a wonderful thing it is, to have a home. There were many years when I did not truly have one.

When I transitioned from childhood to adolescence and began to realize I was gay, I felt like an alien within my family. Suddenly, there was this essential part of me that I feared would make me unacceptable. I felt the need to hide who I truly was. Wise intuition on my part. When I came out to my father at the age of twenty-two, he never spoke to me again. He told my mother that he was ashamed of me. Painful as his rejection was, it only put an exclamation mark upon the previous nine years, when I was consciously trying to stifle any evidence of my queerness, when I was terrified that I would not be loved for who I am.

Most queer people of my generation, and those that preceded mine, know what I'm describing. We know the fear and anguish that came with needing to hide our truth, unable to truly be at home in our families, at our schools, among our friends.

These days the lack of acceptance isn't as total as before, but too many young people are still made to feel like aliens in their homes. And of course, homeless queer youths are doubly exiled— their homelessness being physical as well as psychological. And the youths of color among them, who make up most of the unhoused queer population, have experienced a triple exiling—for they've frequently been unwelcome and unaccepted in white-dominated LGBT spaces. But there is something within each of us that refuses to accept being exiled, that longs and yearns to find a home.

Throughout my years of working with homeless youths, I've observed how many of our young people of color sought such a home within the pageantry of Ballroom. I first became aware of Ballroom culture when I saw *Paris Is Burning* upon its release back in the early 1990s. For me, as for many in the queer community who hadn't previously known about that scene, the film was revelatory. It documented the extraordinary creativity and inventiveness of an exiled people as they reclaimed home and belonging in New York City. The film's heart was its portrayal of the "houses"—the surrogate, chosen families established within the Ballroom community, which collectively competed for prizes at the balls. The houses re-created family structures for their disinherited members, with house mothers and fathers and children. I suspect the film became such a touchstone for so many queer people precisely because we could identify, in our bones, with their craving for homes and families where they could find acceptance.

In 2013, Junior Labeija, one of the stars of *Paris Is Burning* and the iconic MC from the golden era of the Harlem Balls, became a volunteer at the Ali Forney Center. We soon became close friends, and I had the great privilege of learning about the early Ballroom years from one of its pioneers. Junior painted a vivid picture of life for homeless queer kids back in the seventies and eighties. After competing in the pageantry of the balls, the kids would cling to their winning trophies with cold hands while they slept in the subways or on the piers along the West Side Highway.

Junior was one of the unsung heroes who provided the homes that were an essential part of the Ballroom world. Junior had a studio apartment in the Sugar Hill section of Harlem, by Convent and 145th Street, overlooking the renowned Convent Avenue Baptist Church. Sugar Hill was Harlem's most prosperous community: in Junior's words, "notorious for welcoming the most influential men and women of color above- and underground." In 1978, Junior, then about twenty years old, shared his small apartment with up to ten Ballroom-connected homeless youths, whom he describes as a "wolf pack of the most beautiful species" and "the belles of Saint Mary's."

Junior described a scene unfolding from his apartment. "Within my humble abode, some of the most beautiful women (with a little extra) would hang out my window with their voluminous hair, and would be bra-less, with their breasts touching the windowsills. The men in their luxurious cars would screech to a halt, honking their horns and begging to be allowed in the building." (When the Ali Forney Center arrived in Harlem twenty-five years later, we were, let's say, a little more restrained.) But for all their outrageousness, Junior and his companions had claimed the freedom every other person in America had denied them: the freedom to be themselves. Junior was providing a home.

In 2004, we began to put on an annual variety show at the Lucille Lortel Theater on Christopher Street. To honor Ali, we called the show *Luscious*. Queer (and queer-adjacent) performers came forward to support our kids. Over the next few years, Mario Cantone, Murray Hill, Lea DeLaria, Daphne Rubin-Vega, Alan Cumming, and the legendary voguing innovator Willi Ninja were among those who shared their talents with us. It also gave me a forum to speak before hundreds of people, and I began to put my theory to the test. I'd speak about the ways our young people had been thrown away because of their queerness, and of the importance and beauty of our queer community providing homes for them, and about how doing so was core to our dignity and integrity as a people. My hunch proved accurate; the message resonated powerfully. (I remember Willi Ninja tearfully promising to do anything I asked to help our young people, and Alan Cumming being spontaneously moved to empty his pockets after I spoke, giving me all his cash on hand—sixty-three dollars and fifty-seven cents.) Donors and volunteers started to approach us, offering help. The demoralizing sense I'd long held of homeless queer youths being exiled to an outer-Siberia of our community's attention began to thaw.

I should not have been surprised. We queer people, more than anyone, understand that there's no place like home.

# CHAPTER 18

# DAMAGED

B y 2005, youth service organizations were being priced out of neighborhoods like the West Village and Chelsea. But we had a good stroke of fortune that year, receiving funding to open a daytime drop-in center. We started looking for a location and stumbled upon an affordable site near the Hudson River on West Twenty-second Street. It was a small, windowless space: a reception area, a tiny kitchen, a bathroom, a shower, and a half-dozen little rooms on either side of a central hallway. But it felt like a big step forward. It was a place where youths on our waiting list could receive food, medical care, and support until beds became available for them in our residential apartments. And the fact that it was within walking distance of the piers, where so many young people continued to hang out, made the new drop-in site seem like an answered prayer.

The vibe that year was decidedly feminine. Destiny's Child had recently reunited, and their hit song "Lose My Breath" was played at least a hundred thousand times in the new space. I had a small office there, and I would be trying to have meetings or get work done while the song blared on endless repeat in the background, accompanying clients as they vogued and runway-walked up and down the hallway outside my door.

The following year, 2006, our environment got a whole lot more masculine. That summer will always be the summer of the "ag's" (short for "aggressives"). That was the term youths used to describe butch Black lesbians, a whole group of whom collectively began to seek our services. Adorned in uniforms of white T-shirts or tank tops over shiny, baggy basketball shorts, they had a look that was way more Carmelo Anthony than Beyoncé. I enjoyed their addition to our growing community's mosaic of diversity.

By all appearances, Jaye lived up to the "ag" moniker. She had a thin, wiry physique and carried herself with a not-so-subtle air of combativeness, like she wanted everyone to know she would strike back hard if provoked. Jaye wasn't unfriendly—she had lots of friends—but it was clear she was determined to control her environment.

Jaye never spoke with me about her personal life, so I was surprised one afternoon when she joined a discussion about family experiences I was conducting at the drop-in center. Eight of us were gathered in a circle in the meeting room at the far end of our hallway, a colorful assortment of clients' art projects adorning the walls. When I asked if anyone was willing to share how their parents responded to their coming out, Jaye was the first to speak.

"A few days after I came out, my parents took me on a car ride from Philadelphia out into the country. We drove for an hour until we were in the middle of nowhere." Her voice, usually so strong and firm, began to tremble, tears welling up in her eyes. "They drove down some dirt road into a forest. Finally, they said we'd stop to have a picnic. But once we all got out, they jumped back into the car and drove off. They just fucking left me there . . ."

The tears now streamed down her face. "They didn't want me no more. I was all alone in this fucking forest. I didn't know what the fuck to do."

Jaye began furiously rocking back and forth in her chair, like a small dockside boat tossed about in a hurricane. Seeing her distress, I wanted to end the group discussion and try to console her, but before I could intervene, a friend of hers—Tee, another "ag," though gentler and softer-spoken—started to speak, offering her own story.

"My family is totally religious," she said. "When they realized I was a lesbian, I became like nothing, even worse than nothing. Nobody'd have anything to do with me." She too began to cry. "When I heard my grandmother was dying, I went to see her in the hospice. But as soon as she saw me enter the room, she turned her head away. She refused to even look at me." Tee lifted her eyes up to the ceiling, like she was begging God for an answer. "Why won't they love me?" she sobbed.

I looked around the room and saw the other young people becoming upset. Some shifted uncomfortably in their chairs, and one's jaw began to tremble. Then, one after the other, Jaye and Tee slid from their chairs and began crying on the floor, wailing with anguish. Panic seized me. I'd seen young people in our care become very upset, but never like this.

I ran from the room to find two therapists who happened to be on-site. Then, with each therapist attempting to help Jaye and Tee as they continued sobbing on the floor, I fled from the drop-in center.

I paced up and down Tenth Avenue for half an hour, unable to settle myself. It was like the young women's distress had overtaken my body as well. When I finally recovered enough equilibrium to return, I was grateful to find Jaye and Tee had calmed down and were sitting and processing the incident with the therapists.

When we reviewed the matter later, the therapists suggested all of this had been a breakthrough. Jaye and Tee recognized me as a protector, which made them feel safe enough to expose their wounds. Still, I was skeptical. I felt like I had opened doors to emotions these kids were miles away from being ready to address.

I have heard countless young people reveal how their hearts have been broken by their parents' refusal to love them. It is high on the list of the most torturous parts of my job. But as I look back at that distressing autumn day, I realize there was another reason I was so overcome by the anguish of those young women. Without any intention of doing so, they had held up a mirror to my own long-buried pain. I knew something of their anguish, recognized it like I would my own face. I know the damage that is done to an unloved child.

The first memory I hold of my mother is a joyous one.

I am one year old, and she is awakening me from sleep. I open my eyes to see her gazing at me with love, a gentle smile illumining her face.

"Good morning, my beautiful boy," she says. Her voice is warm and smooth as hot cocoa.

I sit up and reach for her arms and hug her.

"You're getting to be a big boy now," she says, still smiling. "Let's go to the kitchen."

I've just been learning to walk, and I toddle out of my nursery toward the living room. My mother keeps pace beside me, leaning over to hold my hand and help me across a hallway. As we pass corners of the house, my father and then my Grandpa Al jump out from hiding and say "Boo!," each with an enormous smile. But I'm not frightened. As I grasp my mother's protective hand, I'm absolutely delighted. It's like doorway after doorway of love is opening to me, and I laugh and laugh and laugh.

The next memory I hold is not joyful at all.

My mother, my little brother, and I are sitting at the kitchen table watching a small black-and-white TV on the counter. Richard Nixon descends the steps from an airplane. This would've been the summer of 1968, when he was running for president. I would have been three years old then, my little brother one, and my mother twenty-three.

My brother sits in a high chair, and my mother is trying to spoon-feed him baby food, but he won't eat. Instead, he screams and cries. My mother looks utterly miserable. She lays her head down on the table, muttering, "I hate this. I hate this so much . . ." I am too young to know what depression is, yet I feel the force of my mother's misery. A dense fog seems to surround her, hiding her joy away. I want with all my heart to help her be happy again but have no idea how.

My mother and father divorced a year later, and she moved out of the house. Over the next few years, my little brother and I would rarely see her. I must have blocked the memories of the pain and confusion I felt at being abandoned; my memories of that time are few. But I do remember how, after my father moved in a new girl-friend on whom I transferred my maternal longings, one afternoon I couldn't find her. Desperate, I ran around the house and through our yard, calling out for her with all my might. After a few minutes I concluded she must have been swallowed up by the earth; vanished forever, like my mother. Feeling certain I would die of loneliness and sorrow, I retreated to my bedroom and curled up on the floor underneath my bed, crying helplessly.

A third memory: I am five. It must be the summer of 1970. My grandmother is driving me out to New Jersey, where my mother lives with her new boyfriend. He is a Greek man, an artist with dark curly hair and a thick accent. When the car arrives, I see my mother sitting on the front steps of a house, her boyfriend hovering behind a screen door, while a half-dozen neighborhood children play with her and their cat. I feel hurt and confused. How can it be that these other children are able to be with my mother and I am not? I haven't seen her for months. As I join them on the steps, I feel like I am nobody special to her, merely one child among the others. It is a rotten feeling, but I fight to keep myself from crying. I fear that if I do, it will only give my mother another reason to prefer the children of New Jersey.

My therapist once explained that childhood abandonment

can be more psychologically devastating than losing one's mother through death. The fact that the mother is still alive but *chooses* not to be with their child is even harder for the child to comprehend.

Despite her walking out on us, I always loved my mother. When I was ten, she got an apartment in New York City, and my brother and I began visiting her on weekends every month or two. Through the remaining years of my childhood and adolescence, it did not occur to me to be resentful or hold her absences against her. I was simply grateful for the times we had together.

As she grew older, her desire to be connected seemed to increase. When I moved into the Catholic Worker, a mile downtown from her apartment, I began visiting for dinner every Saturday—a ritual I kept up for the next twenty years. However, with adulthood came a greater consciousness of the damage I carried. I noticed I would shut down emotionally whenever I was around her. Gary noticed it too. He said I'd "go Stepford," referencing the horror film about the affluent Connecticut town where husbands replace their wives with robot replicas. Some core of exuberance in my personality seemed to evaporate in my mother's presence.

As I grappled with this in therapy, I began to wonder what my mother actually said to me when she left us all those years ago. I had no memories of her leaving, just of her being gone.

I decided to ask one night when we were having dinner. "Mommy, when you left when I was four, did you explain to me that you were leaving? Did you say 'goodbye' to me?"

She looked at me blankly, like I'd asked where she had left her keys.

"No, not that I remember," she said. For a split second, fear seemed to flicker in her eyes.

Then she changed the subject. I don't quite know what I'd hoped to get from her, but in that moment I understood she didn't have the emotional capacity to process what had happened between us. Whatever healing I could hope for would have to come through therapy and prayer.

Let me acknowledge what is obvious. As hard as it's been to deal with my mother's abandonment, I've been privileged to do so in the comfort of my apartment, with a full belly, a warm bed, and a comfortable pillow to cradle my head. Jaye, Tee, and the others had to face the demons out in the cold, sleeping exposed to the dangers of the night. Let there be no illusion that their journeys weren't infinitely more difficult than mine.

But that afternoon when the young women became unglued at the drop-in center, I realized I too was still at war with unresolved rage over my abandonment. It was like we were stuck together in some sadistic hall of mirrors, endlessly reflecting back at us images of our damaged selves.

*"I won't have to worry about crying and suffering no more, I won't have to worry about being disappointed . . . "* When Ali spoke those words at the talent show, they weren't mere sermonizing to the crowd. They were a testament to still-fresh wounds in her own life.

A year before first coming to SafeSpace, Ali received a $10,000 settlement from the assault where she was pushed, with murderous intent, in front of the delivery van that crushed her skull. I later learned from Ines Robledo, a case manager at Streetwork—another drop-in program Ali attended in earlier days—that Ali had hoped those settlement funds would purchase a reconciliation with her mother.

It was all Ali talked about as her eighteenth birthday approached. "I'm gonna get that money and go home, and everything's going to be good again," Ines remembers her saying.

When the money came, Ali returned to East New York brimming with hope. Apparently she had bought gifts for her younger brothers and taken out a life insurance policy with Ali's mother named as the beneficiary. Days later, she was back at Streetwork, her hopes as crushed as her forehead. She refused to answer Ines's questions, except to say the plan hadn't worked out. After that, Ali went silent when it came to her family. When she arrived at SafeSpace the following year, she'd only say her parents were dead.

Since then, I've tried to learn more about this rupture of Ali's hope for a family. Ali's little brother Darrell recalls that Ali showed up with gifts, but doesn't remember Ali's conflict with their mother. But Angie recalled Ali saying that after he'd shared the funds with his mother, she would hang up the phone as soon as she heard her child's voice.

It's possible that I've taken in distorted accounts, refracted through the prisms of Ali's hurt and reticence. Either way, the aftermath remains the same: The money was gone, and Ali was once again unhoused, sleeping on that wretched bench under the Harlem train tracks. Maybe he wondered why his other siblings had been reunited with his mother while he was still homeless. Or maybe, Ali did not need to wonder at all.

Ali wasn't able to exorcise the pain. He couldn't drug it away or resolve it in therapy. He was not some emotional butterfly, able to magically glide above the wreckage of his life. A significant part of Ali's heart was scarred. The damage was real, and it was severe.

But Ali's heartbreak wasn't the end of the story. The great Sufi poet and mystic Rumi wrote a line that, for me, reflects Ali's achievement: *You have to keep breaking your heart until it opens.* There is a mysterious invitation embedded within the heartbreak of us unloved children. What can destroy us also has the power to open us to deeper love.

Ali knew rejection, tears, and devastation. But he was able to fuse that hurt into a determination to love and protect his family of street kids. As walled-off as a portion of Ali's heart needed to be, he still opened it to others. Likewise, losing my mother when I was four left a hole in me that will never be filled: a grinding fear that I am unworthy of being loved. But as I've reflected on my life since my mother died fifteen years ago, I have realized how that experience of abandonment drew me to my work with unhoused people, giving me a profound ability to empathize with abandoned queer kids, to see a connection between their pain and my own.

Over the years I've witnessed numerous youths in our care obtain rewarding lives for themselves despite the heavy burden of their scars. But I'd be dishonest if I didn't acknowledge that many others never overcame the harm. They internalized the message of unworthiness and reenacted their pain in terrible patterns of self-destruction. The wounds borne by Jaye and Tee and countless other discarded queer youths might be enduring.

And yet, several of my most dedicated co-workers have confided to me their own stories of parental rejection—forsaken because of their queerness or abused due to their caretakers' addictions or mental illnesses. There is a harsh beauty in the way we've been able to come together and turn those hurts into a source of empathy.

In this, I see Ali's spiritual DNA imprinted upon the Ali Forney Center. We are a community that has somehow managed to turn suffering into love.

# CHAPTER 19

# DISRUPTING THE NARRATIVE

I n the eighties and nineties, queer people were considered largely untouchable by mainstream politicians. Republicans at their best ignored us, and at their worst scapegoated us to win the conservative Christian vote. Democrats were less inclined to attack us, but kept us at arm's length, like some embarrassing relative you tolerate at necessary holiday functions. Even as late as 2012, Barack Obama, the champion of "hope and change," refused to endorse our right to marry until his vice president, Joe Biden, "gaffed" him into it by admitting his support on *Meet the Press.*

By the 2010s, however, things began to shift. As opinion polls moved in our favor, Democrats and even a few moderate Republicans were more willing to support the civil rights of the LGBTQ community. Yet that newfound support struck me as complicated. Some politicians began to use support for our civil rights to burnish their progressive credentials—often while perpetuating policies that disenfranchised poor people and people of color. Frankly, it enraged me to see such politicians wrap themselves in rainbow flags. *Especially* when they took actions that hurt the young people in our care.

Eight years into the Ali Forney Center's existence, the living conditions of New York City's homeless youths remained dreadful. Most still had no access to shelter. After 2005, when Christine Quinn became the speaker of the city council and a lionhearted man named Lew Fidler was made chair of the council's youth committee, they were able to add 70 beds to the city's youth shelter portfolio, bringing the total number of city-funded beds to 250. But a census soon revealed that more than three thousand homeless youths still lived on the streets of our city, almost half of whom identified as LGBTQ. When the recession struck in 2008, Mayor Mike Bloomberg refused to add any more youth shelter beds. In fact, each year until 2014, Bloomberg tried to cut beds by at least fifty percent in his annual budget proposals, forcing advocates to fight year after year to protect the measly 250 beds.

By then, the Ali Forney Center was offering seventy beds a night, but the numbers of queer kids needing our help grew even faster. By 2010, our list of young people waiting for beds had surged to more than two hundred each night.

It was heartbreaking. A young person would show up at our drop-in center hoping for a bed, traumatized after having been kicked out of their home. Our case managers would spend the next few hours trying to find someplace they might spend the night. Most often they could find nowhere, and we would finally have to advise the petrified young person how to make it out in the streets, telling them which subway lines were the warmest to sleep in, or how to occupy a seat at McDonald's for hours by taking minuscule sips of a coffee or soda. Often, when they realized safe refuge wasn't going to come, the young people would break out in tears, before finally pulling themselves together and heading out to face the night.

Something needed to change. There needed to be an awakening, an opening of eyes to the plight of our young people, far beyond the scope of what we'd accomplished thus far.

In 2010, Facebook was a new phenomenon. My staff frequently mocked my ineptitude when confronting such things as fax machines and passwords and apps. But somehow, I had an intuition that social media might provide a remarkable opportunity to make our young people seen, to get their voices heard.

I met with some of our clients and asked if they would work with me to educate the public. Together we created a social media campaign called Homeless for the Holidays. The kids would take me out into the streets to show me where they slept, describing how they survived without shelter. I'd record their descriptions, photograph where they spent the night, and create Facebook posts throughout the Christmas season with their images and narratives.

Working on that project was grueling. As a "service provider," I'd usually interacted with our young people in shelters, apartments, or drop-in centers, spaces where at least some of their most urgent needs were met, thereby buffering me from the harshest aspects of their lives. Being with them where they faced their repeated battles with the demons of the night was a different experience altogether.

A few days before Thanksgiving 2010, the project began with a young transgender woman named Gennifer, who brought me to the pier where she slept. She tore my heart apart before she even opened her mouth; it was enough just seeing her. She wore a sweet little Minnie Mouse T-shirt—and a black eye from a john who'd beaten her up the night before. We sat down together on a bench where Gennifer slept, sandwiched between the vastness of the Hudson River and the thousands of cars speeding down the West Side Highway.

"I try to be bubbly and joke," she confessed, "but it is really hard when you're hungry and don't get any sleep. I remember one night I was trying to sleep in the piers. But I was just crying and crying all night, wishing God could just take me out of this. I need a change; I cannot go on like this much longer."

Samba was another teen who participated. He grew up in Brazil, but fled to the Bronx to stay in his sister's apartment after their father was murdered. Samba's sister was a "good Catholic" and threw him out when she discovered he was gay, telling him he was going to "the inferno." He took me down into the subways to show where he slept.

"Now I am staying on the A train," he said, a brave smile stamped upon his exhausted face. "It is a long ride from the first stop to the last, so you can get more sleep on that line. Sometimes I do sex work to get something to eat, or to get a place to spend the night. I hate doing sex work, but you gotta do it—it's better than being out in the cold. It's hard sleeping on the trains a lot. You feel so alone. It is too hard."

Over and over again, clients described the pain of feeling alone. The isolation of sleeping in the streets only reinforced their parents' message that being queer rendered them unworthy. Many told me that they felt it would be easier just to die, to bring an end to their despair.

The project required much courage on the part of the young people who were willing to expose their distress to the public, but it generated attention far beyond what I'd hoped. Facebook was still new, and our stark images of the homeless youths with their wrenching testimonies pierced through the glut of selfies and cute pet photos. Our posts were picked up by *The Huffington Post* and *The Advocate*. On Christmas Day they were on the home page of AOL. It felt as if the campaign was helping shake New York's LGBT community awake.

Those were some awfully dissonant times for the LGBT community. We'd made "Pride" our governing construct as we grew in influence and power. But how could we possibly be proud of what our young people were enduring?

A few weeks into 2011, the newly inaugurated governor, Andrew Cuomo, put forth a budget proposal that slashed statewide funding for homeless youth programs by fifty percent. I was appalled. Just six months earlier, his campaign had invited our youths to attend a rally, a gesture that made me think he cared about their needs. When I heard about this budget proposal, I reached out to my contacts in the new administration and got crickets in response. When I put out a statement indicating Cuomo's plan was a disaster, it got hardly any traction. Cuomo had signaled from the jump that he intended to bring marriage equality to New York, and it seemed as if the LGBT press and broader movement were united in lauding him as our great straight savior.

Then an unexpected opportunity fell in my lap. I was invited to speak at an annual gathering of prominent LGBTQ journalists and bloggers in San Francisco. Each year they focused upon a matter of urgency in the queer community, and in 2011, following a wave of highly reported teen suicides, they determined they would center the protection of LGBTQ teens. I couldn't imagine a better forum to address queer media's giving Cuomo a pass.

I was more than a little amused when the forty or so of us began our introductions, seated in a large meeting room at a fancy San Francisco hotel. The hosts invited each of us to say three words that summed up ourselves. One after another, the attendees, many of whom leaned decidedly nerdy, described themselves using words like "radical," "revolutionary," and "change agent." Stifling the urge to giggle at the would-be Che Guevaras peering out from behind their laptops, I took my self-assessment in an entirely different direction. When my turn came, I nibbled my lip in sensuous LL Cool J fashion, smiled suggestively, and said "Nice Italian boy . . ." in my most smoldering voice. (It seemed a good idea to get off to a humorous start, since I would soon be reading the room the riot act.) Everyone erupted in laughter. The next person, a young gentleman from Change.org, offered "distracted all day" for his verbal trinity of self-revelation.

The event organizers had asked that I bring one of our young people to join me in presenting to the journalists. I decided to invite KJ, who was then studying to become an attorney at a law school in nearby Portland, Oregon. It was wonderful to catch up with

KJ—still his calm, thoughtful self nine years after we first met in the church basement.

When the time came for our presentation, I spoke to the group about the massive numbers of homeless LGBTQ youths and the urgent need for the broader queer movement to step up and demand housing for them. Then I vented my frustration at how Cuomo had moved to strip youth shelters of their funding, only to be met with silence by an otherwise fawning queer press. I have no doubt the group felt chastened as they listened to me, but it was KJ who drove the message home. He told the story of fleeing his mother, bleeding and terrified, as she shouted down the stairwell, "You'll be back. The faggots will never take care of you!" Now KJ stood beside a man who'd proved his mother wrong—imploring them not to ignore Cuomo's budgetary assault on hundreds of kids facing the same peril.

In the weeks that followed, an onslaught of articles appeared in the queer press, all casting a harsh, critical eye on Cuomo's plan to cut youth shelter funding. (The press coverage was so extensive that, eight months later, Cuomo's Wikipedia page identified his mistreatment of New York State's homeless youths as one of the four defining issues of the first year of his governorship.)

A month earlier I couldn't get a whisper of a response from the administration. Now, suddenly, I was barraged with daily phone calls from Alphonso David, Cuomo's lieutenant charged with overseeing LGBT and civil rights issues. Only these calls weren't intended to respond to my concerns.

The very first thing Alphonso said to me after "hello" was "You don't know what you're talking about," his tone curt and aggravated.

"I know exactly what I'm talking about," I responded.

Though I tried not to show it, I found the calls intimidating. Alphonso repeatedly warned me to stop criticizing the governor. I knew that the Ali Forney Center relied on hundreds of thousands of dollars in HIV prevention and treatment funding from New York State. Alphonso made it clear I was antagonizing Cuomo and jeopardizing any possibility of a future relationship. Mayor Giuliani had been notorious for stripping city funds from nonprofits that dared criticize him. Now I feared Cuomo might follow suit.

I got some half dozen of those calls over the course of the next week. They annoyed me to no end. The governor struck me as having a special kind of hubris, like someone who punches you in the face to assert his dominance, and then sends his henchmen to harass you if you don't thank him for it.

All of this while Cuomo presented himself as a champion of equality by supporting the right of LGBT people to marry. I have no doubt that my critiques in the press disrupted the governor's chosen narrative, and that's why Alphonso was made to apply so much pressure to shut me up. However, the young people I was charged with representing were being treated as disposable—not so much because they were queer, but rather because they were destitute and seen as powerless. It seemed to me our LGBT community was being manipulated, used like rainbow-colored pawns to make the king appear more progressive than he truly was.

In the end, Cuomo, the great champion of our civil rights, slashed more than $2 million from New York's budget for homeless youths. Service providers across the state were forced to reduce their already tiny operations, and the city was only spared the loss of youth shelter beds because Lew Fidler and Christine Quinn stepped in with city council funds to make up for the cuts. Nonetheless, I felt demoralized at having to battle so hard, only to achieve a draw.

# CHAPTER 20

# MAKING COINS

A s a teenager I made myself voluntarily destitute. Jesus condemned the hoarding of wealth and went so far as to teach that our salvation hinged upon whether we shared our resources with the poor. So I joined the Catholic Worker the day I turned eighteen, moving into a row house in a Washington, D.C., neighborhood that had been decimated from riots after Dr. King's assassination.

That was where I realized that caring for homeless people hardly liberates you from material concerns. We cooked soup daily for the many folks who lived on heating vents near the White House, and, of course, fed the twenty-five people who lived with us. Doing so cost money. We relied on donations that arrived in the mail, but when those donations weren't enough, we went begging.

We'd go door to door to the houses of priests and nuns and monks clustered around Catholic University. It was hard to ring some stranger's doorbell and pitch them on giving money to people they'd never met. I often felt humiliated, especially when the person said no. I remember asking a particularly angry priest for help. His face twisted up in annoyance before he barked "NO!" and closed the door on us. I wished then that I could have melted into the ground. More often than not, though, people were kind to us, and generous.

When I started the Ali Forney Center, I had to make peace once again with being a beggar. The trappings were more prestigious than trudging door to door, but the essential vulnerability was the same.

Our government contracts didn't pay nearly enough to house kids in New York City. For example, the three-bedroom apartments we rented through our HUD contracts cost between three and four thousand dollars a month. However, HUD reimbursed rents based on a national average, which meant we received fourteen hundred dollars per month for units that cost more than twice that. From the start, I had to raise several hundred thousand dollars each year to cover the gap—an amount that soon extended into the millions. It meant putting myself out in the public eye, educating our community about queer youth homelessness in any forum that would welcome me, meeting with foundation officers, speaking at fundraisers, and pushing awareness of the need through interviews with the media.

Having never experienced such visibility, I discovered something uncomfortable: My physical attributes seemed to amplify (and sometimes overshadow) the attention given to my outreach. Ali and the other youths spoke of their sex work as "making coins." I thought about that often, because there were times when the need to "make coins" for the Ali Forney Center seemed to bring me not far from the realm of sex work myself.

Often, I would be invited onstage at benefits held in clubs and bars. Invariably, in those semi-drunken settings, my attempts to address the Ali Forney Center were drowned out by horny men shouting at me to remove my clothes. At least half of the articles written about the Ali Forney Center in the gay press during our first decade mentioned my looks. I was described as "a cutie," "a hottie," "megahunky," "disarmingly handsome," and the list went on.

My attitude toward being treated as a sex object was conflicted. On the one hand, my poor ego swelled at the attention. But I also felt somewhat ashamed. It was hard to imagine Dorothy Day or Cesar Chavez being greeted with shouts to "TAKE IT OFF!" when they advocated for the destitute. But in a time when homeless queer youth were almost entirely invisible to the broader LGBT community, I figured I needed to use every tool in my belt.

I'll never forget a jam-packed Christmas party thrown for us in a beautiful West Village duplex. The lower level of the apartment had a piano and stage, and several hours into the party I stepped up to discuss the Ali Forney Center, only to be met with loud demands that I disrobe. Feeling the pressure to be at least somewhat accommodating, I undid a button on my shirt, smiled, lowered my voice an octave, and said, "I work hard for the money . . ." That whipped the crowd into a feverish frenzy. "Take it off, TAKE IT OFF!!"

Then, one person shouted an offer of a thousand dollars if I removed my pants. From a corner of the room, Raymond's booming voice rose above the crowd. "YOU BETTER NOT!" Later, my coworkers were in hysterics, regaling me with accounts of an enraged Raymond muttering about how he was going to tear through the place "like the black plague."

A particularly outrageous incident occurred during the Great Recession of 2008. With the economy in free fall, I'd recently been notified the Ali Forney Center was going to lose our only source of government funding for the small drop-in center on West Twenty-second Street. Determined to keep the site open, I'd hired consultants with a track record of fundraising for other LGBT nonprofits, who came with the added convenience of their office being located a few floors down from ours. They had this big theory that any donor who'd given us a thousand dollars could up it to five thousand dollars, if only I had dinner with them and made a pitch. An elderly donor had just invited me to his apartment for dinner, so I decided to test the consultants' theory.

My host lived in a large, expensive prewar apartment overlooking Riverside Park. When I arrived, the stooped, skinny, white-bearded man greeted me at the door and led me to his sofa. I immediately noticed an adjacent love seat covered with hundreds of little stuffed animals—teddy bears and dogs and bunnies. The mass of toys seemed puzzlingly out of place in an otherwise elegant apartment. I was confused by the incongruity, but told myself maybe he had a variation of Gary's decorative obsessiveness. (Gary had this tremendous need to be surrounded by thousands of holy cards and religious statues. The apartment we'd shared a decade earlier had looked like the gift shops of Lourdes and Fatima had merged and metastasized inside our walls.)

My elderly host had two steaks in the oven, and while they were cooking, he sat down next to me and poured himself a generous glass of wine. He then proceeded to guzzle it down and refill it four times while I tried to focus his dwindling attention on the Ali Forney Center's needs. This man was eighty-seven years old. I was astonished he could consume so much wine while preparing dinner and remain upright. Finally, he brought me to his dining room and served the food, while switching over to big glasses of whisky.

At last, he revealed his agenda. "Do you know who I am?" he inquired. "I am famous in the gay fetish scene."

I admitted I had no knowledge of his identity. All I knew was that he'd been an executive in the postal service.

"I'm an internationally known 'daddy' of adult babies," he explained.

He pointed to a pile of VHS tapes under a television set and indicated he had starred in many daddy/baby erotic films. Then he opened a cabinet and staggered back with a big stack of Polaroid photos, placing them before me. The photos were of numerous men in their thirties and forties, each one sitting in a diaper on his living room floor while playing with the stuffed animals.

"I get off on having a man stay here for a few days and be my baby," he said. "I put them in diapers and have them play with the toys. When they shit on themselves, I wash them and change their diapers."

I was speechless. What kind of insane situation had I been lured into? I am not one to judge others for their fetishes. I figure God has a sense of humor when it comes to the yearnings we were given. However, I can assure you I had no desire whatsoever to crap in a diaper and pretend I was some little old rich man's "baby."

He leaned close and leered into my eyes. "I find you incredibly attractive," he slurred. "Do you want to come to the living room and play with my toys?"

I was mortified. I said I needed to get home to my husband and thanked him for the meal. He looked disappointed. Moving so close I feared he'd tumble into my lap, he whispered how he was terribly jealous of Raymond. Seeing him move on me, I jumped up, ran to the hallway, and pressed the button for the elevator. He lurched after me, but only caught up as the elevator doors were closing. As the doors shut, he pleaded that I return the next day.

Driving home, I felt thoroughly annoyed and humiliated. I hated being so desperate for money, and also hated that this man saw my desperation as a vulnerability that could be exploited.

My staff found the story hilarious. Seeing it through their eyes, I decided to try to view the evening as comical rather than humiliating. Their hilarity was renewed the following three Christmases, when my elderly suitor mailed me, at our office, large, autographed photos of his smiling face.

I could go on with the horror stories. There was the seventy-something guy who had me drive ten hours to and from the Finger Lakes, suggesting he might join our board and procure big money from his friend Jim Hormel of Hormel Foods. Unfortunately, this was merely a ruse to get me into his hot tub, where I discovered he had no interest in our board, but simply wanted to ogle me as

I sat there stewing in a pot of old man soup. Or the octogenarian who lured me to his apartment overlooking Central Park, where he spent hours promising a major donation while repeatedly trying to grope my thighs. Finally, he said he'd give us $50,000, but only if I removed Ali's name, as he refused to donate to anything sounding like a "Moslem organization."

Looking back on those experiences, I feel as if I'm peering into a different era, a time more shaped by the warping contours of the closet. These men must have been middle-aged by the Stonewall uprising—their adult personalities formed during a time when being gay was utterly taboo, when hiding the truth of oneself was a matter of survival. Add massive amounts of money to the mix, and you've created an ideal recipe for abusiveness. As the acceptance of LGBT people in New York City became more widespread, I noticed that I ceased to experience such egregious mistreatment.

These misadventures always struck me as surreal. Our kids existed in a realm of subway cars and park benches and warehouse shelters. Seeking to provide for them brought me into a world of magnificent apartments, summer homes, and immaculate corporate meeting rooms. It was like each of my feet stood upon two different planets, planets separated by a chasm of economic inequality.

But here's the thing: While I may have been exposed to indignities and no small amount of cognitive dissonance, overall, people replied to my cries for help with remarkable amounts of kindness. I found myself surrounded with volunteers, donors, board members, and organizations more than willing to give their time, care, resources, and love to our youths. For every abuse, there were ten thousand acts of goodness.

One of the most revelatory moments of goodness came in the aftermath of Hurricane Sandy, when our drop-in center was left in ruins.

I never imagined that a storm would destroy our drop-in center. In the buildup to the hurricane, our biggest anxiety was the MTA's unprecedented closure of the subway system. We had nine apartments scattered across three boroughs. With only two days to prepare, we spent the weekend scrambling for ways to keep our sites open and staffed when many employees would have no way to travel to them. The one clue that the drop-in center faced jeopardy came when the city forced a mandatory evacuation of the blocks along the Hudson, warning of a potential storm surge. We gave the kids lists of other homeless drop-in programs and LGBT-friendly spaces in the city, fully expecting to reopen within a few days.

I was stranded upstate when the hurricane made landfall, and for days after as the roads leading to the city were closed. At first I thought we'd escaped the worst—every young person in our care was reported safe. However, on Wednesday, two days after the hurricane, our drop-in center's landlord reached out to inform me that the space on Twenty-second Street had been flooded and would be uninhabitable for a time. Perhaps I was in denial, for I interpreted his message to mean we'd be unable to resume services for a week or so.

On Friday, with the subway system still shut down, our drop-in director, Steven Gordon, and our deputy executive director, Heather Gay, jogged all the way from Brooklyn to assess the center's condition. They discovered the space was *ruined*. More than four feet of water had flooded the entire premises, and mold had quickly sprouted within the unventilated wetness, rendering the air toxic. The computers, phones, medical equipment, the stove, refrigerator, our stored food supplies—all destroyed, along with the building's electrical systems. The drop-in center would be unusable for many months.

At first, I was hesitant to put anything on social media, as if announcing what had happened would make our disaster real. But when the reality of Steven and Heather's report sank in, I pulled out my phone and put a note on Facebook about the drop-in center's destruction. Within minutes, the blogger Joe Jervis reached out, offering to let me post an appeal on his JoeMyGod blog. When I got home, I banged out a few paragraphs about our dire situation.

That one little post opened the floodgates of care. To my astonishment, a mere forty-eight hours later we'd received almost $100,000 in online donations. The response was unlike anything I'd ever experienced. In the next two weeks, I gave more than forty interviews to media outlets who'd reached out to the Ali Forney Center. Our displacement was covered by the Associated Press, *The New York Times,* and almost everywhere else you can imagine. So much extraordinary generosity was unleashed. Kwaku Driskell, our contract manager from the Robin Hood Foundation, ventured to see the site and quickly persuaded his colleagues to give us an extra $50,000. Frank Selvaggi and Bill Shea, two of our most dedicated supporters, hosted a jam-packed benefit where they committed to matching every donation given. The gender-fluid author and social media star Jacob Tobia even raised a substantial amount of support by undertaking a much-publicized (and, no doubt, painful) run across the Brooklyn Bridge in high heels.

Several weeks before the hurricane, I had signed a lease for a new drop-in space in Harlem. I'd long dreamed of being able to offer services overnight, and our space on Twenty-second Street was much too small, with just one toilet and nowhere for the youths to sleep. But I'd expected to remain downtown for another year while raising funds to bring the Harlem building up to code. Instead, our unforeseen displacement forced us to conduct three waves of renovations. The first stage covered the basics, so we could open as soon as humanly possible. The second and third stages took place over the next eighteen months, bringing us into compliance for medical licensing.

We opened the doors to our brand-new Harlem site a few days before Christmas of 2012. It was located on 125th Street, just ten blocks from where Ali was murdered. On that first day, dozens of kids whom we hadn't seen since Sandy showed up, making for a joyous reunion. And that afternoon we did the new center's first intake: a young transgender woman who had not yet initiated her transition. She'd had a "girl's night" sleepover with some friends and forgot to wipe the mascara off her eyes, which had prompted her enraged Christian parents to immediately throw her out of their home. That day, she showed up at our door in the icy December cold with no belongings, not even a coat.

I'm grateful we were able to be there for that young woman, in what must have been among the most desperate moments of her life. And I'm grateful so many people were able to be there for us in our time of desperation.

Another person who once came to our aid was Bea Arthur, the TV superstar. Three years before the hurricane, another storm swept into our lives. Bea was the angel who rescued us—from beyond the grave, no less—during the Great Recession.

It was the summer of 2009, a time when keeping the Ali Forney Center afloat became an ordeal from hell. With the recession, we had lost government funding for our drop-in center, and our biggest housing contract was cut in half. The stock market was in full free fall, so our private donations plunged, and some foundations delayed paying us. Worst of all, the city was usually ten or eleven months behind in reimbursing us for operating the apartments they funded, forcing us to front hundreds of thousands of dollars and essentially function as their bank.

It all combined to create a perfect storm of financial disaster. We had fallen months behind on our rents. Utilities were getting cut off. Paying health insurance was a nightmare, and I was continuously panicked that we'd be unable pay our staff on time. It seemed the Ali Forney Center might end in failure.

The breaking point came that summer. I was driving to work one day in August when I received a call from a landlord threatening to begin eviction proceedings unless we immediately brought our rent up to date. I was too overwhelmed to continue driving. I parked my car at the side of the Palisades Parkway and began to pace back and forth, praying for help.

Catholics believe in something called "the communion of the saints." In times of duress, we ask those in heaven for help, believing that we are connected across boundaries of space and time, of life and death. In my roadside desperation, with cars zooming past, I prayed to my entire cadre of spiritual heroes: Mary, the Mother of God, Saint Thérèse, Saint Francis, Saint Benedict Joseph Labre, Saint Martin de Porres, Charles de Foucauld, Dorothy Day, Thomas Merton, Carlo Carretto, Abba Moses of the Desert, Saint John of the Cross, Bayard Rustin, and Sylvia Rivera. I also called out to others I was certain were in heaven: Ali, Kiki, Cheri, my mother, my grandparents, and Bea Arthur, who had died of cancer several months earlier.

A few years before her death, in 2005, Bea Arthur had shown extraordinary care to the Ali Forney Center. A friend of hers—an accomplished set designer named Ray Klaussen—began volunteering with us and saw how few resources we had for the young people seeking our help. He asked Bea if she would come to New York and reprise a performance of her one-woman Broadway show as a benefit. To my amazement, she agreed to do so. This was Bea Arthur! Star of *The Golden Girls*! Queer icon goddess! The self-proclaimed heir to Judy Garland in the hearts of homosexuals! The champion of feminism across the TV screens of America! I gagged when I heard she'd said yes.

Bea flew to New York City in December. She had such a distaste for cold climates that she didn't own a coat. Instead, she borrowed one from her close friend Angela Lansbury for the journey. I clearly remember the moment of her arrival. She entered the theater about three hours before the performance, holding the puffy, down-filled coat in her hands like it was some terrible burden.

Frankly, I was concerned when Bea entered the theater. She seemed shrunken, disoriented, almost feeble. She bore little resemblance to the formidable star in the promotional photos we were using from her Broadway show of three years before. I feared she wouldn't have the strength and presence of mind to perform for the throngs of people soon to arrive. My fears were exacerbated when she kept muttering over how bad she felt about my carrying her coat.

Klaussen had reassembled the team of top-notch pros who'd worked with Bea on her Broadway show. They descended upon her dressing room with wigs and makeup and a black and blue outfit speckled with sparkling silver jewels.

I remember sitting in the audience in the moments before the show began, feeling anxious. But when the spotlight came on and Bea strode out looking all iconic and regal and bejeweled (not to mention barefoot), I was astonished at her transformation. Suddenly a decade seemed to have been erased. She was sharp, cutting, vital, and hilarious. She excoriated George W. Bush for his administration's homophobia, occasioning thunderous applause, and even shared her recipe for leg of lamb. For ninety minutes, she demonstrated the magical, almost supernatural charisma that's unlocked when a comedic genius meets their audience.

Bea's performance raised forty thousand dollars, an extravagant sum for us in those grassroots days.

The afterparty remains a highlight of Raymond's life. He *worships* Bea Arthur and watches reruns of *The Golden Girls* pretty much every night of his life. We hadn't planned for security, which I realized was a terrible oversight when a horde of obsessed homosexuals began grabbing and pawing at the poor exhausted woman. I asked Raymond, who is built like a defensive lineman, to be her bodyguard. He took firm control of the rabidly excited crowd, making them get in a line, allotting each person thirty seconds with Bea, and sternly forbidding them to touch her. At one point nature called, and Raymond needed to step away to go to the bathroom. Bea wouldn't have it. She grasped his arm with an iron grip and growled, "Where the hell do you think you're going!"

Raymond stayed put. When your idol commands, you hold it in. I would have done no less for Saint Thérèse.

Bea gave interviews afterward, telling the journalists who'd flocked to report on her performance that the Ali Forney Center was saving lives. At the time we were still a tiny, little-known organization. Having a queer icon of Bea's magnitude stand with us ended our obscurity. It was a turning point, a moment when I began to feel more confident we'd make it.

Only when she died, a few months before that day on the Palisades Parkway, did I discover that Bea was secretly battling cancer at the time of her performance three years earlier. What an extraordinary act of kindness, to fly across the country in the middle of winter and put on an exhausting benefit while suffering a debilitating illness. I'll be grateful to Bea until the day I die.

Which was why, in my financial panic, I thought to include the recently deceased star in my frantic prayers. Finally, after I had spent ten minutes pacing the shoulder, my anxiety subsided enough for me to return to my car.

When I arrived at the office, I checked my voicemail and heard a message from one of Bea's closest friends, the film score composer Billy Goldenberg. "How odd!" I said to myself, after I had just included Arthur in my prayers. When I returned his call, Billy made a bizarre proposal. "Carl, I would like you to be the producer of Bea Arthur's memorial service at the Majestic Theater on Broadway."

I told Billy I was honored but baffled by the request. I ran a housing program for homeless queer kids. What on earth qualified me to produce a memorial service for a superstar?

Billy admitted I'd be a figurehead producer. He needed to solicit donations to put on a production worthy of Bea, and he wanted to partner with a tax-exempt organization. Then he dropped the bomb: "We figured it made sense to ask you because the Ali Forney Center is at the very top of the list of beneficiaries in Bea's will."

I felt dizzy, like I might faint. Not even an hour after my prayers of desperation, I learned Bea Arthur had left us $300,000! My mind ticked through the ramifications. We could pay all our months of unpaid bills. We could bring our rents up to date. Thanks to Bea Arthur, we would survive.

There are times in my life when God's loving care seems so undeniably real that I almost become frightened, like it's just too good to be true. This was one of them. When I finished the call, I lowered my head to my desk, whispered, "Thank you, Bea," and began to cry from gratitude.

Nine years later, in 2017, we would open the Bea Arthur Residence: a formerly abandoned building in the East Village that was transformed into an utterly gorgeous long-term housing site for eighteen of our young people. I couldn't have imagined a more wonderful opportunity to show our thanks for Bea's loving-kindness.

I never enjoyed it, but in the end, I'm grateful to have been forced to assume a position of need for our kids. Grateful not only for the generosity it occasioned, but also for the lessons it taught.

I've come to believe that our systems of inequality stem from our fears. We're afraid of being vulnerable to the threats in this world, afraid of being mistreated and degraded, and, ultimately, afraid of death. We are repelled by evidence of our weakness and contingency, and so we arm ourselves, we amass wealth, we exploit, we degrade, we ransack, we oppress.

What a powerful thing it can be to turn the terror on its head. I hated begging for funds; every ounce of my pride was revolted by it. The times when casting myself into a position of need were taken as an invitation to abuse were hard to bear. Even more humiliating were the occasional times I stood before the rich and powerful pleading for help, only to have them respond that our work, or I as the messenger, was unworthy of their support. Thankfully, those times were few and far between.

Sometimes, when I felt myself dreading the need to make yet another plea for help, I would meditate on Ali. It could not have been easy for Ali to need SafeSpace, to need the food, clothing, and medical care we offered. Being at our mercy must have wounded her pride. Yet she was able to embrace the situation with grace. In my mind I can see Ali running to hug Patrick the day she was released from Rikers, gleefully crying out "Patricia!" (her gender-defying nickname for her beloved case manager). I'd think of those nightly calls Ali made to me from prison, the tender yearning for my companionship in her voice. I'd recall looking at the faces of my co-workers on the hateful day I told them Ali was dead and seeing so many tears, those little proofs of love, pouring from their eyes. That radically undefended child didn't recoil from her essential vulnerability; Ali wasn't afraid to reveal her need for our love.

I wonder if there isn't a direct correlation between our intentional willingness to lay down our arms, to renounce our privileges, to embrace our human vulnerability, and what it might take to free others from injustice, oppression, and degradation.

# CHAPTER 21

# OUTSIDE

n 2013, we held a celebration at our new drop-in center in Harlem. Our chef, Jess, along with many volunteers, prepared a mountain of pies and cupcakes and candies for dozens of young people and staff. Then, after everyone was stuffed, we moved the tables back and lined up chairs facing the wall of windows overlooking 125th Street, transforming the dining room into an auditorium.

Staff and clients took turns performing in a talent show. Unlike the big public show we'd put on at SafeSpace, this was an in-house event for our clients and staff. The drop-in center's bearlike director appeared in wig, makeup, dress, and white go-go boots, lip-syncing to "These Boots Are Made for Walkin'." By the end of that performance, the youths were in such a frenzy that many had joined him onstage, a chorus line of would-be Nancy Sinatras high-kicking in glee. Later a young transgender woman wowed us by singing Whitney Houston's version of "I Will Always Love You." When she began the first verse, her long dreadlocks swaying as she moved to the music, I assumed she was lip-syncing. There was no noticeable difference between her performance and Whitney's recording. But no, soon it became clear the voice was hers. When she hit the money note, the long, stretched out "*I . . . I . . . I will always love you . . . uuuuuu,*" we all helplessly leapt to our feet and gave her a standing ovation.

Unfortunately, that joyful evening came to a sad end. We were still a year off from having the funds to keep the drop-in center open throughout the night, and it soon came time to close the building. The luckier youths departed for our apartments, but those on our waiting list had to return to the streets. One teenager, small and timid beneath his wool cap and oversized coat, burst into tears as he prepared to head outside into the cold early April night. Afterward, I asked the staff person who'd consoled him why he'd begun to weep. Apparently after an evening of abundant sweetness and fun, the rotten night awaiting him outside just felt unbearable.

Outside. To be a homeless queer youth is to be forced outside in multiple ways. On the most basic level, they are forced to suffer the physical reality of sleeping outside, like Ali on the bench below the underpass on 125th Street. Yet even before the rupture with their families, many are treated as outsiders.

I think of a Black youth, Laurence—a stocky kid whose hard, "homo-thug" persona was softened by warm, friendly eyes—telling me how his parents had devised an elaborately cruel ritual centered around food. "Our family always ate meals together in the dining room," he said. "But after I came out, I wasn't allowed to sit with them. They made me eat in the basement and wouldn't let me eat on the plates or use their forks and knives. For me it was only paper plates and plastic utensils. They made sure I knew that, in their eyes, I was some dirty diseased faggot they needed to protect themselves from."

Laurence felt so demeaned by this treatment that he chose to live in the streets. It was better to be homeless than to endure such humiliation.

"I left home to save my life. If I'd stayed there, no doubt I would have killed myself."

It's a confession I've heard all too often. When young people are inundated with messages that their queerness irrevocably positions them outside of their families, outside of their homes, outside of goodness, outside of human dignity, and outside the reach of God's love, many internalize their rejection to the point where they fear the only solution is to literally take themselves out.

Benjamin, a preppy white kid with short brown hair and blue eyes, once told me that he'd lie awake at night thinking of ending his life. "I couldn't eat, I couldn't sleep—I was just so afraid of my parents finding out I was gay."

Benjamin's parents were hardcore conservative Christians. When he was fifteen, a store in their northern New England town hung a rainbow flag from its roof. Benjamin was terrified when he saw how much rage this simple act of solidarity provoked in his parents. "They kept going on about how disgusting it was that the storeowners approved of 'those people.' They insisted God is so revolted by homosexuals that he *vomits them out*."

Like Laurence, Benjamin fled from his home. Two weeks before his eighteenth birthday he packed his belongings into several suitcases and got on a bus to New York City. His plan was to sleep outside, in a cardboard box in Prospect Park. Fortunately, Benjamin was able to get a bed with us and remained for more than a year.

I'm struck that the primary metaphor we use for the process of becoming truthful about our queer selves is "coming out." We all come out of the closet, out of the dark spaces of hiding, out of shame. Yet for hundreds of thousands of our children, coming out of the closet leads to being forced outside to the streets. A double helix of chosen act and unchosen consequence, modes of outness bound together.

When I first began to work with these kids, I was bowled over by their integrity, by the tribulations they endured in the service of inner truth. And now, decades later, I recognize in them a blazing spiritual sign. For I understand Jesus to be the God of the outsiders.

We are told Jesus was born outside, in a stable meant for animals.

neighbors forced him out of the synagogue and dragged him to the
edge of a cliff, intending to throw him to his death. Jesus constantly
befriended and embraced sex workers, tax collectors, lepers—those
held by his peers to be shameful outsiders. He denounced religious
systems that segregate people into the categories of righteous insiders and shameful outsiders, and this stance led the leaders of those
systems to call for his death. The Roman soldiers crucified Jesus
"outside the city walls," the Gospels say. And we are told that when
he died in excruciating pain, Jesus cried out from the agony of finding himself outside of God's care: "My God, my God, why have you
abandoned me?"

Jesus acted in radical solidarity, especially toward those considered by society to be unworthy of love. To follow him means joining
one's life and motivations with the oppressed, with the unhoused,
with the enslaved, with the colonized, with the queers. Whenever
anyone is treated as if their life doesn't matter, Jesus goes outside
with them.

*"God loves everyone for who they are!"*
  *"God has mercy on all people!"*
It was June 1997, just days after the talent show where Ali proclaimed his faith in a God who embraces us in our queerness, and
our SafeSpace crew was marching in the Pride Parade. Back then
the parade always got off to a contentious start, for the first thing
we passed was a large crowd of homophobic Catholics who always
stood outside of St. Patrick's Cathedral on Fiftieth Street, carrying
signs that proclaimed we were going to hell.

Ali was never one to remain silent in the face of slurs. He strode right up to the barricade and began to strike poses, blowing lewd kisses toward the detractors and hiking up his blue denim miniskirt to show them his skinny ass.

"Shame!" they cried out. "Shame on you, you sick pervert!"

Ali became enraged. "No, shame on you! Who are you to condemn me? I am a child of God!"

Bill Torres was our group's coordinator. Fearing the conflict might escalate to violence, he ran over and grabbed Ali, pulling her away from the protesters. "Come on, Ali," he counseled, "Don't let those assholes rain on your parade."

"I'm not letting nobody tell me I'm not a child of God!" Ali answered. "Nobody!"

How many times in the years since then, when my own faith has seemed in danger of withering, have I held to that memory of Ali's *confidence* in the radical inclusion of Divine Love? God's heart was the only space Ali trusted he could not be cast out from.

As a teenager, I joined the Church hoping to find support and guidance for the spiritual journey. Spiritual traditions aim to be vehicles of transmission, passing on the hard-won realizations of their founders. But as I grew older and sought what it meant for me to follow Christ as a gay person, I struggled to find Christ's all-embracing love in the churches and spiritual communities I'd turned to for support. Even in the most marginal spaces—in Catholic Worker houses and monasteries—though I met many wonderful and dedicated people, it seemed like the transmission of the spirit of Jesus was blocked by rigid fetishizations of authority and tradition.

More than any church "insider" I ever met, Ali gave me the spiritual transmission I'd been searching for. I learned to fully trust that the queerness of the youths, and my own queerness, were reflections of the queerness of God. The God of love. The God of the outsiders.

Part of me longs for certainty. That longing was satisfied for a time in my youth, when the structures and community of organized religion helped make the journey seem more tangible. When I decided to bring my whole self into my spiritual quest, I was forced to leave many religious certainties behind. Often, my journey of faith has felt like stumbling through the wilderness in the dark of night, wandering into thornbushes, falling into ditches. Yet, the fact that my queerness marginalizes me from my spiritual home has begun to seem a blessing, rather than a curse. This I learned from Ali and the other youths: To be cast outside is to walk on holy ground.

# CHAPTER 22

# BREAKTHROUGH

---

What power does a long-disenfranchised community hold to transform the treatment of its most abused members? How can we locate that power?

The spring of 2011 found me white-hot with rage at Cuomo and Bloomberg over their efforts to slash funds for homeless youths. But after weeks of angry fulmination, I came to a more sobering realization: Our youths were being treated so wretchedly because our LGBT community *allowed it*. The root of the problem wasn't the relative goodness or evil of the mayor or the governor, but rather our own failure to leverage our growing political influence to hold them accountable.

I'd put in much effort to boost our youths' visibility in our broader community, but after all the media attention Cuomo's cuts had generated over the previous two months, I understood that seeing needed to translate into concrete political action. Now I was racking my brain for a plan to make that happen.

My mind kept returning to the birthplace of our LGBT movement, the Stonewall Inn. The riots there had certainly brought about significant political change. Long before I began working with homeless queer youths, I knew they'd performed a pivotal role in the uprising. Hell, it was practically the first thing I learned upon moving to New York City twenty-five years earlier.

\* \* \*

Just a week after I'd arrived at the Catholic Worker, in February of 1986, Gary told me he wanted me to meet two of his friends. We bundled up and walked to the West Village, to a diner across the street from the Stonewall Inn.

"You need to show all due reverence," Gary said as we entered the diner and headed toward the booth where his friends were seated. "They are living icons, they fought in the Stonewall riots."

Gary introduced me to Martin Boyce and Thomas Lanigan Schmidt, both white guys in their mid-thirties. After I removed my coat, Tommy (as I'd come to know him) gave me the once-over and announced, "You look like a Counter-Reformation saint. El Greco would have painted you." Smiling, he continued, "And, no doubt, he'd have wanted you to pose naked."

I flushed with embarrassment. I was twenty, still deep in the closet, unaccustomed to being admired by men. Wanting to seem cool in the presence of these very openly gay guys, I tried not to show my discomfort.

I asked Tommy to tell me more about the Stonewall riots. "Is it true they happened because folks were upset Judy Garland had died?" I asked, repeating a legend I'd heard.

Tommy sneered, "It was the older queens who were into Judy Garland. The respectable, Uptown queens, the Fire Island queens." He was a shortish guy with light-brown hair, a variation on an eight-ies clone-style mustache, and a way of talking that was forcefully adamant, humorously sarcastic, and often quite sexualized. "Us street queens couldn't have cared less. Now, if *Diana Ross* had died . . . or *Martha Reeves*—"

"Or, really, *any* of the Vandellas . . ." added Martin.

Martin and Tommy began to describe the gang of homeless queer teens they had been part of in the West Village in 1969. Back then, Tommy was a homeless refugee from his conservative New

Jersey family, and Martin still lived with his parents but spent his days with the "scare queens" on Christopher Street.

"What's a 'scare queen'?" I asked, confused.

"It was the kids who did 'scare drag,'" Martin answered. "You basically wore male clothes, except for the one feminine piece of your ensemble. Say, a gorgeous scarf, or a bouffant wig, or luscious Chita Rivera eyelashes." For the most diva-esque words—*gorgeous, bouffant, Chita Rivera*—Martin added flourishes with his hands. He spoke in tumbling bursts, like a volcano erupting colorful bubbles.

Tommy explained that back then the police would arrest you for wearing women's clothing, so having just one piece you could remove in a hurry was a survival tactic.

"We were a band of sisters," Martin said. "We looked out for each other, shared with each other, protected each other. Everyone was some kind of Miss Thing: 'Miss Tommy,' 'Miss Martin,' or if you were an out-of-town queen, 'Miss Boston' or 'Miss New Orleans.'"

"Marsha Johnson was our saint," Tommy said.

"Marsha *P*. Johnson!" Martin corrected. It was the very first time I ever heard about Marsha.

"No one could stop Marsha from being herself," said Tommy. "She walked around with flowers and all kinds of stuff in her hair. But she was holy. People knew she was holy. I would see her in the flower district in the West Twenties, and those vendors from India showered adoration on her like she was Shiva. She'd sit in an alley like a goddess, and the vendors would bring offerings of the unsold flowers, piling them all around her. It was the *craziest* thing I ever saw."

"Marsha once saved me from a gay-bashing," Martin chimed in. "Straight guys from Brooklyn or New Jersey would pile into cars and come to the Village to pound the shit out of us. One night I was on Christopher Street, and Marsha came running, crying out,

'Miss Martin, Miss Martin, *hide!*' We hid together under a car while bullies stormed down the street with baseball bats, looking for some poor queen to pummel."

The night of the Stonewall riots, Tommy and Martin were outside when the police started to raid the bar, arresting people for not wearing "gender-appropriate" clothing and escorting them to a patrol wagon. This wasn't an uncommon occurrence, but a different energy had started to rise in the air.

"When we arrived, we saw a crowd," Martin said, "mostly the homeless scare queens at first. We saw the police trying to get this Joan Crawford, 'come fuck me' drag queen into the paddy wagon, and she turned around and slugged one of the cops. Then the crowd was growing larger, and we started moving toward the cops. You could see their confidence start to flicker, and then the cops started moving backward. That thrilled us! We kept moving forward, shouting, throwing pennies and trash at the cops. Finally, the police retreated into the Stonewall Inn, barricading themselves behind the heavy wooden doors."

"There was this scare queen named Miss New Orleans," Martin continued. "She was living on the streets, very poor, very skinny. But, oh, that night she was *irate*. Miss New Orleans dislodged a parking meter right out of the ground! It was like, suddenly, she had *superhuman* strength. Other queens joined her; they used the parking meter as a battering ram and started smashing the big heavy doors apart. Another queen took lighter fluid and set the doors on fire! Oh, I couldn't *believe* what was happening!"

Martin seemed transported as he spoke. It was thrilling to hear about the birth of a liberation movement from those who were there, like sitting in a first-century Roman tavern and hearing stories of Jesus from the mouth of Peter or Mark.

"The police couldn't contain us," Martin continued. "When the cops controlled one spot, we would reassemble somewhere else. We were setting trash cans on fire, people were breaking into stores, we were pushing on cars—all the things that happen in a riot. But it was the scare queens, even more scare than me, who were fighting the hardest. They were the shock troops. I was next to this one queen—oh, I usually hated her, but that night we were sisters. She was throwing garbage at the police, and I wasn't even mad that half the trash landed on me."

I listened, agog.

"Most of us weren't especially political," Martin went on. "But it was the sixties. Revolution was in the air. We saw the Civil Rights Movement, Black Power, feminism, saw all these other groups standing up for themselves, for justice. It was our turn. We were tired of being beaten down."

And this was the part that stuck with me. Tommy said it was important to understand the street queens had been at the center of the riot. "See, the respectable gays, the Fire Island gays, they hated us as much as the straights did. Maybe even more. They were ashamed of us. To them we were nothing but shoplifters, drug dealers, hustlers, street trash. But the riot couldn't have happened without us. We were the ones who had nothing to lose."

Tommy described standing back, looking on in wonder as Miss New Orleans and the other street queens broke open the barricaded doors. "It was like being there at the moment of the Resurrection," he said. "It was like seeing Christ's tomb burst open."

That image captivated me most of all.

Marsha P. Johnson, Miss New Orleans, and their sisters and brothers of the streets had been at the very heart of the uprising that birthed LGBTQ liberation. They brought about political and societal change that benefited the whole queer community. Then, tragically, they were cast away from the care and concern of the movement they helped ignite. They were once again outside the circle of influence. Not unlike our homeless queer kids who also seemed forgotten in the streets.

Street-identified trans women of color were not the messengers that the LGBTQ movement chose to listen to. The reigning glazed media narrative that the burgeoning gay rights movement chose to tell was about the liberating power of "coming out." We would come out to freedom, we would find love and happiness, we'd have hot bodies and hot sex and great clothes and glittering smiles. It was a message for, and by, cis white folks. I don't doubt that we told ourselves this exhilarating story partly to summon the courage to confront the bigotry and hatred we knew awaited us. But if our movement latched onto the promise that coming out was the key to fulfillment, the inconvenient reality was that thousands upon thousands of teens were coming out, only to be thrown out to destitution in the streets.

During those first years after Stonewall, Sylvia Rivera and Marsha P. Johnson had been among the very few people who did respond to the needs of homeless kids. In the early seventies, along with the Ballroom houses, they pioneered efforts to shelter homeless LGBT youth in New York City by opening STAR House, a communal residence for homeless street queens and hustlers. It was a bighearted but precarious endeavor; most of its funds were obtained through sex work, which proved unsustainable, and the communal home stayed open for less than a year.

Now, during the conflicts of 2011, as I sat and thought through this queer history, a lightbulb went on.

What we needed to do was reclaim Marsha and Sylvia's unheeded advocacy that ignited a societal movement. We needed to reassert the centrality of homeless queer youths—both in the media's narrative of our movement's origins and within our ongoing concerns. We needed to collectively unearth the political mandate buried within the truth Sylvia Rivera spoke to me: "They are our children."

In 2011, the political atmosphere was much more primed for change than in the days of the Stonewall riots. We were starting to have significant LGBTQ players in the government that could ignite structural transformation. I was realizing I'd been too much of a lone wolf as an advocate. My personal efforts weren't going to be enough; they needed to be wedded to community organizing. I realized I needed to join with people who could leverage the growing political influence of the LGBT community on behalf of the young people, needed to embody the collective queer *solidarity* that had birthed our movement.

I also thought about the more recent history of AIDS activism, which offered an example of LGBT activists successfully campaigning to acquire massive public funding for medical research and care. Key to their successes were the abilities of radical groups like ACT UP to pressure for governmental response in the streets, antagonizing, even harassing, politicians, while more "respectable" groups such as Gay Men's Health Crisis and the Treatment Action Group were able to lobby behind the scenes, offering strategies the besieged politicians could align with. Could we adopt a similar two-pronged approach?

I began reaching out to activists and providers who agreed to join our efforts to make the protection of homeless LGBT youth a core political priority of our community. We named our endeavor the Campaign for Youth Shelter and decided on a simple set of demands. First, we would call upon elected officials to add a hundred beds for homeless youths each year, until there were no longer waiting lists at the youth shelters. Then we would fight to allow young people to reside in youth shelters through the age of twenty-five, rather than being forced out on their twenty-first birthday. (Since they were allowed to access youth drop-in centers until they turned twenty-five, it seemed cruel and reckless to kick them out of the youth shelters at a younger age.)

I was able to recruit queer political power players like Jonathan Lang of the Empire State Pride Agenda, Steve Askinazy of the Stonewall Democratic Club, and Matt McMorrow of the Brooklyn Lambda Independent Democrats, all of whom had direct access to local politicians. We were also joined by activists like Andy Velez of ACT UP, Jason Walker and Jawanza Williams of VOCAL-NY, and Jake Goodman of Queer Rising, who had honed their organizing skills in radical direct-action campaigns. Rounding out our group were fellow homeless youth service providers like Theresa Nolan of Green Chimneys, Kate Barnhart of New Alternatives, and Jamie Powlovich of the Coalition for Homeless Youth, who could join their voices with mine in speaking to the unmet needs of our youths. Last, but hardly least, the youths themselves—Ali Forney Center clients such as Lex Perez, Skye Adrian, Latifah Blades, and Maddox Guerilla—were able to testify to the necessity for change based on their own lived experiences.

It was remarkable to have such political "insiders" sitting side by side with radical activists and homeless kids as we collectively strategized to bring about change. I suspect that the broad range of participants and skill sets was key to the success we'd go on to achieve.

We launched our campaign on the evening of June 24, 2011, with a press conference in front of the Stonewall Inn. Our small group of queer activists, homeless youths, and even a handful of celebrities— fashion photographer Mike Ruiz, *Breakfast Club*'s proto-grunge goddess Ally Sheedy, and Harmony Santana, a formerly homeless youth and transgender actress then lighting up screens in *Gun Hill Road*—gathered to honor the pivotal role homeless queer youths played in the Stonewall riots. We were even joined by Martin Boyce, my then sixty-year-old friend who had fought at Stonewall all those years ago.

Martin's testimony was powerful. Standing before our LGBT movement's historic birthplace, he once again spoke of Miss New Orleans—how, as the conflict with the cops escalated, she had used a parking meter to demolish the doors of the Stonewall Inn. He described her act of ferocity as a moment of destiny, the lightning rod that transformed a skirmish into a full-blown riot.

Then Martin said he'd come to view Miss New Orleans as a symbol of how the LGBT movement turned its back on the fierce, courageous street queens.

"Years later, I was on Christopher Street on a winter day and saw Miss New Orleans walk past, headed in the opposite direction. She looked lost, homeless, shivering from the cold. I watched as she vanished in the crowd. Oh, it made me so sad to see her like that, this great hero—really the lynchpin of the Stonewall uprising—unrecognized, unprotected, and alone in the heart of the city's queerest neighborhood."

After Martin's moving speech, I stepped up to the microphone.

"For too long we have failed to honor the street kids who ignited the Stonewall riots," I said. "We failed Marsha and Sylvia, we failed Miss New Orleans, we failed Ali Forney, and we are failing the many hundreds of queer kids who will sleep on our city's streets tonight."

I continued. "It is time for us to honor our origins, honor our youths who pay such a brutal price for being queer, honor our dignity as a people. For a community's worth is tested by whether it protects its most vulnerable. From now on, we are going to be united in demanding that our homeless youth be protected. We will no longer allow political leaders to claim to be friends of our community if they force our kids to sleep in the streets."

I closed with Sylvia's assertion.

"*They are our children.* They belong to us and we belong to them."

\* \* \*

As it happened, an hour later, the state legislature voted to make marriage legal for LGBT people in New York. Within minutes, thousands of overjoyed queers flooded the street to celebrate in front of the Stonewall Inn, right where our two dozen activists and homeless kids had stood. Obviously, this was an enormous win for the queer community, but over the next weeks I felt frustrated. Any spotlight our campaign might have acquired was extinguished in the waves of celebration. With time, however, I realized the victory was an unforeseen boon. Suddenly activists and philanthropists had to find a new cause. Many became involved with our efforts, bringing valuable strategic expertise and political connections forged during their long struggle for marriage.

Five months after the humble launch, the Campaign for Youth Shelter garnered enough support to host a substantially larger rally, this time in Union Square Park. But I'll admit, as we first gathered at the band shell on the southern edge of the park, I had an especially bad case of the jitters. It's not easy to simultaneously lead a nonprofit organization and an advocacy campaign. I was afraid of retaliation; I knew very well that I'd antagonized Cuomo and Bloomberg, and I feared they might take out their anger by revoking our contracts. What if I'd miscalculated? What if these efforts ended up hurting our kids?

Initially, the crowd of our supporters seemed sparse as we stood there in the day's fading light—our numbers dwarfed by hordes of oblivious, homeward-bound workers pouring past and descending into the subways. If barely anyone showed up to our rally, it would prove the opposite of what we wanted: It would communicate to the politicians that the queer community remained indifferent to our youths' predicament.

Then came this rumbling sound from the direction of University Place. At first it was barely discernible over the noise of traffic roaring up and down Fourteenth Street. But it steadily grew louder and louder. Then, suddenly, I heard this great eruption of cheers as dozens upon dozens of NYU students—ably recruited by Bill Torres, our volunteer coordinator—came into view, marching toward us. It was wonderful to observe this evidence that our fight resonated with a new generation. By the time the rally commenced, we were joined by many hundreds of attendees: student groups, members of political clubs and religious congregations, queer activists, elected officials. People of every race and gender expression stood together in solidarity. It was an eruption, a gorgeous mosaic of intersectionality, one of the most beautiful sights my eyes have ever seen.

A year earlier, we had struggled to bring media attention to Cuomo's and Bloomberg's cuts. Now we found ourselves speaking before a phalanx of journalists with microphones and TV cameras. I was grateful for the attention to our young people's needs. But if there was a moment that symbolized the distance we'd crossed from Ali dying alone on that cold sidewalk toward becoming a united community, it was that instant when I first caught sight of the crowd parading to join us. It stirred my soul.

In the months that followed, our campaign continued to gain momentum. RoseAnn and George Hermann of the queer synagogue Congregation Beit Simchat Torah assembled a group of LGBT-affirming churches and synagogues to lobby for homeless youth beds. Members of Queer Rising, a radical action group, were arrested blocking traffic outside of Cuomo's offices in protest of his budget cuts. Two of the most influential local LGBT power brokers, Frank Selvaggi and Louis Bradbury, organized an event to support our efforts. Frank went so far as to announce he'd refuse to donate funds to any local politician who didn't support our youths. We gained yet another powerful ally when the Legal Aid Society filed a class-action lawsuit against the city for its failure to provide an adequate number of youth shelter beds.

Alphonso began to meet with the Campaign for Youth Shelter, one of the most apparent signs that the tide was turning. He still harbored such animosity for my public critiques of Cuomo that he initially refused to meet with us if I attended. For that first meeting, I had to sit in an adjoining office like some naughty child. However, Alphonso did put aside his grudge, attending Frank and Louis's event and even consenting to being photographed alongside me. Thereafter we developed a working relationship, and in time even became friends. Over the next few years, the state began to make increases to its youth shelter budget (though the increases were small compared to the big cut during Cuomo's first year in office). Alphonso helped develop a grant with the New York State Department of Labor that proved to be very helpful in connecting our kids to jobs and higher education. And a few years later he would be instrumental in amending state laws so that young people could remain in youth shelters through the age of twenty-four.

By the time of the 2013 mayoral election cycle, our priorities were no longer on the sidelines. Every LGBT political club, as well as the local LGBT newspaper, the *Gay City News,* made adding beds for homeless youths part of their endorsement requirements. During a mayoral forum held at Baruch College to address the concerns of the LGBTQ community, Christine Quinn, then the front-runner, said the response to our young people's unmet needs was "a test of our morality as a city." Bill de Blasio said the spectacle of so many youths left unsheltered was "the LGBT symbol of the Tale of Two Cities," a reference to his campaign theme. Each Democratic candidate pledged they would implement our platform of adding a hundred youth shelter beds per year.

When de Blasio won the election, he kept his promise. New York

City went from providing 250 beds at the time of his election to more than 800 as of 2020. The additional beds were transformative. Our waiting list was cut in half, and the younger kids in our care were able to access shelter far more quickly than ever, usually within twenty-four hours. The scale of the investment was breathtaking. The six hundred new beds represented an expenditure of $30 million per year for a population that had long been treated with complete disregard.

Our victory transformed the landscape for all of New York City's homeless youths, not just the LGBT ones. Think of it: Our queer community was able to compel a radical reformation in the city's care of its most impoverished youths. I was so proud.

I generally believe it's wise to be humble about one's identities, both personal and collective. No group of people is without flaws, just as no individual is perfect. But here, as a queer person, I feel able to boast wholeheartedly. Along with the courage of the Stonewall rioters and the ferocious determination and compassion with which our community responded to the needs of those with AIDS, those months when I watched us come together and fight to protect our kids demonstrated what was best and strongest and most beautiful about our LGBT community.

We are a community attacked and vilified by many religious believers. We are called "groomers," we are slandered as being some-how inherently harmful to children. And yet how can anyone with a shred of spiritual awareness not see the sacredness of what we accomplished?

In the eyes of the world, the happenings in the lives of the rich and powerful and glamorous are considered of utmost importance. Their whims, their clothes, their sex lives, their conflicts, their life-style blogs and social media brands, even the décor of their kitchens and bathrooms, devour public attention.

I believe that what matters to God could not be more different. Those who are poor, outcast, regarded with contempt: They are the ones who are most beloved in God's eyes. For decades the homeless queer youths of our city were treated as the wretched of the earth—beaten, bullied, scorned, harassed, persecuted, left outside to die in the streets. By fighting to protect them, our LGBT community became a vehicle of justice and love—and, as I see it, an instrument of Divine will. Together we broke through the door that separated our young people from the collective concern and brought them inside.

It was like seeing Christ's tomb breaking open.

# CHAPTER 23

# THE HOLIDAY OF THE MEGA-DIVAS

t was November 2016, the day after Trump was elected president. As I led the bimonthly meeting of our program directors, I looked around at the faces of my co-workers—Latin Americans, transgender and nonbinary people, Black folks, immigrants. Almost everyone sitting around the table belonged to one or more groups who'd been vilified by Trump and his supporters. All around the room, eyes were marked by shock, sorrow, and horror. I feared for our group, for these people I cared so deeply about, and for the direction that our nation was heading. In a morose time, I wondered where we might again find some joy.

A week and a half later I was in my office, finishing the day's final emails. Most of the staff had departed for the day, so I was surprised when Alex Roque, then our extraordinarily talented director of development, excitedly entered my office. He'd just received a call from a representative of an unnamed "major A-list celebrity" who was considering spending Thanksgiving with the youths of the Ali Forney Center. They asked about the location of our largest housing site and requested photos of the dining room. While he was telling me this, another call came through, this time from the representative of a second anonymous superstar who wanted to bring holiday gifts to our kids the day after Thanksgiving.

As Alex and I sat there wondering who they could be, the phone rang again. I saw Alex's eyes widen, and when he put the phone down, he burst out, "Oh. My. GOD! The one who wants to join us for Thanksgiving Day is *Madonna!*"

My heart stopped. Good thing this didn't happen between 1989 and 1993, for in those years my gay-boy Madonna fandom burned so white-hot that I probably would have required hospitalization if she'd invited herself over for dinner. Even now I was swooning.

Another call came through. As Alex listened, he stared at me and mouthed, "Oh my God, oh my God . . ." He hung up. "This is insane! The other celebrity is *Lady Gaga!*"

Over the next hour, a blizzard of calls ensued as representatives from both camps scrambled to prepare for the visits. Alex would have Madonna's rep on the phone and need to put her on hold for Gaga's rep, and vice versa. Each insisted upon absolute secrecy, promising that the visit would be canceled if we breathed a word to *anyone,* even to our co-workers. Consequently, we were unable to alert the respective reps of the other celebrity's plans.

But how could it possibly be a coincidence that two of the reigning mega-divas of the past quarter century would be on our phone at the same time planning visits? It had been ten years since Bea's benefit, the last time a superstar of comparable magnitude had visited.

"Maybe it's not a coincidence," I speculated. "Maybe they are tag teaming to see if we can be trusted to keep our mouths shut."

"But Madonna and Gaga haven't got much love for each other," Alex noted. A few years earlier, Madonna had made no secret of her feelings that Gaga had copied her playbook, being especially critical of how "Born This Way" utilized chord progressions similar to "Express Yourself." Gaga responded by asserting that her musical skills were superior to Madonna's. Each diva's army of fans took up the fight, blanketing social media with disparagements and rabid denunciations.

"Maybe this is a response to Trump's election," I mused. "Maybe they want to show their fans that even feuding superstars need to stand together to support the folks Trump is attacking."

Within a few hours we solidified a game plan. Madonna would visit our largest housing site—our twenty-bed facility in Sunset Park—along with two of her children and an entourage of some half-dozen others, including a bodyguard, publicist, boyfriend, and driver. Her personal chef would cater the meal. Gaga would arrive the following day, bringing truckloads of gifts to the drop-in center, accompanied by her mother, several friends, and a film crew from the *Today* show.

On Thanksgiving, before Madonna's team pulled up, we gathered as many of our residents to the Sunset Park residence as possible, promising that a very famous woman would soon join them. Madonna made us collect and lock up everyone's cellphones, even mine. I sat in the living room, waiting with a dozen young people, all of them feverishly speculating about who the famous person might be.

"Tell us! Tell us who it is!"

My lips were sealed.

"I bet it's Beyoncé!" said one.

"No, it's probably Hillary Clinton," another declared.

Alex was the only one allowed to keep his phone, so he could be in communication with Madonna's camp. He kept running into the room to whisper breathless updates into my ear. "She's half an hour away . . ." "She's on the BQE . . ." "She's just around the corner . . ." Finally, the doorbell rang. With the staff and youths assembled in the front hallway, I opened the door, and Madonna stepped inside, her entourage shuffling in behind her.

"Oh my God, it's *Madonna*," one of the youths squealed. The rest of us stood there in silence, completely flabbergasted to have the Material Girl herself standing in our humble doorway. Even I, who knew she was coming, stood there utterly dumbfounded. (Frankly,

I was surprised at how young she looked. With her blond hair and smooth, unwrinkled skin, it was like staring back into 1990. Whether she was still doing "mad Botox," as Andrew had insisted years ago, or something else, it was clearly working for her.)

"Well, are you going to invite us in, or what?" Madonna asked with her signature attitude, delivered with a smile. Several of the youths, unable to contain their excitement, began to jump up and down. I led the group inside and we all took our seats around the big table in the adjoining dining room, where her personal chef and assistants laid out their platters of food.

And then there she was, a living icon of my youth, sitting with her kids and ours, calmly eating Thanksgiving dinner while our clients spazzed and gagged with amazement.

One young man was so excited by Madonna's presence across the table that he couldn't stop his head from bouncing up and down, like an overenthusiastic cockatoo. For most of the meal Madonna was low-key, calmly engaging in small talk with the young people. At one point several of the kids begged her to vogue.

"I came here to share a meal with you, not to put on a performance," she replied.

But when they continued pleading, she begrudgingly stood for twenty seconds, clutching her handbag and shaking her plaid-covered butt, serving up banji-girl realness with all the requisite haughty petulance. The young people's mouths gaped open. They seemed too awed to know how to react.

After the turkey and stuffing and macaroni and cheese had been devoured and the pies reduced to crumbs, Madonna had us all go around the table, one after another, and share what made us grateful. I was absolutely tickled to see America's pop-queen bad girl channeling her inner third-grade schoolteacher.

Finally, we all gathered for a group photo and Madonna departed with her entourage, leaving us all somewhat staggered with awe at what had just gone down. No sooner had the door closed than the young people begged for the return of their cellphones, upon which they promptly scattered to brag on the internet about how they'd just met *Madonna*.

Lady Gaga came to our Harlem drop-in center early the next afternoon, arriving with her mother, Cynthia, and two huge SUVs packed with gifts. Again, the kids had no idea what was about to unfold. She strode into our crowded dining room, her blond hair pulled back in a tight ponytail, dressed in skintight black jeans and a T-shirt emblazoned with BE BRAVE in bold red letters. When she called out in a loud voice, "Hey, guys, it's me, Lady Gaga!," utter pandemonium ensued. Many of the youths erupted in screams. Others dissolved into tears. It reminded me of a particularly frenzied Pentecostal revival service. Clearly, the Mother Monster had won these kids' adoration as thoroughly as Madonna had acquired mine twenty-five years earlier.

The next few hours were an extravaganza. First Gaga, her mother, and her assistants organized the huge piles of scarves, hats, socks, and makeup, handing them out to all the individual youths, some of whom continued crying, while others held up their phones to film the spectacle. As she handed out the gifts, many of the youths stammered out confessions of their undying devotion.

"When my parents pushed me out for being gay, all I had was you, and *Born This Way* on auto-repeat," one bearded young man told Gaga. She hugged him, and tears streamed from his mascara-lined eyes.

"Thank you for being alive," she said as the two emerged from their embrace.

After the gifts were distributed, Gaga gathered everyone into a big circle on the floor.

"I'm going to teach you to meditate," she said. "I suffer from a mental illness, PTSD, and meditating has really helped me learn how to cope better." As she explained how to use a mantra, I noticed several of the young people struggling to sit still. It was touching, and a bit comical. How could any of them focus when their legend was only a few feet away on the carpet?

Afterward, Gaga perched herself atop our upright piano and serenaded us with a rousing acoustic rendition of her new single, "Million Reasons." She then spent an hour posing for selfies with every young person and staff member (making me most grateful that a few months earlier we'd enrolled our youths in a program to provide them with free phones).

While the visit was underway, the work of welcoming homeless youths to our drop-in center continued. A young man had arrived for the first time and was sitting in a counseling room down the hallway with one of our staff for his intake—an hour-long session where we learn who the new client is and take note of their most pressing needs. The newly arrived youth, like so many who've been forced to contend with rejection and homelessness, confided that he had struggled with thoughts of suicide. He told our worker that when he felt hopeless, he listened to Lady Gaga to find the strength to hang on.

When the intake was completed, the staff person said, "By the way, if you'd like to meet Lady Gaga, she just happens to be in our dining room *right now*." The young man leapt out of his chair, smoke nearly coming from his heels as he ran to Gaga as fast as his feet could carry him. He broke down sobbing in her arms.

Later that afternoon, both divas, within minutes of each other, posted news of their visits on social media. The queer blogosphere was soon filled with millions of voices going on about how every

LGBT teen in America was jealous of the kids at the Ali Forney Center.

It turned out that neither superstar was aware of the other's visit. As hard as it is to believe, their simultaneous acts of kindness and generosity were a total coincidence. How's that for a holiday miracle?

# CHAPTER 24

# A TRUCK STOP ON I-94

I n spring 2009, I received a cryptic call from a man named Anthony. In a thick New Jersey accent, he told me that he had something very urgent to share, but he needed to provide the information by email. Only then would he speak further. I was a bit unnerved, wondering if he might be putting me through some elaborate sales pitch. But curiosity prevailed, so I shared my contact info.

It turned out Anthony's motives were pure. He wanted to raise awareness of a tragedy he'd witnessed, though his story was more devastating than anything I could have imagined.

He wrote about a boy named "Caleb" who lived in upstate New York. Caleb came out to his parents shortly before his sixteenth birthday, prompting a vicious beating from his father, who subsequently threw Caleb out of their home. A month later Caleb returned, only to be met at the door by his mother. She warned him to stay away. His father had threatened to "kill the little faggot and bury him in the backyard" if Caleb ever came home.

Over the next few months Caleb survived in the mountainous forests of rural Delaware County. He was seldom seen. A couple on a camping trip caught a glimpse of him stealing food from their tent. Later, a policeman saw him hitchhiking. But the last person to see Caleb alive was Anthony, the man who had called me. Anthony was the conductor of the train that Caleb jumped in front of to end his life. He wrote that they had looked into each other's eyes in the split second before Caleb's body was crushed.

Reading Anthony's testimony, my mind initially chalked up the boy's suicide as another consequence of the anguish of familial rejection. Only later did I consider another factor: how difficult the boy's survival must have been in a rural area without any shelters for homeless youths. The sheer isolation and lack of resources must have only added to his despair.

It had taken years to build up the Ali Forney Center and push New York City's government to offer enough shelter for its homeless youths. I hadn't given much thought to what was available for young people in other parts of the country. Sure, almost half of our clients came to us from other states, and especially from the Deep South. But I'd assumed their main reason for coming to New York was to escape anti-LGBT hatred in the more conservative parts of the country. It hadn't occurred to me that many came from areas without any shelter whatsoever.

One particular encounter shocked my eyes open. I was in a church basement in a town called Anoka, near Minneapolis, Minnesota, meeting with a group of parents and progressive ministers who were considering creating a shelter for LGBT teens. It was a heartbreaking situation. A few years earlier, a group of conservative Christians had forced a ruling upon the city's school district, preventing LGBT issues from being talked about within the school system. In the aftermath, LGBT students were targeted for bullying and teachers declined to intervene, afraid they would lose their jobs if they stepped in to defend the persecuted teens. In the less than two years since, nine LGBT students in the district had committed suicide, many of them after enduring harassment from their peers.

As we sat in a meeting room below the church on an assortment of folding chairs and tattered sofas, a minister told me that a census of the local school district had identified more than a thousand students dealing with homelessness.

"Are there any youth shelters nearby?" I asked.

She shook her head. "In the whole state of Minnesota there are only ten youth shelter beds, all in Minneapolis. And those beds are *always* filled."

"So, what do the police do when they come across a homeless kid?"

"Since there's no shelter for the kids the police usually drop them off at a truck stop on I-94, figuring they'll either prostitute themselves to the truck drivers or hitch rides to Chicago and become that city's problem."

My mouth gaped open. These people had brought me here to advise them on an impossible situation. What could I possibly say?

The next day I visited the one youth shelter in Minneapolis, the ten-bed facility the minister had mentioned. It was located in a well-maintained house in a suburban neighborhood with lawns and trees. The program director introduced me to a young woman who'd spent months living on the city's streets before a bed opened for her. I asked what it was like being homeless in the frigid winters of that northern Midwestern city. She was sixteen years old with a sweet, round face that reminded me of my long-deceased SafeSpace co-worker, Cheri Hamm. Her eyes quickly welled up as she described her experience.

"Most nights were not so bad, because I found a bus driver who let me spend the night riding with him. He was really kind. He let me lay down in the back and sleep while he drove his route across the city. But he was off two nights each week, and those were horrible. I had to sleep in a cardboard box, out in the streets. I remember one night I was shivering so bad, I was sure they'd find my body frozen in that box. It was really, really scary, I was crying *so* hard. I really thought I was going to die."

I returned to New York deeply shaken and began researching what was available on a national level. There were fewer than six thousand beds for homeless youths in the entire nation, most of them concentrated in a handful of large cities. Many states had no more than five or ten beds. To this day, the overwhelming majority of unaccompanied homeless youths in the United States—which a very conservative estimate would number at least 500,000—have absolutely no access to youth shelter.

Now I was haunted, thinking of Caleb being reduced to stealing food from campsites, of the young woman in Minneapolis feeling *grateful* for the ability to sleep on a city bus. That winter I decided to look at our Homeless for the Holidays project through a national lens. I interviewed some of our youths who'd come from other states, asking what it was like to survive in areas without any youth shelters.

Their accounts were harrowing—and, in a larger sense, revealing. A seventeen-year-old was thrown out of his rural Georgia home for being a "faggot" and had no way of getting to Atlanta, where he might have found shelter. He spent three days in the woods near his home, depressed, immobilized with anxiety, with no food or water, until he finally collapsed from hunger and dehydration and had to be hospitalized.

Another young man fled his father's homophobic abuse in a small Texas city with no youth shelter. Like the girl from Min-neapolis, he rode the city buses all night, until some strange man drove up to the bus stop and offered to let him sleep at his place in exchange for sex. The sixteen-year-old boy was repulsed by the idea, but finally gave in, unable to bear the thought of another long, sleepless night on the bus.

Then there was a young woman taken in by a twenty-five-year-old man, who allowed her to sleep on a mattress in his basement on one condition. Her "contribution to the house," he explained, would be that she sleep with him and his friends. As many as five of them would line up at night and take turns raping her. Then in the morning he'd drive her to school. Telling me this in a cold park near our drop-in center, the two of us surrounded by darkness except for the glaring light of a streetlamp above, she looked me in the eyes and confided in an even tone, "I was only fourteen. I didn't know anything about sex. I knew homework, video games, chores."

To work with homeless kids is to be confronted with the particular evil of how their innocence is so often ravaged and stolen. But I cannot recall a starker example than this sweet transgender girl telling me how she'd think about homework and video games while being gang-raped. We wrongly let ourselves off the hook if we isolate this evil to the wrongdoings of individual perpetrators. Young people are lured into such situations because we, as a broader society, have failed to provide them with a safety net.

Somehow, I never stop being astonished at the self-delusion built into our American psyches. We tell ourselves we are this great beacon of justice in the world. We imagine we are a civilized, decent people, all while leaving our most helpless, vulnerable children to fend for themselves in our streets, bus stops, and forests. Our leaders talk of protecting children, wrapping themselves in sanctimonious ideals of "family values." Perhaps we need such cognitive dissonance and denial merely to keep functioning while so many suffer around us.

I cannot tell you how many times I've heard funders and even fellow activists tell me something along the lines of *I'm not really interested in providing shelter. Shelter merely puts a Band-Aid on the homeless problem. I want to see long-term solutions; I want to see the root causes addressed.*

I want to scream when I hear this.

I do understand why funders have a hard time getting enthused about shelters. Warehouse shelters have often been frightening, violent, dehumanizing places, and should be recognized as such. However, the Ali Forney Center and many other providers have demonstrated that youths can be sheltered in safe, dignified, home-like environments. The Ali Forney Center has even expanded beyond shelters, to the point where it now offers long-term transitional housing and is in the process of developing permanent supportive housing. But I would never use those programs to denigrate the necessity of emergency shelter. Long-term housing programs usually have intricate eligibility requirements. Gaining access to them tends to be a slow bureaucratic process, taking months to achieve.

As for the "Band-Aid" metaphor, it is grossly inadequate. The condition of being unhoused isn't a paper cut—it's a gaping wound. When a queer kid is homeless, they face violence, sexual assault, addiction, and incarceration. Their health, even their lives, are at terrible risk. Providing shelter is not like applying a bandage. It's more like a tourniquet that prevents a young person from bleeding out. When a kid shows up at your door asking for help, they need somewhere safe to sleep that very night, not a six-month process that leaves them languishing in the streets, or a theoretical blueprint for eliminating structural causes of homelessness.

Every city in our nation must have a safety net in place for homeless children. Every rural region should as well. And given the enormous prevalence of LGBTQ youths suffering homelessness, I believe every local queer community has a responsibility to plan for how their young people will survive. Our community centers, our queer-affirming churches, and LGBT-affirming elected officials all must take part in advocating for shelter and an infrastructure to support their long-term needs. Surely any responsible community is obligated to protect its most vulnerable members.

Housing people decently is an expensive proposition, and a significant contributor to the success of the Ali Forney Center was our ability to leverage local queer political influence to gain public funding. It must be acknowledged that such LGBT political muscle doesn't yet exist in most cities and regions in the country. In my view, that puts a particular onus on the large national LGBT advocacy organizations to lobby for federal tax dollars to support local youth housing initiatives. We LGBT people pay billions of dollars in taxes; it is up to us to demand that our fair share is returned to our neediest youths.

# CHAPTER 25

# THE GIFT OF TEARS

J ESUS WOULD STONE HOMOS. STONING IS STILL THE LAW.
So proclaimed a sign in front of ATLAH World Mission-
ary Church, an ornate redbrick building three blocks south
of our Harlem drop-in center. The church's pastor, James David
Manning, had gained notoriety a few years earlier when he used a
sign outside the church to post deranged messages accusing Barack
Obama of being a pimp and of murdering his grandmother. By 2014,
he had turned his focus to hate speech targeting LGBT people. The
church's neighbors were already upset, and this latest call to violence
was the breaking point.

Around that time, a woman who lived directly across the street
reached out to me, saying she felt compelled to take a stand. Stacy
Parker Lamelle, a dark-haired woman in her thirties, proposed
launching an online fundraiser for the Ali Forney Center to combat ATLAH's vile message of religious intolerance. I was happy to
partner with her. ATLAH was a five-minute walk from our drop-in
center, on a busy stretch of Lenox Avenue. I hated picturing our
young people walking past a sign that advocated violence against
them. Over the next two years, Stacy and I worked together on several benefits. By the fall of 2015, Stacy and other local activists had
raised over $17,000 for our program.

Unfortunately, her friendly neighborhood kindness and support
did not rub off on Manning. That fall, he posted a new message on
the church's yard sign: MUSLIMS HATE FAGS. THEY THROW FAGGOTS

OFF BUILDINGS. THE BIBLE SAYS THROW THEM OFF TOO. Stacy wasn't having this. She decided to take a more forceful stand and organized a rally of people from the community, gathering in front of ATLAH to protest its despicable sign.

It was quite a scene. Several hundred protesters, some of our staff and youth advocates among them, assembled in the evening's darkness in front of the imposing building. Many carried signs proclaiming LOVE NOT HATE, and the rest of us chanted those same words. Thirty minutes after we'd begun, Manning came out into the church's courtyard, accompanied by about two dozen of his supporters and a handful of children who appeared to be nine or ten years old. Our two groups were separated by a wrought iron gate encircling the church.

It was the first time I saw Manning in the flesh. A Black man in his late sixties with a toad-like, jowly face, the pastor was dressed elegantly in a white shirt, tie, long black overcoat, and brown homburg hat. His words, however, clashed with his formal couture.

"*Faggots!! Lezbos! N\*\*\*\*\*S!*" he shrieked in a high-pitched voice. "*Demon possessed freaks, your breath smells like BUTTHOLES!!!*"

He was shouting into a microphone, with loudspeakers amplifying his obscenities and overpowering our chants. I was horrified that our youths were hearing this. I looked at them; some appeared shocked, while others looked enraged.

"This is a lot to deal with," I said to the young people. "Please, if you want to leave, feel free to do so. I don't want you to have to be exposed to this man's craziness."

But they decided to stay. Maybe it felt like a rare opportunity to physically confront the religious demons that had tormented so many of them—the ghosts of their past embodied in the snarling, corpulent minister on the other side of the gate.

Now, here's the heart of the matter, at least in my eyes. Because of his vulgar and buffoonish eruptions, it is easy to write off Manning as a deranged, fringe fanatic. And yet, as a Catholic, I must ask myself: How different are his wild condemnations of LGBT people from the beliefs of many mainstream religious leaders? How different are Manning's hateful messages from those coming from some of the leaders of my church?

In 2019, Cardinal Dominik Duka of Prague proclaimed the LGBT movement to be "satanic." That same year, Archbishop Marek Jędraszewski gave a homily at the Krakow Basilica, warning congregants of a "rainbow plague" that "wants to conquer our souls, hearts, and minds." Even the usually sweet-hearted and sometimes astonishingly welcoming Pope Francis once saw fit to compare transgender people to nuclear weapons, accusing them of pushing an ideology "that does not recognize the order of creation." While these leaders have not joined Manning in calling for overt violence against us, how can anyone with even the most limited knowledge of recent history deny the inevitable consequences of dehumanizing a persecuted minority, of likening them to an infectious disease or weapon of mass destruction? *Kill a fag today, Cardinal O'Connor says it's OK.*

The young people at the Ali Forney Center pay a brutal price for such words. For, at its root, the crisis of LGBT youth homelessness is a crisis of religion. Nine out of every ten youths who come to the Ali Forney Center tell us it was their parents' religious beliefs that drove them from their homes.

This tsunami of family rejection is a tragedy not only for the discarded kids, but also for parents forced to navigate the rift between their love of their children and adherence to their belief systems. Obviously, parents bear responsibility if they harass their kids and kick them out of their homes, but the Church bears no less responsibility for creating an environment where so many parents are made to feel ashamed of their LGBT children and are led to see them as evil.

These beliefs are encoded within the Catholic Catechism, which describes the lovemaking of LGBT people as "acts of grave depravity," "intrinsically disordered," and "contrary to natural law." It goes on to describe the condition of being attracted to persons of the same sex as "objectively disordered." I cannot say this plainly enough: These words lead to child abuse. They create a war zone between huge numbers of religious parents and their LGBT children. In my time running the Ali Forney Center, I often felt like I was overseeing a battlefield triage unit, frantically attempting to bind up the bloodied young victims of this ideology.

And heartbreakingly, the battle doesn't end when kids are driven from their homes. These hate-filled messages can affect kids far into their adult lives, with the voices of parents and ministers insisting that the longings of their hearts are evil, that their very selves are abominations. These are the kinds of lies that destroy a child.

In Old Testament times, some of Israel's neighbors worshipped a vicious, bloodthirsty god they called Moloch. Moloch demanded child sacrifice, and to appease the brutal deity, his devotees handed over their children to be killed. "But go and learn what this means," Jesus said, "*I desire mercy, not sacrifice.*" Parents may imagine that they are adhering to a moral path when they reject their LGBT children, but this torrent of kids sacrificed to the streets proves they follow Moloch, not Christ.

Rashon was a big presence at the Ali Forney Center, because of both his large, pear-shaped body and his equally outsized personality. For about five years he was part of our family, living in our housing sites, a constant fixture at our drop-in center, and the boisterous MC of our in-house balls and talent shows. Whenever I came by the drop-in center, he'd come running as soon as he saw me, enveloping me in a great big hug.

One afternoon, Rashon told me about his upbringing. His

grandmother had raised him from the time he was seven. "There's nothing like a grandmother's love," he recalled wistfully, his high-pitched, melodious voice sounding like a mournful flute. "She raised me like I was her own. I thought she loved me unconditionally."

Rashon's grandmother was very religious, and the church was at the center of their lives. "She had me in everything you could think of. I was in Bible study, Sunday school, the men's choir, the junior choir, the usher board, the missionaries, the junior missionaries, *everything*."

Then his voice got low and solemn.

"I came out to her when I turned seventeen. When I told her I was a gay Black man, she just totally disowned me. Just like that, right then and there. Afterward all she could say to me was, 'I rebuke this demon.'" Rashon looked down for a moment, and then continued, "I love my grandmother dearly. I love her to this day. But how can you disown your child?"

Something in Rashon was too sweet, too vulnerable, to cope with the withdrawing of his grandmother's love. I saw the devastation in his eyes, heard the heartbreak in his voice. In the space of a moment, he went from being her beloved child to being a demon. He was ruined by it.

After Rashon aged out of the Ali Forney Center, he descended deeper and deeper into drug addiction. When he died six years later, in August of 2021, we concluded it was likely from an overdose. I was at an auto-repair shop when I learned of Rashon's death from posts on Facebook. I hid myself in a cubicle and wept, feeling ruined by Rashon's loss and by the ever-accumulating wreckage done to so many children I've cared for.

I could fill the pages of ten books with nothing but the miserable, evil stories young people have told me of being cast out in the name of God. The scope of their suffering is wider than we can

THE GIFT OF TEARS

imagine. Those who uphold the teachings that cause this tidal wave of religious rejection have blood on their hands.

Every child exposed to religious indoctrination about the sinfulness of homosexuality is endangered, even those whose parents would never dream of casting them out.

Jane Clementi's son Tyler died by suicide in 2010, following a humiliating incident where his college roommate livestreamed video of Tyler having sex with another young man. The death was reported on nationally as an example of cyberbullying. When I had the chance to speak to her, though, Jane mentioned a discovery she'd made in the days after her son's death. Drowning in grief, she was going through Tyler's belongings and came upon a Sunday school lesson from when Tyler was twelve or thirteen.

"I found these mimeographed sheets of paper where there were church teachings with missing words, and the kids had to fill in the blanks. I saw one page where it said, 'homosexuality is BLANK.' And Tyler had to write, A SIN."

Jane knew she was looking upon the groundwork of shame that had caused her son to end his life. "How can any child have to write such things about themselves?" she asked. Then she paused, as if to summon the strength for what she would next confess.

"Carl," she said, "that is my biggest regret in life, that I sent my sons to a church that would teach them that."

After the priest sex abuse scandals erupted into public view in 2003, I couldn't set foot in a Catholic church for seven years. I was just too disgusted by the lies, cover-ups, and corruption. I told myself that I would practice authentic spirituality through my efforts to care for homeless youths and tried to shake the dust from my feet.

Still, there was something in me that couldn't find peace; a yearning that kept my soul restless. In my youth I'd found the deepest, most intimate communion with God in daily silent prayer, in the hours when I was still and alone with God. I knew in those moments, not in some conceptual way but in the depths of my being, that God is all-loving, all-merciful. My life's work has been an attempt to materialize that inner experience of love, to bring it to life outside of me. But over the decades, walls of distrust had grown inside my heart. The homophobic cruelties at the Catholic Worker, the abandonment of thousands of kids in our care for religious reasons . . . these rejections led me to doubt my foundational experience of a God of love. They gave rise to a corrosive voice within me that insisted: *See, see, belief in God gives birth to a swarm of toxicity. Let go of your fantasies. Face up to the fact that this "God" is nothing more than a cover for control and abuse.*

But in April of 2015, during the week of my fiftieth birthday, I was staring out my bathroom window when I suddenly felt overcome by the beauty of the early morning light. This brought back memories of my adolescence, when I'd wake up at 4:00 A.M. each day to pray on my father's porch. Those mornings were among the most joyous times of my life. Alone with God, face-to-face in silent intimacy, the darkness of the night slowly giving way to light—and in so doing seeming to dramatize my own awakening to Divine love. Now, as I peered out the window some three decades later, I felt like I had thrown away the most precious gift of my life.

The love I discovered in God when I was younger was wild and boundless. But as I grew up and grew into my queerness, I had to reckon with some heavy questions. How could leaders of a religion devoted to a God of love vilify my community? Why must they value their dogmas over the lives of God's queer children? How could the spiritual tradition that nurtured my early years of service be the very same entity that so recklessly brought devastation upon the young people in my care?

Now an answer began to present itself: What if I was not meant to turn away from this conflict but in fact *called upon* to confront it? What if I was meant to witness the devastation inflicted on LGBT youths and use my voice for truth, to cry out that such cruelties are not the way of Christ?

As I watched the sunrise on the morning of my fiftieth birthday, I recognized a longing within myself to return to that spiritual practice that had once felt like my direct connection to God. But I knew if I was going to resume a daily habit of contemplative prayer, I had to face my inner demons. I began to arise each morning to sit in silent prayer again. For the first few weeks it was rough going: sitting there trying to sort through a swarm of feelings of disappointment and betrayal by the Church and to reach beyond them to regain trust in a God of love. But eventually, I began to feel some of the blockages loosen. Sometimes, when I had flashes where I once again *knew* God's love, I would even begin to weep, feeling overwhelmed.

It is embarrassing to admit to so much crying in this book. In my insecurity, sometimes I've wondered if I ought to title it *An Insufferable Torrent of White Tears*. But my tears place me in direct continuity with the first Christian contemplatives: the women and men who fled to the desert in the third century A.D., seeking silence, humility, and purity of heart. These early spiritual leaders saw "the gift of tears" as a sign of God's grace. Weeping, for them, was the natural physical outcome when our small, finite beings truly encountered God—not merely the narrow god of our human projections, but the living God of infinite love. The mystics shed tears of repentance, tears of suffering, tears of wonder, and tears of joy. And they believed their hearts were washed clean and purified by those tears.

The desert fathers and mothers sought to live at the farthest margins of their society, seeing the wilderness as the place where wisdom might be discovered. Nowadays I suspect these marginal places are different. If we want to find wisdom about our society and about ourselves, we must step outside the displays of power and respectability that we spend so much of our lives cultivating. Listen to those who have been discarded. Listen to what makes you cry. I tell you: Wisdom is there.

Recently Ali's friend Angie told me about a time when she and Ali argued about faith. "When my grandmother was dying," she said, "I remember Ali was talking to me about God. And I said, 'What kind of God is that, that would take away my grandmother? Have I not suffered enough?' Ali sat there and told me, 'You never question what God does, cause God knows why he does the things that he does. If your grandmother is dying, it's because it's time for her to go.'

"I said, 'Wow, that's pretty harsh!' And he was like, 'No, you're gonna cry, and it's OK to cry, cause that's why God gives us tears: So we can wash away our pain. And Miss Thing, you need to cry, because you're a bitter bitch!'"

As usual with Ali, her deepest truths came wrapped in a package of shade. The truth I have learned, ever so slowly, from Ali and my many other guides, is the important discipline of becoming present to the sufferings of others and to my own. Not to flee, not to run, not to avoid or numb, but to have the courage to feel the pain, cry the tears, and then try to respond with whatever is mandated by love. And to be honest with myself when I fail.

Here is where I've landed in my spiritual practice. I continue praying silently every morning and night. Once a week, I spend a day in quiet solitude at a small hilltop cabin an hour from our home, staying there from morning to nightfall. I pray Lauds and Compline from the breviary, the Catholic prayer book used by monks and nuns. This makes me feel connected through the ages to the desert people, those marginal lovers of God. I attend Mass sporadically. I continue to struggle with a sense of betrayal and anger toward the leaders of the Roman Catholic Church. However, over time, I've noticed that meditation makes me conscious of my essential human solidarity with those who frustrate me, for in the silence I am compelled to face my own capacity for rejection, cruelty, and betrayal.

I've also started doing what I can to end the harm perpetrated in the name of religion. I've written op-eds and given speeches in welcoming churches. I've sent open letters to Cardinal Timothy Dolan, my local bishop, and even to Pope Francis, inviting them to visit the Ali Forney Center and speak with the young people whose lives have been devastated by their teachings. Those invitations were not accepted, but they remain in effect.

Thomas Merton wrote of an "eternal conflict" within Christianity— a conflict between those who become self-righteous and judgmental of the sins of others and those who learn to humbly accept their essential unity with their fellow humans. I hope the Church will come to such humility and repent of the terrible harm it has done to queer people, especially queer children. I don't know if I will live to see that. All I know is I cannot imagine how the harmful elements of the Church can be healed if I cannot uproot the rage and division in my own heart. I'm tired of being angry. God help me, I don't want to end up a bitter bitch.

# CHAPTER 26

# CELEBRATION

t is April of 2013. A shy, thin young man tentatively stands in front of a crowd of almost a hundred people in our drop-in center's large dining room—peers, staff members, and volunteers. He is dark-skinned and looks small in an oversized red sweatshirt, like some nervous, newly ordained priest approaching the pulpit for the first time. Seeing his trepidation, I suspect he's never performed in front of a crowd.

I wish I could remember his song, but I cannot. What I do remember is his fear, which froze and silenced him after one or two notes had quavered out of his trembling lips. And I remember how the young people responded. They could have mocked him with shady remarks. (Teens can be merciless when someone shows signs of weakness.) But that's not what happened.

"You can do it!" Rashon called out. Rashon was still alive then, serving as the MC of the talent show. "You can do it." Then other young people began to join with Rashon, chanting "You can do it!" in unison. When the boy still stood there, petrified, Rashon walked over and hugged him. "It's OK, you can do it," Rashon repeated.

The boy in red regrouped. He stammered a few more words of his song, then froze again. Rashon walked up beside him, placed his beefy arm on the boy's bony shoulder, and began to sing along. Dozens of the other kids rose to join them, standing beside the boy, singing with him, demonstrating their unity, their solidarity, with the trembling young man. He finally found the courage to finish the song. When he was done, everyone cheered, and many of the young people joined Rashon in embracing him.

It was one of my favorite moments at the Ali Forney Center. What happened during that talent show was the worthiest outcome of our work—providing our young people the foundation they need to support one another, to stand up for their communities and offer one another the courage to sing.

Another musical celebration comes to mind, though this one had no element of reluctance.

It was a warm, sunny afternoon during the summer when "Baby Boy" played on endless repeat. Taking advantage of the lovely weather, most of the young people from our drop-in center had left us to hang out on the piers. With the place almost empty, it was mercifully quiet, and I took advantage of the rare absence of Ms. Knowles's stylings to make some necessary calls.

I was on the phone when the quiet was broken. I heard a voice—an awful noise, like the deranged bellowing of a nauseated hyena. After placing the call on hold to investigate, I walked out of my office to find a tall young man in a white T-shirt and bright orange shorts pushing a mop across our hall, blissfully singing along to whatever was sounding within his headphones.

I walked up and tapped him on the shoulder. "I'm Carl," I said, introducing myself.

"Hi, I'm Lamont," he replied, removing his earphones and shaking my hand. His eyebrows were shaped high and arched, giving him a somewhat stern appearance, softened by a warm, friendly smile.

"I don't think you realize how loud you're singing," I offered. "I'd be super grateful if you could lower the volume a bit."

He bashfully resumed his mopping duties in silence, as I walked away with a smile.

Lamont Joseph was then twenty years old. He'd lived in the

Brooklyn neighborhood of Crown Heights until a few weeks earlier, when he came out to his parents. Lamont's father told him he couldn't accept his son's queerness and threw him out of the home. Lamont spent a week sleeping in the Utica Avenue subway station, keeping a knapsack filled with his belongings in a storage locker at a nearby McDonald's, where he worked and was able to shower.

"I felt like I was being tortured," Lamont explained when I asked about sleeping in that subway station. "But I also felt hopeful. I knew I'd made the biggest sacrifice I'd ever had to make. I was pretty sure my life would be going uphill from there."

Lamont struck me as an optimistic guy. But maybe he just knew himself, knew his inner strength.

After a week, Lamont had found the Ali Forney Center and moved into the first apartment we'd opened, in Hell's Kitchen. "I couldn't believe how nice it was," Lamont recounted when he and I caught up recently. "I felt like I was living in *The Real World*." But even more so, he marveled at living in an environment where his queerness could be celebrated. "I thought I'd found the Promised Land."

That fall, Lamont returned to Crown Heights to resume his sophomore-year studies at Medgar Evers College. Crown Heights was then quite notorious for being among the city's more homophobic neighborhoods, and the hostilities had created an environment on campus where students and faculty feared being out and open. "Pretty much everyone was on the DL," Lamont said. Hostilities notwithstanding, Lamont had become accustomed to openly living his truth. He had no interest in returning to the closet at Medgar Evers.

Lamont began speaking to other students about how to change the environment. He proposed they start a support group for LGBT and allied students. The response was far from enthusiastic. Some were worried the club would bring unwanted attention to the gay students, and with that attention, danger. Others said, "Keep that shit for the white colleges," he remembers. "Like by making space for gay people I was betraying my race. It was so annoying, and so stupid."

Despite the resistance, Lamont forged ahead. He put up posters advertising the club, although someone soon ripped them down. At the first meeting, it was just Lamont, one other student, one faculty advisor, and two security guards the school stationed there due to concerns for the participants' safety. Still, they continued to meet weekly. Over time the threats and criticisms diminished. At the end of the school year, they had more than twenty ongoing participants. By the time of Lamont's graduation two years later, between forty and fifty students were attending the meetings. They went on to host campus-wide events that attracted more than two hundred partici-pants. Lamont and his friends succeeded in carving out a space of acceptance in what had been overtly hostile territory.

Recently I asked Lamont where he'd found the inspiration to start the support group, and how he summoned the courage to do so in the face of ferocious opposition.

"It was from being at the Ali Forney Center," he answered. "From being in a community of people who were willing to endure any-thing to be true to themselves. That gave me the strength and pride I needed." Hearing that made me prouder than I know how to say.

Lamont is now a dancer and a choreographer, often using his creative freedom to express love for his Afro-Caribbean heritage. (He studied for a time with Raymond, participating in free dance classes Raymond offered to queer street youths in a church hall off Christopher Street.) After graduation, Lamont began to teach dance at Medgar Evers, and for four years the college hosted Lamont's Bloodline Dance Company.

In March of 2017, late in the afternoon of a cold, gray day, I drove to a snow-covered Brooklyn to attend a performance by Lamont's company. They put on a masterful show. I was especially impressed by the dancers performing on huge stilts, towering high above the stage, in a Trinidadian dance form known as Moko Jumbie. Seeing them way up in the air, moving with grace and beauty, I felt as if I was seeing a reflection of what Lamont had himself accomplished.

Earlier, I wrote that Ali and I belonged to a generation on the front lines of the battle to bring acceptance of queer people into the public sphere. Warriors on the first line of attack are the ones who suffer the greatest losses, but sometimes, a few prevail. They break through the enemy lines. They capture new territory, and their astonishing victories make it safer for the others who will follow. Sitting there in that auditorium, I celebrated Lamont as one of those victors.

Lamont's story came full circle in 2020. His agent sent him to an audition, and the next thing Lamont knew he was dancing alongside Beyoncé in *Black Is King*, her Afrocentric tribute to Black pride, strength, and beauty. When I asked what it was like dancing with Queen Bey herself, Lamont answered, "I felt like Alice waking up in Wonderland. It was magical."

As for me, I don't need Beyoncé's endorsement to view Lamont as a king.

A few weeks following the talent show with the trembling boy, I was flying out to the West Coast to attend KJ's graduation from law school.

After KJ stayed with us in the Ali Forney Center's first church basement shelter, he was placed in one of New York City's newly opened LGBT foster care group homes. While residing there, he co-authored the city's first policies on the treatment of queer youths in its foster care system. Then he'd worked as a job developer for a few years, helping homeless and foster care youths enter the workforce.

Those efforts to empower others and change unjust systems naturally informed KJ's decision to pursue law as his vocation.

However, as I sat there on the long flight to Oregon to visit KJ, something was troubling me.

A few days earlier, I had had an unsettling encounter. I'd been walking along a park on West Twenty-eighth Street when I noticed several homeless men semi-collapsed against one another next to the public restroom, a handful of empty pints of vodka strewn below them. As I came closer, one of the men stood up. He was a Black man, his facial hair graying, shabby and unkempt, his thin body wrapped in a tattered black coat. I assumed he was about to ask me for money and reached inside my pants pocket for some quarters.

Then he made a gesture I recognized. He stretched his arms down to his thighs and turned his opened palms toward me, presenting himself. Then, tilting his head to the side, he flashed a big smile and said, "Carl, it's me, *Randy!*"

I hadn't seen Randy in fifteen years. He'd been one of the young people who hung around SafeSpace during Ali's time.

Randy never attracted much attention. He hadn't brimmed with charisma like Ali or Inkera. He wasn't loud and demanding like Angie, and he never erupted in rage like Kiki or Ricardo. Those youths had dominated our focus, sometimes for better and sometimes for worse. It was common for a kid like Randy, all unassuming and passive, to be relegated to the back corners of our attention.

"It's me, Randy!" he repeated. "From SafeSpace. Don't you remember me?"

"Of course I remember you, Randy," I said, smiling. I reached out to shake his hand. "How are you doing these days?" I immediately winced at the question.

Randy looked down at the empty vodka bottles. "I'm OK." He shrugged. "Probably could be doing better."

Randy did not ask me for money, but I couldn't bear to leave him empty-handed. I found a twenty-dollar bill and handed it to him. "Thank you," he said. "Thanks for everything you all did for me at SafeSpace. I'll never forget it."

As I flew out on that long westbound flight, I couldn't stop thinking about Randy, and the distance between our intentions and their results. Despite his words of thanks, I couldn't help wondering why things had turned out so poorly for him, if we hadn't done enough to help. To this day, I am baffled at why some of our kids were able to rise above their circumstances and others were trampled under them. I feel like I've had precious little control over who has succeeded and who has failed.

Donors, philanthropic foundations, government funders—everyone wants me to tell them "success stories." They want to hear how our interventions paid off in our young people achieving rewarding lives. I certainly understand the craving for such testimonies. The world can seem like a bottomless pit of suffering and need, and people rightfully want to invest their money somewhere where it will make a difference. But in my heart of hearts, I feel that success stories are diversions, a product of our desire to avoid recognizing the complexities of brokenness and our complicities in the systems that cause harm.

It is easy for us to identify with the courage and fortitude of a Lamont or a KJ. It is much harder to put ourselves in the circumstances of someone like Randy. But I've come to feel there is something crass, gross, and superficial about the demand for "success." It is an ice-cold, capitalistic way of evaluating worth. If we can't see our solidarity with those whom society judges to be "failures," then we don't understand what solidarity really is.

The next morning, I put those thoughts aside so I could be present in celebrating KJ's triumph. What an amazing vision: this young transgender man, one of our very first residents, beaming with pride in a cap and gown, his law degree in hand.

When the ceremony was done, I went searching for KJ in a large courtyard where hundreds of students and their families were gathered. It took some effort to locate him in the crowd, as he is not especially tall, but at last I found him and we wrapped each other in a big hug.

"It means a lot to me that you came all the way out here," he said, a beaming smile on his face.

"There's nowhere I'd rather be," I told him.

Afterward I joined KJ, his father, boyfriend, and several of his friends for a meal at a Thai restaurant. What a joy it was to listen as he regaled us with battle stories from law school and assessments of his job prospects. In many ways KJ was the same person I'd met a decade earlier: still calm, cool, a touch sardonic. He still looked into your eyes when you spoke, and his brow still wrinkled with concentration. Yet when I looked at him, his face bathed in the afternoon sunlight flooding through the restaurant windows, I thought how different this young man seemed from the seventeen-year-old with the scabbed-over scalp I'd first met in a windowless church basement. The hurt and trauma that enveloped him then was gone. He seemed joyful and at peace. KJ was surely alive.

After the meal, KJ walked me to my car and gave me a farewell embrace. "You and the Ali Forney Center saved my life," he said.

I cringed. The language of "saving" generally makes me uncomfortable.

"KJ," I replied, "you worked really hard to make this happen. *You* saved your life."

He looked at me intently, and his voice dropped in volume until it was barely a whisper. "What happened to Ali could have happened to me. It didn't because you all were there for me."

* * *

It's strange. For me, the joy of victories never eliminates the pain of defeats. When I returned home from KJ's celebration, the encounter with Randy stayed with me. I couldn't stop picturing his gesture: the arms stretched down, the palms opened toward me, the tilted head. Why was it so familiar? Then it came to me. His pose was identical to one in a painting by William Blake. In that painting, the risen Christ appears in a blaze of light to his disciples, who have fallen to their knees in amazement. Only one disciple seems able to look upward. However, he doesn't look up at Christ's face, or at the aura of glory that surrounds him. Rather, his eyes are fixed on the wounds still visible on his teacher's down-stretched hands. He recognizes God as the wounded God, the God whose wounds remain even in Paradise.

At the beginning of this book, I raised a question that I have wrestled with for a long time: *How do we absorb profound rejection and loss without being buried alive under their weight?* I can't say I've found an answer. I know there are wounds that cut too deep to ever heal entirely, scars that must always remain. In my own life, my mother's abandonment and the pain of losing Ali have become essential parts of who I am. What, then, can healing mean when there are wounds that cannot be overcome?

I do not believe the scar tissue from Ali's murder will ever be extricated from my heart. I don't even want it to be. Sometimes anguish is what love feels like; it is the physical and psychological expression of affection contending with loss. But I can integrate the horror of Ali's death with the joy of Lamont's and KJ's triumphs, can recognize how they are pieces of the same whole. And I can recognize the seemingly smaller triumphs, like that night in the dining room when Rashon and the others stood with the trembling boy and gave him the courage to sing. That sweet moment in our drop-in center offered a radiant image of wholeness, of frailty and triumph bound together by love. For me, it is a symbol of what is best about us.

We may be wounded, sometimes irrevocably, and sometimes even fatally. But when we can nonetheless stand together in loving solidarity, holding each other up, we rise above the ashes of our brokenness. When such a thing happens, it deserves to be celebrated.

CHAPTER 27

# A GOOD HAUNTING

---

V isiting our residential apartments, I am often moved by our young people's bedrooms. Some choose to cover their beds with stuffed animals, teddy bears, little heart-shaped pillows, and Hello Kitty dolls. It feels like I'm looking at evidence of their need to reclaim an innocence that was robbed from them.

Throughout this book, I have called the persons in our care "kids" and "young people," yet so much of our work was about preparing them to face adulthood. After enduring the traumatic ruptures of family rejection and homelessness, many of our clients simply were not ready to support themselves by their twenty-first birthday. Often, they would age out of our apartments and return to the subways, too afraid of suffering homophobic and transphobic violence to seek housing in the adult shelters.

Ali was twenty-two years old when she died. Dion was twenty-four. Kiki, too, was twenty-four. I knew I could never feel any closure about their deaths so long as New York City failed to provide safe housing for youths in that age range. We had extraordinary success in 2014 when Mayor de Blasio agreed to add hundreds of new youth shelter beds, but they were all designated for sixteen-to-twenty-year-olds. The city refused to add any for those who were twenty-one to twenty-four.

Making that happen was a long slog. In 2017, we persuaded New York State to amend its laws to allow young people to reside in publicly funded youth shelters until they turned twenty-five. But the state left it up to each locality to determine if they would raise the age, and I was outraged when the de Blasio administration refused to implement the decision. Finally, in 2018, shortly after being elected speaker of the city council, Corey Johnson forced the change with a veto-proof majority of votes.

I assumed that when we got over that hurdle, I would feel a certain degree of inner peace—the reward of arriving at a destination after a grueling journey. Something in me needed to see that the conditions that had doomed Ali were being rectified, as if that one final change might quiet the voice inside me that blamed myself for not doing enough to protect her. Instead, to my surprise, I felt burned out, drained of vigor and motivation, depleted. It was as if all the effort, all the struggle, all those years of fighting to change the conditions for homeless LGBT youth in Ali's name, had built a protective scaffolding around my heartbreak, harnessing it for transformative power. But now, having accomplished my most important goals, the scaffolding had crumbled away, and I was forced into a confrontation with the brokenness that lingered within my heart. No matter what we built, Ali was still gone.

When, after the better part of a year, the burnout and exhaustion didn't lift, I realized the time had come for me to step down as the leader of the Ali Forney Center. I'd never wanted to be in charge indefinitely, and I knew that our young people deserved someone whose heart was wholly present and focused on responding to their needs. In June of 2019, I announced to our board that I would step down in eight months.

Even after my announcement, the inner turmoil didn't go away. Numerous times that summer I was jolted awake by nightmares that I had been exposed as a horrible, despicable person. Over the years, being the leader of the Ali Forney Center had become the bedrock of my identity, an answer to the pain of my childhood and my lingering doubts about my worth as a person. Letting go of the role felt like a huge portion of my persona was withering away.

It was a lonely time to feel demoralized. That summer marked the fiftieth anniversary of the Stonewall riots, and all of queerdom seemed exhilarated. There were parties, massive celebrations. I was even given the honor of speaking before thousands at the opening ceremony of World Pride at the Barclays Center, but I still felt disconnected from what was going on around me.

When Pride Sunday arrived, I joined our Ali Forney contingent for the march. I was waiting for our section to enter the parade on a jam-packed Midtown street, alongside dozens of co-workers, youths, and a smattering of board members and volunteers. The atmosphere was festive, with the usual dizzying array of rainbow flags, feather boas, and semi-naked bodies adorned with glitter. But the wait seemed interminable—we stood in our designated holding area for more than six hours.

Suddenly, I heard an unforgettable, robust female voice with a quintessential Queens street accent calling my name. I *knew* that voice but couldn't recognize the middle-aged woman from whom it emerged.

"Carl, it's me, Angie!" she exclaimed.

It was Ali's close friend, Angie Echevarria! I hadn't seen her for twenty-two years—the last time being at Ali's memorial service. Angie was the one who prompted Ali to exclaim that he'd do fish in a can, on a bun, or in a salad, but he'd *never* do her. She had been sitting right next to Ali in the SafeSpace lobby when he said I looked so old and busted, I'd have to pay for sex on Christopher Street. Of all the kids falling out in reactive hysterics, Angie had laughed the loudest. That's what I remembered most about Angie: her very loud, emphatic voice. Now she was here—as a staff member, it turned out.

I remembered signing the hiring paperwork for an Angela Echevarria that spring, but it didn't register who she was. I'd only ever known her as "Angie." What a wonderful turn of events, to discover that one of Ali's closest friends was now employed at the Ali Forney Center as an outreach worker.

A few months later we arranged to meet. We came together on a warm September evening at our Harlem drop-in center, shortly after dinner.

Angie told me that she had become homeless in 1986 at sixteen years old and found refuge in a residential program in Spanish Harlem called Project Enter, one of the small youth organizations that didn't survive into the nineties because of the Covenant House juggernaut. Project Enter was where she met Ali, all the way back in 1987. He showed up there at the age of twelve—seven whole years before I met him.

Angie and Ali remained close friends over the next ten years. She remembers them making a pact: Each year, no matter the obstacles, they would come together to celebrate each other's birthday.

One of her fondest memories was a night she and Ali spent together at the notorious Carter Hotel, a hellacious fleabag of a place just off Times Square (and the three-time winner of TripAdvisor's "Dirtiest Hotel in America" survey). Angie had rented a room for the Pride march in 1997, and she ran into Ali that evening while wandering Times Square. When she asked where he planned to spend the night, Ali told her he would probably sleep on the steps of Saint Mary the Virgin.

"The steps of Saint Mary's?" Angie replied. "You're buggin'! Come spend the night with me at the Carter."

Ali demurred. "Oh, Miss Thing, they're gonna think we're a couple!"

"What do *you* care what people think?" Angie shot back.

Ali relented. "We walk in," Angie recalled, "and of course Ali says, 'Oh, we're *newlyweds*.' I laughed so hard I was crying. Later the Asian woman from the front desk comes to our door with this fruit platter and says, 'Here, for your honeymoon.' And I just started laughing. And after she left, Ali says, 'You better *shush*, Miss Thing. You better *never* tell no one!'"

Angie had been troubled, as I was, by changes in Ali during the last weeks of his life. By then Angie had aged out of our drop-in center and gotten a full-time job doing harm reduction at NYPAEC, one of the other programs Ali frequented. She noticed the uncharacteristic eruptions of rage and was alarmed by Ali's newfound standoffishness. "I saw Ali deteriorating. But anytime I asked questions about how he was doing, he said I was too nosy."

Ali had been banned from NYPAEC after fighting with the youth who wouldn't return Regine's loan. But on December 4, the night he was permitted to return, he and Angie did street outreach together. After finishing their shift, they stopped by a Starbucks on Eighth Avenue and Sixteenth Street, where Angie invited Ali to join her for a cup of coffee. "He was like, 'Miss Thing! Coffee is a *white woman* thing! You know I don't do that!'"

It was cold outside. Angie felt uneasy about leaving Ali to a night of sex work and drugs. She suggested Ali stay at her place on Staten Island. Ali declined, saying he had to "make coins." But Angie didn't want to give up, so she reminded him that her birthday was approaching. Couldn't they go out to dinner first to celebrate, like they always did on each other's birthdays? "Ali just turned to me with this sad, sad look and said, 'Bitch, you're so fucking needy.'" This time, he didn't seem to be joking.

Unable to convince Ali to join her, Angie made the journey to Staten Island alone. It was the last time she saw him alive, for Ali was killed that very night.

*  *  *

Twenty-two years later, the pain of Ali's death was still so raw that Angie began to cry as we sat together in the center bearing her dearest friend's name.

"Why didn't I just make Ali come home with me, Carl? Why? Maybe he'd still be alive." I had no trouble understanding her feelings of helpless, anguished regret, for I had them too.

Ali promised Angie that if he ever died, he'd come back to haunt her. She said the promise had been borne out, but that it was "a good haunting." She often reflected upon their time spent reaching out to other homeless youths in the streets—right up until the night of Ali's death. Ali "shined" then, she said, shined with goodness and caring. That luminous, inextinguishable memory of her friend's goodness had influenced her decision to spend her career helping homeless youths ever since. Angie had done extensive street outreach, served as a case manager, supervised a syringe exchange program, and even worked at Covenant House.

Over the years, Angie had twice applied for jobs at the Ali Forney Center but hadn't been called in for an interview. Recently, she saw we were hiring outreach workers, but was reluctant to try again. However, she told me how that night Ali had appeared in her dream and said, "Miss Thing, you better submit your résumé!" Two days later, she was called in for an interview and was hired on the spot.

Angie found a great deal of meaning in doing street outreach for an organization bearing Ali's name. "It's how I keep my Ali alive," she said, her voice swelling with pride. Angie now often worked with homeless Latin American immigrant youths terrified of being deported by ICE. Instead of reaching out to social service organizations, they slept hidden alongside the tracks in a dark tunnel beyond a subway station. (A painful reminder of the relentlessness of oppression—how it continues to morph into new forms, how the work of confronting it is never done.)

We sat sharing our memories of Ali for more than two hours.

When we began, the setting sun flooded the plant-filled office with light, but now Harlem had gone dark beyond the windows. It was time for Angie and her co-workers to head out into the night, searching for young people in need. I thanked her profusely for sharing such intimate memories of Ali. She looked me in the eyes and said that she could never thank me enough.

"Back in those days, *nobody* cared about homeless youth," she said, "much less homeless LGBT youth. We were like an omen, like a bad taboo." To her, the fact that a movement to house, heal, and affirm queer youth had risen from the ashes of Ali's death was nothing short of a miracle.

After I left Angie and headed out into the Harlem night, I found myself crying tears of gratitude and joy. Angie had brought Ali back to me—brought back Ali's words, Ali's voice, Ali's wisdom, and Ali's spirit—with a vividness that I never dared hope to relive.

Now, all these years later, as my homebound car rumbled down 125th Street and headed up the Palisades Parkway toward home, I realized the demons that had tormented me for the past year were scattered. The malaise was gone. What a blessing, that I got to know and cherish Ali and find myself included among the dispossessed children whom Ali loved.

Furthermore, I saw, with shining clarity, the meaning of these years of work. They were an act of devotion to the radical witness of Ali's life, an act of honoring and striving to reciprocate the greatness of her care, of sowing and tending its incendiary seeds of fire. For when the structures that govern our lives treat any group of human beings as disposable, the very act of affirming they are worthy of love becomes a birthplace of resistance.

May Ali—and the God whom Ali loved so fiercely—accept my humble offering.

# NEAR PARADISE

---

*They will resurrect you in a hot-ass minute.*
—BRIAN TYREE HENRY, *The Late, Late Show*

It is odd to find myself growing older. How can I possibly be in my late fifties? Inside, I still feel like a child, with an immense plain of time stretched in front of me. It is jarring to realize that more than half of my earthly life has passed. I find myself beginning to contemplate my coming death.

As a teenager, I longed to see the face of Christ with my own eyes. I spent many, *many* hours in prayer and meditation, desperate to catch a glimpse of my beloved God. That longing has changed. For I have seen the face of the crucified Christ, over and over again, for decades. I saw Christ when Cheri was choked with tears in the SafeSpace kitchen. I saw Christ when Ali sat with me in sorrow at the subway station, and when I looked into the stunned, grief-stricken eyes of KJ, Rashon, and so many other young people as they told me how it felt to be abandoned by family and sleep in the streets.

For the better part of my life, I have looked upon the broken Christ, the Christ of the persecuted, the Christ bound to us in our desolation. Now my deepest yearning is to see the healing of their wounds, the binding up of what was broken, the wiping away of every tear, the "making all things well."

But to be honest, my capacity for hope often feels strained by the cruelties and wreckage I've witnessed. Sometimes, the idea of Paradise has seemed a sentimental fantasy—a sweet, childish attempt to bandage over the gaping wounds of oppression and suffering.

My gnawing doubts notwithstanding, I still continue to hope.

It is a brilliantly sunny afternoon, and I am on West Thirty-sixth Street, walking east toward Ninth Avenue. I notice a Black man approaching me in the blinding light. I can tell he is a construction worker from the hard hat atop his head and the tool belt hanging from his waist. He must be working on the new skyscraper being built on that block.

Only when he is arm's length away do I recognize his face.

*Oh my God,* I realize. *It is James Burke!*

James Burke, who sat with me on the Cyclone at Coney Island. James Burke, who exuded happiness whenever we were together, like he was safe in the presence of his protective older brother. James Burke, who devastated me when he aged out of SafeSpace, standing for days across the street, staring helplessly at our windows and sucking his thumb. What a miracle, for him to appear before me now, years later—strong, healthy, intact, *alive*!

"Carl!" James cries out joyfully, having recognized me in the same instant.

"James!" I answer, amazed and overcome.

Only after James disappeared did I realize how deeply impacted I'd been by him—by his quietness, by the simplicity of his presence, by the unguarded, joyful love that emanated from him.

"James!" I repeat, in a delirium of joy and wonder, "I am so happy to see you! I was so scared for you when you aged out of SafeSpace. Are you OK?"

I was never able to get more than one word from James in response to my questions. I doubt I ever heard more than "yes," "no," or "OK" come out of his mouth. This day is no different.

"Yes," he replies, the same old smile overflowing across his face.

I point down at the tool belt. "You're working as a construction worker?"

"Yes."

"Do you have a place to live? Are you off the streets?"

He nods his head, still smiling.

"James, I cannot tell you how happy I am to see you, to know you are doing well for yourself."

He stands before me, silently beaming that radiant smile. I am running late for a meeting, so I give him one of my business cards and ask that he keep in touch. I shake his hand, fearing it might be uncomfortable for a straight construction worker to be hugged by a big gay guy near his worksite. But as I start to walk away, James Burke reaches out, grabs my shoulder, and pulls me into a tight embrace. It feels like a culmination of all the embraces of my life, and a magnificent sign of the great embrace to come.

Since the time of my adolescent mystical awakening, there have been brief, flashing moments when I am able to truly *see*. I have recounted some in this book: riding the subway with James, Ricardo, Milagro, Precious Jewel, and Ali, and seeing them as infinitely beloved; seeing the youths in that first Harlem apartment lined up in front of the mirror as they struck their flamboyant poses; seeing the surging crowd of NYU students coming toward us; seeing Rashon and the others singing along with the frightened kid at the talent show; and seeing Ali in the bright spotlight, crying out, "My God will love me for who I am." There are moments in life when a fog lifts, when some mystical veil is torn and, however obscurely, we see life with the eyes of Paradise. Such moments are not everyday occurrences—usually I've gone years between them.

Being reunited with James Burke on West Thirty-sixth Street felt like one of those holy moments. It fed my hope that what's broken in the world might be repaired, what has been hurt might be healed, what has been fragmented might be made whole.

All those years ago, I couldn't bear to look out my window when James stood outside on the sidewalk, staring helplessly up at our building. It was as if all the world's pain and vulnerability had condensed itself into his lonely, forlorn figure. I knew James loved me, and yet I turned away from his gaze. I should have gone out and hugged him, should have accompanied him again to the adult drop-in center. I should have done something, *anything*, except turn away.

It is said that no one can look upon the face of God and live. The assumption is that if we saw God fully, in all of God's power and glory, we would be annihilated by shock and terror. But I don't believe that's the reason. Rather, I believe it is because we cannot look upon the totality of God's radical love without dying of shame. If we knew the true extent to which we are responsible for one another and obligated to carry one another's burdens, we would be unable to bear our guilt. I wonder if our blindnesses aren't part of God's mercy: slowly, gently allowing us to begin opening our eyes to the infinite worth and value of each person we encounter.

Many faith traditions believe there will be a final judgment, an evaluation of our lives, before we enter Paradise. That God will judge us for every good work, every misdeed, every kind act that we failed to perform. I spent years lacerating myself for turning away when James stood outside my window. But when James Burke and I hugged on the sidewalk that afternoon, I did not perceive any judgment in his embrace, only love.

As James held me in his arms, I reckoned it is not God who judges us; rather, we judge ourselves. When we stand before the face of God, we might see clearly the depth of our betrayals, our injustices. But we can also find something vastly truer: that God only sees us with love. Every meager shard of goodness we've been able to coax out of our poor hearts is returned to us a thousandfold, pressed down and flowing over.

I saw James Burke one more time, a week or so later. He was on his lunch break when I ran into him by the salad bar of a deli on Ninth Avenue and Thirty-sixth Street. I bought lunch for James and myself and invited him to eat with me at the Ali Forney Center's office nearby. He was full of smiles to see Milly and Bill, co-workers whom he remembered from SafeSpace. Then James removed his hard hat and set down his toolbox, and the two of us took our seats at a small table in my room. As we quietly ate our lunch, I had no exalted "seeing." No veils were torn. I was simply delighted to be with my friend once more.

I hope I get to see James Burke again.

# AFTERWORD

Each year, as many as 4.2 million youths and young adults experience homelessness in the United States. Of these, 700,000 are estimated to be unaccompanied minors, which means they are not accompanied by a parent or guardian. Forty percent of them are estimated to be LGBTQ. LGBTQ youths are more than twice as likely to experience homelessness as straight youths.

Homeless LGBTQ kids face higher rates of violence in the streets and shelter system. They experience higher rates of trauma, mental illness, and substance abuse. This specific group of youths are especially vulnerable to victimization in large, warehouse-style shelter settings. Some even endure attempts at conversion therapy in religious shelters.

The Ali Forney Center has grown to become the largest and most comprehensive organization offering dedicated housing and support to homeless LGBTQ youths, in the United States and in the world. We offer emergency and long-term housing, medical and mental health treatment, substance abuse and vocational and educational services. We have developed programs to respond to the specialized needs of transgender and nonbinary youths. More than two thousand young people receive our support each year.

If you are interested in helping, please visit our website at aliforneycenter.org.

Furthermore, as I have been completing this book, the United States has suffered a virulent spate of right-wing legislative efforts to

deprive LGBTQ people of their human rights and equal treatment.
The transgender community and LGBTQ youths have been especially targeted. These efforts are reprehensible for many reasons, not
the least for how they further stigmatize LGBTQ youths, thereby
escalating the challenges too many parents have in accepting their
children. The political climate today is driving many more young
people into homelessness. Such attacks demand to be responded to
with political engagement, and I urge my readers to contact their
elected officials and insist that they support our queer communities
and our children.

# ACKNOWLEDGMENTS

To all the people who helped me bring this book to life, thank you.

This couldn't have been done without Adam Bucko, who persuaded me to write this all down.

My editors, Derek Reed and Leita Williams, your expert guidance has been invaluable in making my story more vivid and revelatory. My agents, Charlotte Sheedy and Jesseca Salky, thank you for championing this book and working so arduously to help me shape it. And Wylie O'Sullivan, thank you for your skillful and enthusiastic assistance in assembling my proposal. Thanks also to the many others at Convergent and Random House who touched this book, including Tina Constable, Campbell Wharton, Jessalyn Foggy, Alisse Goldsmith-Wissman, Rachel Tockstein, Luke Epplin, and Julie Ehlers.

There were numerous people who were so kind and generous with their time as they read through and offered feedback on drafts or portions of the book, including Ally Sheedy, Jim Forest, Fr. James Martin SJ, Jonathan Montaldo, and especially my BFF: the fierce and opulent Junior Labeija, who read through every word of every chapter of every draft. (I love you, Ms. Labeija!)

I am also incredibly grateful to those who shared their memories of Ali with me: Darrell Bodie, Nancy Tricamo, Patrick Thomas, Kristin Miscall, Michael Togbah (aka Dutchess), Kate Muldowney, and Bill Torres. And especially to Ali's dear friends Inkera Jordan and Angela Echevarria, you were immensely helpful in opening dimensions of Ali's life that were previously unknown to me.

To those who spoke to me of their experiences at SafeSpace and the Ali Forney Center, including Jovon Vaughn, Lamont Joseph, and Ksen Pallegedara Murray, thank you.

There were so many people who shared in the work this book describes. I identified many more in the early drafts of this narrative, and a painful part of the editing process was my editors' insistence that so many names would cause confusion for my readers. They suggested that I acknowledge them here. So here goes:

To Andie Simon, Liza Sutton, Tisha Riley, Glenda Andal, John Wright, Cheri Hamm, John Nelson, Donna Klassen, Rolando Hernandez, George Boria, Edwin Madeira, Earl Williams, Melvin Bermudez, Kurt Shaw, Kristin Miscall, Joleen Nell, Liza Zaretsky, Vidal Lopez, Deborah Sills Iarussi, Jimmy Rao, Erik Mercer, Adam Melaney, Rene Ortiz, Teri Messina, Yola Norville, Stacy Siff, Tracy Skinner, David Conroy, Fleming Braxton, Harold Hamilton, Sarah Germany, Rebecca Harrington, Douglas Walker, and all my co-workers at SafeSpace. You taught me so much about dedication and compassion. It was a joy and a privilege to work with you.

I am so grateful to those who came with me from SafeSpace to start the Ali Forney Center: Carter Seabron, Kijana West, Gil Colon, George Santana, Lynn Walker, and Jennifer DeSimone. And of course, special love and gratitude for Joey Lopez, Bill Torres, Milly Velez, and Nancy Tricamo, all of whom were with us at the start, knew Ali personally, and remained working with us for most of my tenure. You were each so crucial in imprinting Ali's values and spirit upon the Ali Forney Center.

To Lisa Cowan and Linda Manley, your assistance in helping me through the nuts and bolts of creating a new nonprofit organization was utterly invaluable. I'd have been lost and adrift without you, seriously.

Lisa Wong and Amin Smalls, thank you for daring to take on the seemingly impossible task of persuading landlords to rent their apartments to homeless youths and helping us obtain our first living spaces.

Leslie Carter, Michele Mumford, Michele Maraziti, Marisol Davila, Wil Fisher, Jama Shelton, Pleas Ferguson, Eric Hartman, Steven Gordon, Marcia Bernard, Finn Brigham, Shawn Brown, Corby Serrano, Stacey Lewis, Dahana Louis, Anastasia Teper, Rhodes Perry, Troy Philadelphia, D'Angelo Johnson, Beth Wolf, Francetta Lane, Paul West, Andria Ottley, Keisha Jackson, Jasmel Delgado, Noam Tidhar, Sophia Frontino, Aliyah Vinikoor, RJ Supa, Gregg Parratto, Cole Giannone, Shilpa Ramesh, Tyler Neasloney, Walter Castenada, Gloria Soto, Sugi Salazar, Eva Embers, Paul Clark, Joanna Rivera, Jess Tell, Cheryl Thompson, Kemba Williams, Agatha Edwards, David Vacek, Avi Bowie, Tracee Brown, Delores Royster, Laura Palmer, Deonne Dowden, Allison Ellis, Kahmia Moise, Erika Usui, Shawnell Connell, Kathryn Sedgwick, Sheraine Gregory, Naz Seenuath, Russell Gregory, Ariel Young, Noman Fayyaz, Segun Owomoyela, Terri Squires, Kim Rajamani, Ryan Barnard, Seyyed Naghavi, Zachary Cohen, Steve Cruz, and my many hundreds of other co-workers at the Ali Forney Center—I thank each of you for your efforts to provide our young people with homes where they could be loved for who they are, and for opening your hearts to absorb so much of their trauma. I especially want to thank everyone who spent long, sleepless nights awake so our young people might sleep in safety and peace.

There are numerous people who have volunteered with our young people and/or who volunteered their labor and talents to help us support them. A huge thanks to Fay Simpson, Ed Di Guardia, Ray Klaussen, Katie Kenisberg, David Calafiore, Omar Reyes, James Heatherly, Brian Hetherington, Jeff Davis, Kevin Hertzog, Jeffrey Gray, Justin Sayre, Linda Simpson, Ryan Davis, Jeffrey Self,

David Raleigh and Rick Bahl, Ari Gold, Alan Cumming, Billy Porter, Linda Simpson, Murray Hill, Melissa Sklarz, Mario Cantone, Sandra Bernhard, Edie, Trai La Trash, Lea DeLaria, Willie Ninja, Tovah Feldshuh, Cole Escola, Frankie Grande, Justin Vivian Bond, Antony and the Johnsons, Nick Perkins, Ocean Morisset, Matthew Oberstein, Adam Rosen, Jerry Hathaway, Madonna, Lady Gaga, Bea Arthur, Billy Goldenberg, Mike Ruiz, and the thousands of others who offered their time, talent, skill, and love.

To the individuals who served on our board: Tony O'Rourke Quintana, Franklin Stevens, Richard Tazik, Peter Soares, Krishna Stone, Robert Sember, Ilsa Jule, Desmond Smith, Paul Ramsey, Richard Pargament, Jeffrey Banks, Vikki Barbero, William Floyd, Joe Evall, Andy Ward, Miles Afsharnik, Neil Koenigsberg, John Polly, Jon Mallow, Carlton Sapp, Jason Rudman, William Greene, Tom Ogletree, Kathryn Zunno, Martin Farach-Colton, Keith Vessell, Alberto Arelle, Mark Lane, Billy Dume, Greg Johnson, Ed Wells, Marie McKenna, Joanna Bratt, Lee Eslyn, Tai-Heng Cheng, Anthony Hird, Martin Jackson, John Quinn, Julie O'Shaughnessy, Mariam Adams, Pete Vujasin, Dan Sternberg, Ana Beatriz Sani, Collin Spencer, and all the others, thank you for selflessly giving your time, resources, and ingenuity.

To those who reported on and documented the plight of our young people: Tina Rosenberg, Margot Adler, Kai Wright, Steven Thrasher, Beth Fertig, Paul Schindler, Rachel Aviv, Alex Morris, Nichole Christian, Melissa Russo, Dominic Carter, Chelsea Carter, Noah Michelson, Cal Skaggs, Reuben Kleiner, and Verena Dobnik. And to Cathy Renna and Chris Constable for their assistance in bringing media attention. I thank each of you for considering the lives of our young people worthy of attention during a time when that attention was largely withheld.

There are countless names of those who joined in our advocacy for our young people and helped plan rallies, circulate petitions, and organize campaigns that transformed New York City's treatment of homeless LGBTQ youths: Matthew McMorrow, Jonathan Lang, Erin Drinkwater, Theresa Nolan, Jake Goodman, Natasha Dillon, Andy Velez, Steve Askinazy, Jason Walker, Jawanza Williams, Carrie Davis, George and RoseAnn Hermann, Wade Davis, Ross Murray, Allen Roskoff, Eunic Ortiz, Rod Townsend, Melanie La Rocca, Emanuel Xavier, Martin Boyce, Danny Garvin, Skye Adrian, Maddox Guerilla, Latifa Blades, Ethan Geto, Michael Czaczkes, Cathy Marino-Thomas, Edie Windsor, David Dunn Bauer, Everett Arthur, Kate Barnhart, Jamie Powlovich, Jason Cianciotto, Sassafras Lowrey, Sylvia Rivera, Wilhelmina Perry, and everyone else, thank you.

My gratitude goes out to the elected officials and their staff who performed vital roles in legislating that transformation: Alan Gerson, Christine Quinn, Tom Duane, Brad Hoylman, Ritchie Torres, Corey Johnson, Carlos Menchaca, Daniel Dromm, Costa Costantinides, Bill Perkins, Keith Wright, Rosie Mendez, Diane Savino, Linda Rosenthal, Erik Bottcher, Richard Gottfried, Jerry Nadler, John Liu, Kenneth Fisher, Jumaane Williams, Scott Stringer, Alphonso David, Dirk McCall, Elvin Garcia, Joey Bernard Pressley, Michael Mallon, Robert Atterbury, John Blasco, Laura Popa, Arturo Garcia-Costas, Daryl Cochrane, and especially my hero, the lionhearted Lew Fidler.

And of course, none of this could have been accomplished without those whose financial generosity made our work possible. To Henry van Ameringen and T. Eric Galloway, Brian McCarthy, Frank Selvaggi and Bill Shea, Ellen, Joe, Sarah, and Will Higdon-Sudow, Kevin, Meg, and Alex Okane and Victoria Lamberth (Okane), Louis Bradbury, Steve Bell, Jon Stryker and Slo Randjelovic, Frank Godchaux, Linda Gottlieb, Mitchell Gold, Gabriel Manzon and Tony D'Angelo, Robert Johnson, Joe Serrins, Leonard A. Lauder, David Dechman and Michael Mecure, Ted Snowdon and Duffy Violante, Gary Knapp, Alan van Capelle and Matt Morningstar, the

Paul Rapoport Foundation (and Jane Schwartz and Ona Winet), the Robin Hood Foundation (and Kwaku Driskell), the Calamus Foundation (and Brian O'Donnell), the David Bohnett Foundation (and Michael Fleming), the JD Lewis Foundation, the Gill Foundation, the Lily Auchincloss Foundation, the Oak Foundation, the New York Community Trust, and the many thousands of others who have shared their resources with our young people—my gratitude for your generosity knows no bounds.

The holiday season is a hard time for young people who go without family and endure homelessness. I want to extend my deep thanks to all those who put heartfelt effort into giving our young people abundance and love during the holidays. I must especially recognize the following:

Eliza Byard and the staff of GLSEN, who, for years, chose to forgo the costs of a fancy holiday party so those funds might instead purchase gifts for our youths.

Neil Schaier, who, with great inventiveness and love, constructed a great many participatory games for the annual holiday carnival at our drop-in center.

Zoe Elizabeth Mavridis, who for many years organized her friends into a hardworking crew of gift-buying, candy-providing angels of holiday kindness.

Craig Smith, who, with the support of Ian Bruce, has for years purchased extravagant gifts for each and every one of the young people in our care (this is in addition to Craig having been among our most generous donors and serving as a member of our board).

All the many staff and volunteers who missed holidays with their families so that they might give a semblance of family to our young people.

And everyone else who went above and beyond in their efforts to give our young people joyful holiday experiences.

And a special thank you to leaders of other organizations who came to the Ali Forney Center's aid in times of trial:

Clarence Patton, of the Anti-Violence Project, who leapt into action after two of our young people were attacked outside a police precinct near one of our residences in Brooklyn, arranging a meeting with the captain of the precinct where we expressed our outrage and accompanying the young people and me to file reports.

Kevin Jennings, then of the Arcus Foundation, who quickly obtained a generous grant for us when we were reeling from funding losses after the federal sequestration in 2014.

Glennda Testone and the LGBT Community Center, who, after our drop-in center was destroyed by Hurricane Sandy, magnanimously offered us space to care for our young people at the Center while we rushed to ready our new space.

And finally, there are some people who have been so integral to our work that I would like to offer a special mention to.

Ali Mroczkowski, you were far and away the most steadfast volunteer during our first decade, cooking hundreds of nutritious meals (to the point where you had our young people *requesting* edamame!) and serving as one of our first life coaches. When I think of the goodness and generosity that made the Ali Forney Center possible, your face is the first that pops into my mind.

David Mixner, you have been an extraordinary friend to the Ali Forney Center, and to me. David has written, produced, and performed in multiple shows based upon his remarkable life, sharing most of the proceeds with our young people. In addition, he has reached out to government leaders to express his outrage when they took action to harm our youths, and furthermore has brought many donors to us. I love you, David!

Kyle Merker, you have been invaluable to us as we grew from a small, grassroots organization to a large professional entity, first as our fiscal manager, then as a board chair for many years. I value your skill, dedication, and friendship immensely.

Marti Gould Cummings, you have performed and advocated for us for many years, and have been an extraordinary board member. I thank you for always being there for us with your wonderful spirit.

Bishop Laurence Provenzano, Rev. Charles McCarron, Rev. Andrew Durbidge, Mary Beth Welsh, and the Episcopal Diocese of Long Island, you all have been tremendously supportive, providing us a low-cost space to shelter our young people for more than a decade. During a time when religion-based hostility toward LGBT people has been so pernicious, your community has been a steadfast witness to love.

Joe Jervis and his JoeMyGod community. Joe, you gave us a spotlight in a time when queer youth homelessness was largely ignored. Again and again you came to our aid in times of need, making me feel like a great army of sweet, generous bears had our back.

Steven Herrick, your remarkable work and vision made the Bea Arthur Residence a reality, and your support, assistance, and advice with our other building projects to create homes for our young people has been invaluable.

Erin Law, you were such a great chair of our board during my last years in leadership. In a time when I felt increasingly beleaguered by the stresses and pressures of my job, your kindness, support, levelheadedness, and ingenuity were a godsend.

Nadia Swanson, you have been my partner in providing technical assistance and support to other homeless LGBTQ youth providers across the country and around the world. I am deeply grateful for your goodness, skill, and wisdom.

Heather Gay, thank you for spending a decade overseeing our programs during a period of tremendous growth and remarkable challenges. I so appreciated how you were a voice of advocacy for our young people and our staff, especially your efforts to center the needs of our trans, nonbinary, and BIPOC communities. I loved working with you.

Alex Roque, you have been such an extraordinary fundraiser in our second decade, and such a strong, brave, and visionary leader as my successor. It meant the world to me to be able to recommend you as the next leader of the Ali Forney Center with so much confidence in your intelligence, strength, goodness, and courage. That's all!

Gary Donatelli, thank you for your goodness, friendship, and love. In so many ways your inspiration opened the way before me.

Raymond Brown, you have been my much better half. Thank you for the hundreds of delicious meals you cooked for our kids, for always letting me know you believed in my abilities when I was tempted to doubt them, and for putting up with all my drama for all these years. I love you helplessly.

It humbles me to acknowledge that there are still thousands who are more than richly deserving of my thanks. To all of you who shared in our work and helped manifest Ali's heart and spirit, I conclude with these words of Saint Thérèse:

*"Only in heaven will you know what you mean to me. For me you are a lyre, a song . . . much more than a music box; even when you say nothing!"*

PHOTO: GREGORY KRAMER

CARL SICILIANO spent several years in the 1980s living and working among the homeless in Catholic Worker communities in Washington, D.C., and New York City. He also spent nine months living in monastic communities, first at the Benedictine Grange in Connecticut and then at the Monastery of Christ in the desert in New Mexico.

After coming out of the closet in 1987, Siciliano spent seven years in New York City working with homeless people and people with AIDS. In 1994 he became the director of SafeSpace, a drop-in center for homeless teens, where he met Ali Forney.

In 2002, in the aftermath of Ali's murder in the streets of New York City, Siciliano founded the Ali Forney Center, which he (with the help of many others) built up to become the largest, most comprehensive organization in the United States and the world dedicated to homeless LGBTQ youths. Its programs have been widely recognized for their innovation and excellence.

In 2020, Siciliano stepped down as the executive director of the Ali Forney Center but continues helping oversee their work to assist and support providers of housing for homeless LGBTQ youths across the United States and around the world.

Siciliano's writing has been published in *The New York Times*, *HuffPost*, *The Advocate*, and *The Journal of Adolescent Health*.

Siciliano was granted the New York Public Library's prestigious Brooke Russell Astor Award, which is presented annually to an "unsung hero who has substantially contributed to improving the quality of life in New York City." Furthermore, he was honored by President Barack Obama as a Champion of Change. Siciliano resides in upstate New York with his husband, Raymond, their six parrots, two dogs, pig, and assortment of chickens.

## ABOUT THE TYPE

THIS BOOK was set in Caslon, a typeface first designed in 1722 by William Caslon (1692–1766). Its widespread use by most English printers in the early eighteenth century soon supplanted the Dutch typefaces that had formerly prevailed. The roman is considered a "workhorse" typeface due to its pleasant, open appearance, while the italic is exceedingly decorative.